"Everyone thinks China is different, and in many respects it is. However in this important book, America's preeminent watcher of China's economy, Nick Lardy, makes a compelling case that the market has mattered more than the direction of the state for China's success. Everyone concerned with the future of China in the global economy should carefully consider Lardy's thesis."

—Lawrence H. Summers, Charles W. Eliot University Professor at Harvard University, former US Treasury Secretary and Director of the National Economic Council

"For three decades, Nick Lardy has consistently recognized the cutting edge changes in China's economy. He has done it again. At a time when the new conventional wisdom is that the Chinese dragon is deploying 'state capitalism' to challenge the international market economy, Lardy has mined the data to discover China's real driving engine: its private sector. The Chinese private sector is now the dominant creator of growth, jobs, trade, and return on assets. Chinese private companies are now even the innovative source of foreign direct investment abroad. Lardy concludes by pointing to areas—especially the services sector and a few key administered prices—where China needs to complete the transition to market competition. Lardy's analysis will support the work of China's reformers, even as it frustrates the latest Cassandras of capitalism in the West."

—Robert B. Zoellick, former World Bank President, US Trade Representative, and US Deputy Secretary of State

"Nick Lardy is one of the world's leading experts on the Chinese economy. His book makes a deeply researched and rigorously analyzed case that China's economy has increasingly relied on market forces to allocate resources, and that privately owned businesses have played a growing and important role in China's success. This book is critical reading for anyone trying to gauge China's economic prospects and challenges the proposition that China's economic performance has been attributable to centralized control of decision making in the economy."

—Robert Rubin, cochairman of the Council on Foreign Relations and former US Treasury Secretary, founder of the Hamilton Project

"*Markets over Mao* turns conventional wisdom on the Chinese economy inside out. Nick Lardy's meticulous empirical analysis dispels the popular notion that a creaky state-directed economy is about to collapse. Instead, he paints a compelling picture of the staying power of China's market-based dynamism. This book is a must read and a long overdue wake-up call for vast legions of China doubters."

—Stephen S. Roach, senior fellow, Yale University Jackson Institute for Global Affairs, and senior lecturer, Yale School of Management

"Nicholas Lardy, one of the world's leading experts on China's economy, challenges the argument frequently made that China's high growth rate over the past decade was the result of state-led industrial policy and the increasing role of state enterprises. He shows instead that this economic performance has been the result mainly of market forces and China's large and growing private sector and that the reforms announced at the Third Plenum of the Chinese Communist Party in November 2013 indicate that this trend will continue in the future. Specialists on China and nonspecialists simply interested in better understanding the Chinese economy will both gain insights from this book and the careful research that went into producing it."

—Dwight H. Perkins, Harold Hitchings Burban _____ University

MARKETS OVER MAO

THE RISE OF PRIVATE BUSINESS IN CHINA

—

NICHOLAS R. LARDY

PETERSON INSTITUTE FOR INTERNATIONAL ECONOMICS

WASHINGTON, DC | SEPTEMBER 2014

Nicholas R. Lardy, called "everybody's guru on China" by the *National Journal*, is the Anthony M. Solomon Senior Fellow at the Peterson Institute for International Economics. He joined the Institute in March 2003 from the Brookings Institution, where he was a senior fellow from 1995 until 2003. He was the director of the Henry M. Jackson School of International Studies at the University of Washington from 1991 to 1995. From 1997 through the spring of 2000, he was also the Frederick Frank Adjunct Professor of International Trade and Finance at the Yale University School of Management. He is author, coauthor, or editor of numerous books, including *Sustaining China's Economic Growth after the Global Financial Crisis* (2012), *The Future of China's Exchange Rate Policy* (2009), *China's Rise: Challenges and Opportunities* (2008), *Debating China's Exchange Rate Policy* (2008), and *China: The Balance Sheet—What the World Needs to Know Now about the Emerging Superpower* (2006). Lardy is a member of the Council on Foreign Relations and of the editorial boards of *Asia Policy* and the *China Review*.

PETERSON INSTITUTE FOR INTERNATIONAL ECONOMICS
1750 Massachusetts Avenue, NW
Washington, DC 20036-1903
(202) 328-9000   FAX: (202) 659-3225
www.piie.com

Adam S. Posen, *President*
Steven R. Weisman, *Vice President for Publications and Communications*

Graphics typeset by Kevin A. Wilson, Upper Case Textual Services, Lawrence, Massachusetts
Cover Design by Fuszion
Cover photo by © Shansekala, © David Franklin
Printing by Versa Press, Inc.

Printed in the United States of America
16   15   14   5   4   3   2

Library of Congress Cataloging-in-Publication Data
Lardy, Nicholas R.
Markets over Mao : the rise of private business in China / Nicholas R. Lardy.
    pages cm
Includes bibliographical references.
ISBN 978-0-88132-693-2
1. Government business enterprises—China.
2. Privatization—China. 3. China—Economic policy—1976-2000. 4. China—Economic conditions—1976-2000. I. Title.
HD4319.L37 2014
338.6'10951—dc23
                                        2014011127

This publication has been subjected to a prepublication peer review intended to ensure analytical quality. The views expressed are those of the author. This publication is part of the overall program of the Peterson Institute for International Economics, as endorsed by its Board of Directors, but it does not necessarily reflect the views of individual members of the Board or of the Institute's staff or management.
The Peterson Institute for International Economics is a private, nonprofit institution for the rigorous, intellectually open, and honest study and discussion of international economic policy. Its purpose is to identify and analyze important issues to making globalization beneficial and sustainable for the people of the United States and the world and then to develop and communicate practical new approaches for dealing with them. The Institute is completely nonpartisan. The Institute's work is funded by a highly diverse group of philanthropic foundations, private corporations, and interested individuals, as well as income on its capital fund. About 35 percent of Institute resources in our latest fiscal year were provided by contributors from outside the United States.
A list of all our financial supporters for the preceding year is posted at http://piie.com/supporters.cfm.

Contents

Tables

Figures

Boxes

Preface

It is widely known that China's economic growth over the past three and a half decades has been without historical precedent. The reason for this phenomenal and sustained growth is more controversial. There is a widespread view that China's government has succeeded through "state capitalism." Adherents of that view believe that China largely eschewed reliance on market forces in favor of retaining direct ownership of the commanding heights of the economy. Despite China's undeniably growing private sector, it was assumed the government exercised substantial indirect control of the rest of the economy by allocating credit via the state-owned banking system.

Nicholas Lardy compellingly overturns this view. He argues that China has maintained extraordinarily rapid growth since 1978 primarily because of the freeing of the private sector and the shrinking of the state—that is, markets over Mao, as he memorably characterizes it. Market forces came to play an ever larger role in resource allocation, and private firms emerged as the most dynamic element in China's economy. In fact, Lardy shows that private firms became the major source of economic growth, virtually the sole source of job creation, and the major contributor to China's still growing role as a global trader. China has grown because it has grown more capitalist. Thus it does not represent an alternative model to capitalism, at least in terms of what parts work.

In addition, the evidence marshaled in this book disproves the often asserted view that the decade of leadership of former President Hu Jintao and Premier Wen Jiabao (2003–13) increased the role and importance of state-owned firms. Yes, the Hu-Wen government promoted industrial policies that appeared to advantage state-owned companies at the expense of private as well as foreign firms. But Lardy's comprehensive analysis shows that these efforts were largely unsuccessful. The financial performance of state-owned companies improved only briefly and temporarily relative to that of private firms but then declined so sharply for most of the decade that by 2012 the efficiency of state-owned industrial firms had fallen to only one-third that of private firms. By 2013, China's growth was even more dependent on private companies than when Hu-Wen took over.

For Lardy, the critical test of the new Chinese leadership on economics will come in services, where inefficient state firms remain completely dominant. Lardy's major contention is that freeing private business in this area can contribute significantly to Chinese economic growth, even as the economy moves away from the credit- and investment-driven growth path of recent years. Lardy argues that China's current leadership of President Xi Jinping and Premier Li Keqiang seeks to further transform the role of the government, ceding even greater space to the market; their statements to date, notably in the Third Party Plenum released in November 2013, support this view. The Xi-Li government seems likely to focus its efforts on less distortionary government priorities, such as meeting increasingly urgent popular demands for cleaner air and water and safer food supplies, providing a stronger social safety net, and making economic growth more inclusive. Lardy documents their public commitments to further enhance the role of the market by eliminating the few remaining price controls—including bank deposit interest rates, which continue to distort the allocation of resources—and by reducing the regulatory barriers that impede the entry of private firms into services.

The Institute has a long history of studies on the Chinese economy. Nicholas Lardy, Anthony M. Solomon Senior Fellow at the Institute, has led our work in this area, beginning with his 1994 book *China in the World Economy*. More recently, as China has become even more important to the global economy, the Institute has increased its research and outreach on China. We have published eight policy briefs and working papers on China-related issues in the last two years, created a dedicated blog "China Economic Watch" on Chinese economic policy, and now publish a regular "China Rebalancing Watch." Other books include these multiauthor studies: *China: The Balance Sheet—What the World Needs to Know Now about the Emerging Superpower* (2006), *China's Rise: Challenges and Opportunities* (2008), and Arvind Subramanian's *Eclipse: Living in the Shadow of China's Economic Dominance* (2011). Later this year, we will publish *Bridging the Pacific: Toward Free Trade and Investment between China and the United States* by C. Fred Bergsten, Gary Hufbauer, and coauthors.

The Peterson Institute for International Economics is a private, nonprofit institution for rigorous, intellectually open, and honest study and discussion of international economic policy. Its purpose is to identify and analyze important issues to making globalization beneficial and sustainable for the people of the United States and the world and then to develop and communicate practical new approaches for dealing with them. The Institute is completely nonpartisan.

The Institute's work is funded by a highly diverse group of philanthropic foundations, private corporations, and interested individuals, as well as income on its capital fund. About 35 percent of Institute resources in our latest fiscal year were provided by contributors from outside the United States. A list of financial supporters for the preceding year is posted at http://piie.com/supporters.cfm.

The Executive Committee of the Institute's Board of Directors bears overall responsibility for the Institute's direction, gives general guidance and approval to its research program, and evaluates its performance in pursuit of its mission. The Institute's President is responsible for the identification of topics that are likely to become important over the medium term (one to three years) that should be addressed by Institute scholars. This rolling agenda is set in close consultation with the Institute's research staff, Board of Directors, and other stakeholders.

The President makes the final decision to publish any individual Institute study, following independent internal and external review of the work. Interested readers may access the data and computations underlying Institute publications for research and replication by searching titles at www.piie.com.

The Institute hopes that its research and other activities will contribute to building a stronger foundation for international economic policy around the world. We invite readers of these publications to let us know how they think we can best accomplish this objective.

ADAM S. POSEN
President
June 2014

Acknowledgments

This book would not exist without the support of Ryan Rutkowski and Nicholas Borst. They made it possible to efficiently exploit the flood of statistical data from not only the National Bureau of Statistics of China but virtually every other government agency in the finance and economics domain. I also benefited from a discussion with members of a study group convened at the Peterson Institute in January 2014 to discuss a draft of the manuscript, a group that included Nathaniel Ahrens, Steve Barnett, Nicholas Borst, William Cline, David Dollar, Patrick Douglass, Carla Friedman, Carla Hills, Matt Goodman, Yukon Huang, Albert Keidel, Deborah Marks, Marcus Noland, Adam Posen, Ryan Rutkowski, Arvind Subramanian, Damon Silvers, Edwin Truman, and Nicholas Vernon. Both Fraser Howie and Dwight Perkins sent detailed, helpful comments on the draft manuscript. Formal peer reviewers of the next draft of the manuscript—Richard Cooper, Yiping Huang, David M. Lampton, and Dennis Tao Yang—also offered important comments that helped to shape the final manuscript. Many other individuals offered assistance along the way with matters large and small, notably Andrew Batson, Carsten Holz, Scott Kennedy, Barry Naughton, Thomas Rawski, Marcus Rodlauer, Dan Rosen, David Stockton, and Janet Zhang.

As the manuscript took shape I had the opportunity to present the findings of the study to audiences at the Peterson Institute, Stanford University, a conference in Beijing organized jointly by the People's Bank of China and the International Monetary Fund, an Institute for International Economic Studies conference in Tokyo, the China Development Forum organized by the London School of Economics, at meetings in both the United States and China of a Track II Economic Dialogue organized by the National Committee on US-China Relations and the China Center for Economic Research at Peking

University, a conference in Taipei organized jointly by the Johns Hopkins University and the Center for China Studies at National Chengchi University, and a conference in Beijing organized jointly by the Peterson Institute and China Finance Forty Forum. Comments made and questions raised at these meetings led to substantial improvements in the study.

Adam Posen, the president of the Peterson Institute, has been a strong supporter not only of this study but the Institute's work on and interaction with China more broadly. Steve Weisman, the Institute's vice president for publications and communication, led a talented team, including Susann Luetjen, responsible for production and design, and Valerie Norville, who edited the manuscript.

Introduction

China's growth since economic reform began in the late 1970s is unprecedented in global economic history. No other country has grown as rapidly for as long. By 2013 China's economy was 25 times larger in real terms than in 1978. As a result, China's share of global GDP more than quadrupled, from under 3 percent to 12 percent.[1] Along the way it overtook a half-dozen advanced industrial countries in aggregate output to become the world's second largest economy.[2] Similarly, it abandoned the autarkic trade and investment policies that had been pursued under Mao Zedong to become the world's largest trading economy and the second largest recipient of foreign direct investment. Of course, its huge population means that its rankings in per capita terms are much lower. China has nonetheless moved up in terms of per capita income. In 1980 the World Bank (1982, 110–11) classified China, along with about 30 of the world's poorest countries, as a low-income economy. By 2013 the Bank put China in the upper-middle-income category, with a per capita income ahead of 55 countries classified as either low income or lower middle income.[3]

This study examines the role of markets and the private sector in China's

---

1. IMF, *World Economic Outlook*, October 2013.

2. In 1980 the economies of Canada, Italy, France, Germany, the United Kingdom, and Japan were all larger than that of China. By 2013 China had surpassed them all, sometimes by substantial margins. For example, China's economy is now about four and a half times the size of Canada's.

3. World Bank, *Development Indicators*. The World Bank ranks China as 97th in per capita GDP out of 179 countries covered.

economic transformation.[4] Three major themes emerge. First, China achieved extraordinarily rapid economic growth after 1978 primarily because market forces came to play an ever larger role in resource allocation. This thesis counters the argument, recently but widely advanced, that the real engine of Chinese economic progress has been the government's adoption of an economic model that eschews reliance on the market, preferring instead to retain direct ownership of what is sometimes referred to in China as the commanding heights of the economy (经济命脉) and to exercise substantial indirect control of the rest of the economy by directing the allocation of credit via the state-owned banking system.

Second, this study finds little support for another frequently expressed view, namely that President Hu Jintao and Premier Wen Jiabao dramatically increased the role and importance of state-owned firms during their decade of leadership (2003–13).

The third theme of this study is that the major sources of China's future growth will be similarly market rather than state driven. The new leadership of President Xi Jinping and Premier Li Keqiang likely will further enhance the role of market forces, as endorsed by the Third Plenum of the Eighteenth Party Congress in the fall of 2013. Vested interests may seek to thwart this initiative, but it is unlikely that President Xi and Premier Li will follow the Hu-Wen leadership in abandoning fundamental economic reform and attempting to use industrial policy to promote growth that some see as ever more reliant on state firms. Nonetheless, enhancing the role of the market so that China can continue to outperform global growth and play an ever expanding role in the global economy will require important changes in China's institutional arrangements, especially in the role of the state in the economy.

The central finding of this study is that the economic reform process that began in the late 1970s has transformed China from a state-dominated economy into a predominantly market economy in which private firms have become the major source of economic growth, the sole source of job creation, and the major contributor to China's still growing role as a global trader. Not only does this study find little support for the view that state firms grew in prominence during the Hu-Wen decade, it demonstrates that private firms continued to displace state firms throughout the period. Going forward, however, China must deregulate to increase competition in those portions of the economy where state firms have been protected and complete the reform of factor prices, especially the prices of energy and capital that continue to impede the efficient allocation of resources throughout the economy.

One foundation of China's transformation from a state-dominated to a predominantly market economy, the displacement of government-determined by market-determined prices, is outlined in chapter 1. On the eve of reform,

---

4. The term "private" in this study generally refers to the universe of household businesses (i.e., self-employed), registered private companies, and firms in other registration categories in which the majority or dominant owner is private.

almost all important prices were set by the State Price Commission, with little regard for supply and demand in the market. As a result, there was little connection between firm profitability and efficiency of resource use. The chapter also demonstrates that most markets are now competitive; prices reflect supply and demand rather than market power exercised by a few big firms. The transformation to price determination in competitive markets was accompanied by a fundamental change in the financing of investment. The system in which firms remitted all profits to the Ministry of Finance and the State Planning Commission determined the main investment priorities, which were funded through the state budget, was replaced by a system in which the most important source of investment finance was the retained earnings of firms, followed in importance by bank credit. In an increasingly competitive market environment, the most productive firms had larger retained earnings and therefore were able to grow more rapidly by using these earnings to finance expansion. Thus the gradual shift to a market-based allocation of resources contributed significantly to the acceleration of economic growth starting in the 1980s. Finally, chapter 1 documents China's transition from a system of urban job assignment with bureaucratically determined pay scales and lifetime employment to a far more market-driven system for the allocation of human capital.

Chapter 2 provides an overview of the enduring problem of state-owned enterprises in China. The drag of the state sector was partially masked in the first half of the 1980s, when reforms in agriculture led to an unprecedented spurt of growth of farm output. Two reform initiatives are examined. The first was the substantial downsizing of state-owned firms in the second half of the 1990s and the first part of the next decade, when bankruptcies, mergers, and privatizations cut the number of state-owned industrial firms by three-quarters, leading to the loss of tens of millions of jobs in the state sector. The result of this restructuring was a decade-long substantial improvement in the financial performance of state-owned industrial firms.

A second major initiative was the creation of the State Asset Supervision and Administration Commission (SASAC) in 2003. The creation of SASAC, which focuses on the largest state-owned group companies, coincided with the launch of several major industrial policies that many see as stacking the deck in favor of state-owned firms and thus marking the resurgence of the state's role in China's industrial sector. The analysis in chapter 2, however, shows that the profits of SASAC firms as a share of all nonfinancial firms' profits in China peaked in 2006–07 and have since fallen sharply. And SASAC firms' return on assets has also declined since the middle of the 2000s and is now far below their cost of capital. These findings undermine the notion that SASAC has been able to transform the performance of China's largest and most important state-owned companies.

Chapter 3 documents the dramatic transition that has occurred in the ownership structure—away from an economy in which state or collective firms produced almost all economic output to one in which private firms produce about two-thirds of output. A corollary of this transformation is that almost all of the growth of urban employment since 1978 has been in private firms. Employment in state and collective firms has shrunk by several tens of millions and now accounts for less than one-fifth of urban employment. Private firms have become the main source of economic growth, the sole source of increasing employment, and the major contributor to China's growing and now large role as a global trader.

This dramatic transformation is the result of three factors. First, state policy toward private economic activity evolved from one of substantial discrimination in the early years of reform to one that, with a few important exceptions, now approaches neutrality—that is, state policies provide almost equal treatment of firms regardless of ownership. Second, private firms earn substantially more on their assets than state firms. This means that the ratio of retained earnings to assets of private firms is higher than in state-owned firms, providing relatively more funds for expansion and thus faster growth. Third, the access of private firms to bank credit has improved so much that on average new bank lending to private firms in 2010–12 was two-thirds more than to state firms. Thus the often repeated assertion that the voracious credit appetite of state firms has squeezed out private firms from access to credit is fundamentally misleading. Finally, chapter 3 reviews studies of the role of the Chinese Communist Party in the private sector. These studies show that entrepreneurs join the party for prestige and to promote their firms' business interests. Although millions of entrepreneurs are now party members, this has not become a channel through which the party exercises leadership over the private sector.

Chapter 4 looks to the future. Although the role of the market has increased, more should be done. While state firms are contributing a declining share of China's output, their claim on bank credit and investment resources has not shrunk commensurately. And the return on assets of state firms on average is well below their cost of capital, clearly signaling that state firms remain a significant drag on economic growth. A few key administered prices distort the allocation of resources. And regulatory barriers impede the entry of private firms into the few domains, mostly in services, where state firms retain near complete control and productivity is particularly low.

President Xi Jinping and Premier Li Keqiang have clearly signaled that they will seek to further enhance the role of the market through liberalization of the few prices the state still controls and through deregulation that will increase competition, particularly in services. These changes would mirror the dramatic opening of the manufacturing sector that began in the 1980s, which has led to a dwindling role of state firms. If Xi and Li can overcome the vested interests that have opposed these reforms in the past, government firms in the service sector will have to step up their game; otherwise state firms' share of services will shrink. Either outcome would be positive for China's economic growth.

The evidence reviewed in this study provides scant support for those who have labeled China's development as one of state capitalism (Bremmer

2010).[5] While those using this and similar phrases, such as "authoritarian capitalism," "corporate Leninism," or "regulatory capitalism," do not have a uniform view of China's development strategy, they share the belief that China's transition to a more market-oriented economy has been interrupted or perhaps even abandoned in favor of a strategy involving much more state-directed allocation of resources (James McGregor 2010, 2012; Lee 2012; Hsueh 2011). According to those who see China as an exemplar of state capitalism, this change of strategy emerged early in the President Hu and Premier Wen period and then accelerated as the global financial crisis unfolded beginning in 2008.

There is little doubt that the stimulus program that the Chinese state launched in response to the global financial crisis was bold, allowing the Chinese economy to sustain an impressive growth rate averaging almost 10 percent in 2009–10, even as the United States and many other advanced industrial economies endured the worst economic conditions since the Great Depression.

China's stimulus, however, was much less state-centric than is commonly charged. It did entail a substantial acceleration of infrastructure spending by the Ministry of Railroads and by several thousand so-called local government financing vehicles. The latter are responsible for the construction of roads, subways, water supply and sewage treatment systems, and other urban infrastructure. States play a major role in infrastructure investment in most market economies, so a temporary sharp ramp-up in these programs should not be the basis for judging that China's transition to a more market-oriented economy has been suspended or abandoned.

The second largest contribution to the increased pace of investment that sustained China's growth in the global crisis was predominantly private—an acceleration of the residential housing boom that predated the crisis. As I have written elsewhere, this boom is in part the result of government policies that (largely inadvertently) have made private housing a preferred asset class for China's high-saving households (Lardy 2012). China has almost certainly overinvested in housing for at least the past five years. A future moderation in private housing investment constitutes a significant macroeconomic risk because housing-related demand for steel, cement, aluminum, copper, and other building materials as well as household appliances and to some extent even automobiles has become one of the most important drivers of China's economic growth. But an increasingly risky boom in private residential housing is hardly evidence of a more state-directed economy.

The third largest component of increased investment was in industry and services. But the common image of state-owned enterprises massively increasing their borrowing from state-owned banks at the expense of private firms is misleading. State firms did increase their borrowing, but the evidence presented in this study shows that the investments these firms undertook

---

5. *Economist*, "The Rise of State Capitalism: The Emerging World's New Model," special report, January 21, 2012.

were generally not well chosen, thus contributing to the decline in the return on assets of state firms in recent years. Private firms were also big borrowers during and immediately after the global financial crisis. In contrast with state firms, private-firm investments generally were well chosen. As a result, the return on assets of private firms continued to rise during the global financial crisis. Consequently, private firms' contribution to China's economic growth has continued to expand while that of state firms has slumped.

The analysis in this study is based on a wide range of official data compiled and published by the National Bureau of Statistics of China and many other government agencies. The case that these data are sufficiently accurate to support the conclusions reached is outlined in box 1.1.

Box 1.1 How reliable are Chinese economic data?

This study relies on official Chinese economic data to draw conclusions about the rise of market forces. Are these official data sufficiently reliable to support the findings of this study?

The quality of Chinese economic data varies enormously but has been steadily improving. Some data, such as China's statistics on registered urban unemployment, are clearly flawed, not because of measurement errors but because the universe of people considered to be in the urban labor force is limited. Both the numerator and the denominator in this calculation are restricted to individuals with permanent urban residency status. Thus in spring 2009, when China's exports were extremely weak due to the global financial crisis and more than 20 million individuals employed in export processing factories on China's southeast coast had lost their jobs, China's unemployment rate remained virtually unchanged.[1] Most of the individuals who lost their jobs were migrants and thus not usually included in counts of the urban labor force. So the registered urban unemployment rate may be statistically accurate according to the Chinese definition, but it is not useful if one is interested in measuring, for example, the effects of an external shock on domestic urban employment.

On the other hand, central bank data on loans and deposits and various measures of the money supply are quite accurate.[2] Banking is a highly regulated system, the small number of banks makes measurement easier than measuring the value added of China's millions of enterprises and more than 100 million farm households, the unit of measure of loans and deposits is quite simple, reported amounts are easily checked through audits of financial institutions, and there is no obvious incentive for the central bank to misreport data on the money supply.

As the quality of economic data has improved, statistical authorities have been willing to increase the frequency with which the data are released. In the 1990s, for example, the State Administration of Foreign Exchange (SAFE) released only

(box continues next page)

---

1. Tan Yingzi and Xin Dingding, "20 million migrants lost jobs: Survey," *China Daily*, February 3, 2009. Available at www.chinadaily.com (accessed on April 14, 2014). The official unemployment rate moved from 4.2 percent in the fourth quarter of 2008 to 4.3 percent in the first quarter of 2009. Twenty million jobs represent 6 percent of the reported urban labor force at the time.

2. This judgment is based on many years of use of these data and on the absence of any suggestion by outside critics that these financial and monetary data have been misreported or manipulated.

Box 1.1   How reliable are Chinese economic data? *(continued)*

annual balance of payments data, typically with a long lag, but in 2010 it started to release quarterly data.[3] And the time lag in publication steadily shrank.
More importantly, the granularity of the data has increased steadily. The current
account in the 1990s, for example, was disaggregated into only four types of
transactions: trade in goods, trade in services, income, and transfers. But in recent years, SAFE has disaggregated trade in services into 13 separate categories.

Nonetheless, skepticism about the reliability of Chinese data, particularly GDP
data, abounds, based both on the difficulties of measuring GDP in a rapidly growing economy where the structures of production and expenditure are changing
rapidly and on the view that the statistical authorities sometimes shade the data
to please their political masters. Outside analysts have spent much effort in con-
structing alternative measures of Chinese economic growth, relying on inputs
such as power use and rail transport. However, careful analysis by economists at
the San Francisco Federal Reserve Board has shown that official GDP data for 2012
are consistent with other indicators, including data that are reported outside of
China, and do not appear to have overstated Chinese economic growth, as some
had suggested (Fernald, Malkin, and Spiegel 2013). However, because of technical
difficulties in the measurement of housing services, official data probably somewhat understate the level of GDP. But this shortcoming does not appear to have
a significant impact on the reported official growth of GDP (Lardy 2012, 157–61).

Compared with measurement of GDP, which is technically complex, measurement of the variables used in this study is relatively straightforward and sufficiently accurate to support its findings. For example, chapter 3 presents data on
the return on assets of private and state firms over a 15-year period. The data
show returns in 2012 of 13.2 percent and 4.9 percent, respectively, for the two
ownership types. But the conclusion that private firms make much more effective use of capital does not hinge on the precision of the numbers, but rather that
private firms appear to be roughly two to three times more productive in the use
of capital than state firms. The true advantage of private firms might be either
somewhat more or somewhat less than shown by the data. But the underlying
data are not so weak that the true ratio would lead to a revised conclusion about
the relative efficiency in the use of capital in firms of the two ownership types.

The greatest challenge in tracing the rise of the private sector in China over
the past almost four decades is not the accuracy of the underlying data but
keeping track of the numerous changes in coverage and definitions that Chinese

(box continues next page)

---

3. In 2012, SAFE also published the quarterly data back to 1998.

Box 1.1   How reliable are Chinese economic data? *(continued)*

Chinese statistical authorities have introduced over the years and being sensitive to the different definitions and coverage employed by the many agencies that compile and release data. Great care has to be taken to ensure that analysis is based on apples-to-apples comparisons. Many of these problems are discussed in the text and, for those who are interested, in greater detail in chapter notes.

Those who believe that even the more straightforward data used here are somehow distorted, either by false reporting from below or by manipulation by national statistical authorities, need to answer a simple question. On virtually every metric examined in this study, private firms have consistently outperformed state firms. They grow faster, employ capital more efficiently, create more jobs, and increasingly generate more exports than state firms. Even if it were possible, why would the government understate the economic performance of state companies and overstate the economic performance of private companies for a period of more than 30 years?

1

State versus Market Capitalism

On the eve of China's economic reform in the late 1970s, private economic activity and the role of the market were severely limited and the role of the state and state-owned enterprises was pervasive. The State Planning Commission set output targets for major products, which in the case of industrial goods were produced almost entirely by state-owned firms, and arranged for the supplies of raw materials and intermediate goods needed to meet these production goals. Almost all prices—whether for agricultural products, investment goods, or retail commodities—were set by the State Price Commission. The Ministry of Finance provided funding through the government budget for investment in most of these state firms. Overall, more than a third of total output was allocated through the unified state budget, an extraordinarily high share for a low-income economy with minimal transfer payments to its citizens. Typical of planned economies, China had a mono-banking system, in which a single, wholly state-owned financial institution controlled almost four-fifths of all deposits, was responsible for more than 90 percent of all loans, and simultaneously served as the central bank (Lardy 1998, 61).

China's nonagricultural economy was heavily dominated by state-owned firms, a legacy of the system of central economic planning introduced in the mid-1950s. In industry, state-owned enterprises in 1978 accounted for only about one-quarter of all firms, but the balance of firms were collectively owned, which almost invariably meant a considerable degree of ownership and control by provincial or local governments. Moreover, state-owned firms accounted for four-fifths of industrial output and seven-tenths of industrial employment. State firms controlled the lion's share of industrial fixed assets as well. As will be demonstrated in chapter 3, state-owned units also dominated most components of the tertiary sector, although in some cases collective, quasi-governmental units also had a significant presence.

Agriculture was organized in collective units called communes, which were required to deliver a large share of their output to state-owned procurement agencies at prices set by the State Price Commission. In rural China there were tiny family-controlled private plots, but severe restrictions on marketing the agricultural output from these plots meant production was almost entirely for self-consumption rather than the market.

This chapter traces a momentous shift in the roles of the state and markets in allocating resources in the Chinese economy. It examines markets for products and factors of production. Product markets have been dramatically transformed, with price formation almost entirely determined by supply and demand rather than the government. The picture for factors of production is more complex. Labor markets have been largely transformed but retain some nonmarket elements from the prereform era. The market for capital is the most state controlled, and markets for other factors of production such as electricity, water, refined petroleum products, and natural gas—a group of commodities the Chinese refer to as "products of a resource character"—remain subject to various administrative controls.

Product Markets

In the late 1970s, bureaucrats in the State Price Commission fixed the prices of all important goods. Created when central planning was first introduced to China during the First Five-Year Plan (1953–57), the commission set the prices at which rural collective units were compelled to deliver fixed amounts of various types of agricultural output to state procurement agencies. It also set prices for all important consumer goods, sold almost entirely through state-owned retail establishments, and it set the prices of all important producer goods, including machinery and equipment, coal, and other ores and minerals. These producer goods were allocated according to plans drawn up by the State Planning Commission.

Equally important, these administered prices were set with scant regard for actual market conditions. The State Price Commission set prices not to equilibrate supply and demand but primarily to enhance the government's control of resources in the economy. For example, the bureaucrats set low prices for forced deliveries of agricultural products to the state for two reasons. First, the government pursued a low-wage policy in urban areas to boost profitability of state-owned firms, particularly manufacturing companies, which were located predominantly in urban areas. These firms were required to surrender virtually all their profits to the Ministry of Finance, thus the low-wage policy boosted fiscal revenues as a share of GDP. Low wages were made possible in large part by low prices for grain and other staple foods in urban areas. Second, the government wanted to ensure especially high profits in industries that were heavily dependent on inputs from the agricultural sector—food processing, textiles, apparel, and cigarettes. Again, supernormal profits in these industries fed directly into higher fiscal revenues for the government and thus more control over economic resources.

Similarly, the government set low prices for coal, energy, and many other industrial raw materials. Again the goal was greater government control of resources. If the price of coal had been determined by market supply and demand, state industries such as steel and electric power would have paid more for this critical input, thus reducing their profitability. While on a net basis market pricing of coal, energy, and raw materials might have been a wash for the overall profitability of state firms, the government's low-price strategy for industrial raw materials concentrated profits in a smaller number of state firms producing final goods rather spreading profits over a larger number of firms, including those producing raw materials and intermediate inputs. The government believed this concentration facilitated revenue collection and thus enhanced state control, enabling it to pursue a big-push industrialization strategy.

Most of these features of central planning were still in place in 1978, though the chaos of the Cultural Revolution (1966–76) had reduced the role of planning compared with the 1950s. As reform got under way in the late 1970s, price-setting bureaucrats had little idea of what market equilibrium prices would be for most products because those markets did not exist. Since China's leaders had pursued an extremely autarkic trade policy for more than a decade, they also had little or no knowledge of world market prices, which might have provided some guidance for setting domestic prices. The most important consumer goods—grains, edible vegetable oil, cotton cloth, and even bicycles—were rationed in urban areas, just as they had been in the 1950s. State units, whether factories or government offices, distributed coupons to their employees, and these coupons as well as the appropriate amount of cash had to be presented at state-run outlets to acquire such goods. Machinery and equipment and other producer goods were subject to what was referred to as "unified distribution" (统一分配), a key part of the system of material supply planning introduced in the First Five-Year Plan (1953–57). In practice, this meant that the State Planning Commission directly allocated hundreds of important raw materials and investment goods, such as coal, timber, cement, steel products, and metal cutting lathes. Based on estimates of various technical coefficients, the Planning Commission allocated to each major state enterprise the inputs necessary to meet the output targets specified in each enterprise plan. The plan also specified the allocation of the output of each major enterprise (Lardy 1978, 15).

As economic reform began, rigid state price controls gradually eroded. Rural free markets, which the state had suppressed during the Cultural Revolution, were gradually reopened. Once delivery quotas to the state were met in local areas, the government allowed farmers in these localities to sell their surplus on these rural free markets. Similarly, in the early 1980s the government began to liberalize retail prices for a growing range of consumer goods. But the biggest breakthrough came in 1983, when the state established a two-tier structure for the pricing and distribution of coal, steel, machinery and equipment, and other producer goods (Wu and Zhao 1987). Under this scheme, enterprises were still required to deliver planned levels of output to state agencies at state-fixed prices but could sell their above-plan output in parallel markets in which prices were freely determined by supply and demand.[1]

Under this scheme the government kept the overall physical quantity of each product subject to the material allocation system more or less constant. Given steady economic growth, the share of output allocated at government-fixed prices gradually declined as firms channeled incremental output entirely onto the market, typically at much higher prices (Naughton 2007, 92–93). The marketized share of production grew dramatically, and by 1993 the material allocation plan was formally abolished (Naughton 2007, 101).

The resulting transformation of the domestic price environment is captured in table 1.1, which shows, for three broad commodity categories, the share of transactions measured by value at market, state-guided, and state-fixed prices for various years from the beginning of reform in 1978 through 2003. State price setting eroded most rapidly for agricultural and consumer goods. By the mid-1980s over half of all farm gate sales were at market-determined prices, and retail commodities were not far behind. The state initially retained substantially more control of producer goods prices; market-determined prices did not dominate the sales of these goods until the 1990s. By 2002–03, market-determined prices prevailed in about 95 percent of all transactions involving both retail commodities and agricultural products and 87 percent of all transactions for producer goods.

By 2001, the number of products subject to government price fixing was quite small—13 commodities, 9 services, and 5 types of public utilities. For consumer goods, the main items still subject to state price fixing are salt and pharmaceuticals. The government also controls the prices of fuels such as gasoline, diesel fuel, aviation fuel, and natural gas; prices of electric power, water, and other utilities; railway freight rates; and prices of postal and telecommunication services (Lardy 2002, 26–27). Of course, government control or regulation of the prices of some of these commodities and services is commonplace in other market economies.

Even where government-administered prices have been retained, some are now fixed in a very different way from the past. In the 1980s, for example, the government maintained rigid and highly distorted prices for both crude oil and refined petroleum products. The State Price Commission fixed the domestic price of crude oil at about one-sixth the international level. But in the late 1980s the government began to ratchet up the domestic crude oil price, and a decade later, when convergence to the international price was largely complete, it adopted a formal policy of changing the fixed price of

---

1. The declining importance of state-fixed prices was also reflected in bureaucratic shifts. In August 1982 the State Price Commission, an independent agency reporting directly to the State Council, was downgraded to become the State Price Bureau within the State Planning Commission. The Planning Commission itself later became the State Development and Planning Commission and later the National Development and Reform Commission.

Table 1.1 Price formation in the reform era by commodity type, 1978–2003 (percent)

Year	Retail commodities			Agricultural commodities			Producer goods		
	Market	State-guided	State-fixed	Market	State-guided	State-fixed	Market	State-guided	State-fixed
1978	0	3.0	97.0	6.0	2.0	92.6	0	0	100.0
1985	34.0	19.0	47.0	40.0	23.0	37.0	13.0	23.0	64.0
1987	38.0	28.0	34.0	54.0	17.0	29.0	n.a.	n.a.	n.a.
1991	69.0	10.0	21.0	56.0	20.0	22.0	46.0	18.0	36.0
1992	n.a.	n.a.	5.6	n.a.	n.a.	10.3	n.a.	n.a.	19.8
1995	89.0	2.0	9.0	79.0	4.0	17.0	78.0	6.0	16.0
1999	95.0	1.0	4.0	83.0	7.0	9.0	86.0	4.0	10.0
2000	95.8	1.0	3.2	92.5	2.8	4.7	87.4	4.2	8.4
2001	96.0	1.3	2.7	93.9	3.4	2.7	87.6	2.9	9.5
2002	96.1	1.3	2.6	94.5	2.9	2.6	87.3	3.0	9.7
2003	95.6	1.4	3.0	96.5	1.6	1.9	87.4	2.7	9.9

n.a. = not available

Note: The numbers represent the percentage of transactions, measured by value, at the three types of prices.

Sources: Lardy (2002, 25); Beijing Normal University (2003); Li and Wang (2006, 104–106); Dougherty, Herd, and He (2007, 310).

crude oil on a monthly basis to keep it roughly in line with the international price. Shortly thereafter, in mid-2000, the government began a policy of ad hoc adjustments of the prices of refined petroleum products to keep them from diverging too much from international prices and in January 2009 adopted a formal policy of adjusting these prices whenever an index of global crude oil prices changes by more than 4 percent in any 22-day working period. But the government has typically not mechanically raised refined product prices by the full indicated amount when the international price of crude is above $80 per barrel (Lardy 2012, 107–108).[2] The link between domestic and international pricing was further tightened in 2013, when the National Development and Reform Commission (the successor to the State Planning Commission) began to change domestic prices of refined products every 10 working days and also eliminated the 4 percent threshold requirement previously necessary to trigger a price change.[3] Despite the government's continued control of prices of crude oil and refined petroleum products, it is fair to say that the highly distorted prices of the past have given way to a more market-oriented price regime.

Labor and Capital Markets

Prior to the late 1970s there was no market for labor in China. In urban areas the Ministry of Education or government labor bureaus at the local level assigned jobs to almost all potential workers when they left school at whatever level. In rural areas the population was organized into collective production units, either agricultural communes or collective enterprise units known as township and village enterprises. Labor mobility and labor turnover were nil. Spatial mobility was highly constrained; rural residents rarely were able to leave their home villages to seek alternative employment. In urban areas job assignment was lifetime. In 1978 in urban China, the combined number of workers who voluntarily left their jobs or were fired was less than 0.05 percent of the labor force. "A worker was 10 times more likely to retire and four times more likely to die on the job than to quit or be fired" (Naughton 2007, 181).

In urban employment there was also no wage flexibility and thus no linkage of wages to productivity. Beginning in the mid-1950s the government determined wage levels for nonagricultural jobs based on a complex classification system that considered occupation, region, industry, ownership (state versus collective), administrative level (central versus local), and size and technological level of the workplace. Factory workers were divided into 8 wage grades and administrative and managerial workers into 24 levels (Cai, Park,

---

2. The domestic price of crude oil is determined by a global index reflecting crude oil prices for North Sea Brent, Middle East benchmark Dubai, and Indonesian Cinta crude oils.

3. National Development and Reform Commission, "Notice on Further Perfecting the Price Formation Mechanism for Refined Petroleum Products," March 26, 2013. Available at www.ndrc. gov.cn (accessed on August 6, 2013).

and Zhao 2008, 169). Once a worker was assigned a wage grade or level based on these criteria, wage increases were strictly a function of seniority. Based on the number of employees of various types, the government specified the annual wage bill in the plan for each major state enterprise.

The emergence after 1978 of labor markets characterized by labor mobility and turnover, as well as a linkage between productivity and wages was very gradual. In rural areas by the early 1980s, farmers were allowed to start individual nonagricultural businesses. But initially government regulation still prevented farmers from leaving their home villages, giving rise to the phrase "leaving the land without leaving the village" (离土不离乡) (Cai, Park, and Zhao 2008, 170). In 1983 the government for the first time permitted rural residents to engage in long-distance transport and marketing of agricultural products, slightly expanding the opportunities for nonagricultural employment. A year later farmers who ran their own businesses or worked in enterprises in small towns were allowed to register as nonagricultural households in those towns. Also by the middle of the decade, the government allowed farmers to seek employment in township and village enterprises (TVEs) in nearby towns, facilitating the continued, rapid expansion of employment in TVEs.

As a result of these and other reforms, the number of migrant workers expanded, and a larger and larger share migrated over longer distances. The earliest official data show that in 1982 only 7 million residents, less than 1 percent of China's population, had migrated and were employed outside their native county.[4] This number rose to 22 million by 1990, 79 million by 2000, and 163 million in 2012. Including 99 million who migrated within their native county, the total number of migrant workers for 2012 was 263 million, a fifth of China's entire population. Of these, 99 million were employed in urban areas within their native county, 87 million were employed outside their native county but within their native provincial-level administrative unit, and 76 million had found employment outside their native province.[5] These migrants are predominantly, but not entirely, of rural origin. In 2000, for example, 15 percent of migrants who were employed outside their native province were of urban origin. These long-distance, city-origin migrants tend to be relatively highly educated (Liang and Ma 2004, 484). These data demonstrate that spatial mobility, both rural to urban and intraurban, increased dramatically during the reform era, thus coming a long way toward fulfilling one of the criteria for concluding that China has developed a vibrant labor market.

---

4. In the 1980s China had about 2,000 counties.

5. The underlying data in this paragraph are based on the Chinese census, which defines migrants as those who at the time of a census have been living for at least six months in a place other than where their household is registered. Data for 1982, 1990, and 2000 are from Liang and Ma (2004). Data for 2008 and 2012 are from National Bureau of Statistics of China, *Report on the 2012 National Migrant Worker Investigation Survey*, May 27, 2013. Available at www.stats.gov.cn (accessed on May 28, 2013).

In urban areas the state took steps to gradually phase out the system of permanent employment in state-owned enterprises beginning in the mid-1980s when it dropped the system of lifetime job assignment for factory workers and introduced five-year labor contracts for new employees. This gave enterprises the flexibility in deciding whom to hire. But the state, fearing urban unemployment, still imposed strict limits on firing workers during their contractual period. Contract workers accounted for only 4 percent of total employment when the system was first introduced, but by 1995 this had grown to 39 percent, presumably meaning that almost all new enterprise hires in this period were contract workers (Cai, Park, and Zhao 2008, 172).

But the real end of the permanent employment system in state-owned enterprises came in 1995 when, under the slogan "seizing the large and letting go of the small" (抓大放小), the government began a massive downsizing of state-owned companies. Thirty million state workers, almost two-fifths of the total, lost their jobs as small and medium-sized state-owned firms were closed or privatized. The share of job losses in the collective sector was even larger, resulting in a dramatic shrinkage in public sector employment (Naughton 2007, 184).

The last domain in which the state ended the system of labor assignment was for college graduates. As early as the 1980s, some college graduates began to seek employment through job fairs and direct negotiation with potential employers. By 1992 only about half of college graduates were assigned to jobs through the plan of the Ministry of Education, and by 2001 this share had fallen to less than 5 percent (Beijing Normal University 2003). In March 2002 the State Council endorsed a Ministry of Education proposal to formally end the system of job assignment for college graduates, replacing it with a market-driven recruitment process (Qu and Jiang 2006, 48).

The 1980s also marked the beginning of wage flexibility in urban production units. This began in the state sector when firms were allowed to retain part of their profits rather than remitting them in their entirety to the Ministry of Finance. One of the approved uses of these funds was to pay bonuses to workers. However, the government still regulated bonus amounts, and the traditional government pay scales based on occupation, region, and other factors still largely determined worker compensation. By mid-1992 the government gave state-owned enterprises more autonomy to set their internal wage structures, and in 1994–95 the Ministry of Labor issued new regulations allowing firms even more flexibility in setting wages, including the authority to allow wages to grow more rapidly than profitability as long as the increase in wages did not exceed improvements in labor productivity (Cai, Park, and Zhao 2008, 169, 171).

In addition, the state had no control of the earnings of self-employed workers and made little or no attempt to influence the wages of workers in registered private firms. These categories of employment, discussed in detail in chapter 3, grew slowly in the 1980s. By 1990, in urban and rural China combined there were only 72.75 million self-employed and private sector workers, accounting for 8 percent of the total labor force, including farmers (National Bureau of Statistics of China 2004, 122–23).[6] But, stimulated by reforms discussed in chapter 3, the number of private workers grew rapidly during the past two decades. By 2010, private sector employment, where wages were market determined, reached 281.5 million and accounted for almost two-fifths of total employment.[7] In addition, there were an estimated 136 million workers in urban limited-liability companies, shareholding limited companies, and foreign-funded enterprises where the majority or dominant owner was private and where wages also were market determined.[8] Thus in total, by 2010 about 415 million nonagricultural workers, or 55 percent of China's total labor force, were employed in units where the market determined wages.

While largely transformed, China's labor market falls short of being fully marketized because of continuing controls on place of residence through the household registration system. Introduced in 1955, this system impedes the movement of labor from rural to urban areas by restricting the ability of registered rural residents to attain the right to live permanently in urban areas. In 2012 China's urban population was 712 million (52.6 percent of the country's total population). Of these, only 480 million, 35.3 percent of China's population, had an urban residence (户口) permit.[9] Holding an urban residence permit not only conveys the right of permanent abode in urban areas but also the right to the full range of social benefits. Thus migrant workers living in cities generally are not eligible to participate in China's five social insurance schemes (pensions, health care, unemployment, workers' compensation, and maternity leave), and if they migrate with their families, their children usually cannot attend urban, publicly funded primary and secondary schools.[10]

In summary, China has transitioned from a system of job assignment with bureaucratically determined pay scales and lifetime employment to a far more

---

6. The total is the sum of 14.91 million and 6.14 million self-employed in rural and urban areas, respectively; 1.13 million and 0.57 million employed in registered private enterprises in rural and urban areas, respectively; and an estimated 50 million employed in township and village enterprises that were registered as individual businesses or private enterprises (Naughton 2007, 286).

7. The total is the sum of 25.41 million and 44.67 million self-employed in rural and urban areas, respectively; 33.47 million and 60.7 million employed in registered private enterprises in rural and urban areas, respectively; and 117.2 million in township and village enterprises that were registered as individual businesses or private enterprises (Zhang 2011, 137).

8. An estimate of this number for 2011, 131.3 million, is presented in chapter 3 and summarized in table 3.8. Using the same methodology for 2010 yields an estimate of 136 million.

9. "Reform to bridge the gap," *China Daily*, December 19, 2013. Available at www.chinadaily.com (accessed on December 15, 2013).

10. The share of migrant workers employed outside their native county who were covered by social insurance schemes in 2012 was as follows: pension, 14.3 percent; health, 16.9 percent; unemployment, 8.4 percent; workers' compensation, 24 percent; and maternity, 6.1 percent. National Bureau of Statistics of China, *Report on the 2012 National Migrant Worker Investigation Survey*, May 27, 2013. Available at www.stats.gov.cn (accessed on May 28, 2013).

market-driven system. Employment is now via voluntary contracts between workers and employers, wages are by and large market determined, and formal lifetime employment has disappeared. There is evidence of massive labor mobility both within and across counties as workers search for better employment opportunities than are available in their native place. However, labor mobility would be further enhanced by relaxing and eventually abolishing the household registration system.

Has the transformation toward market determination in the allocation of labor been matched by changes in China's allocation of capital? Critics charge that China's banks systematically misallocate investment resources, mainly by concentrating their lending on state-owned firms, and that stock and bond markets remain too small and flawed to improve the overall allocation of capital. This view became particularly salient during the global financial crisis, when it was alleged that most of China's massive increase in bank lending was allocated to state-owned enterprises (Fan and Hope 2013, 4).[11]

As will be laid out in detail in chapter 3, state-owned firms' share of output has steadily eroded since 1978. By 2011 state firms produced only 26 percent of industrial output, with virtually all the rest produced by private firms, including privately owned foreign firms. The transformation is even more dramatic in manufacturing, where state firms' share of output is only 20 percent (National Bureau of Statistics of China 2012b, 54, 503, 513).[12]

But in finance, the state remains totally dominant. The share of bank assets controlled by what the Chinese government categorizes as the five large-scale commercial banks (all listed and majority state owned) has gradually receded and is now just under half. But most of the balance of Chinese bank assets are held in smaller institutions in which the state is the majority or dominant owner. Among the domestic banks, only rural banks, city commercial banks, and perhaps Minsheng Bank, which together accounted for about 15 percent of the assets of the banking system in 2012, can realistically be considered private (Hamid and Tenev 2008, 455; China Banking Regulatory Commission 2013, 164). And the share of assets in the more than 100 foreign banks operating in China has been stuck at around 2 percent for more than a decade, the lowest share of foreign bank assets among a group of 21 emerging markets surveyed by the Bank for International Settlements (BIS).[13] China's banking

---

11. "In 2009 SOEs were the recipients of some 85 percent of bank loans associated with the government's 4 trillion yuan emergency stimulus package." Andrew Moody and Hu Haiyan, "Debate heats up on role of govt giants," *China Daily*, July 8, 2013, p. 13.

12. Industry consists of manufacturing, mining, and utilities. In 2011 the share of output of utilities (supply and production of water, electric power, and gas) and mining produced by state-owned firms was 90 percent and 52 percent, respectively, and utilities and mining accounted for 6 and 13 percent of the value of industrial output.

13. China, at 2 percent, was tied with Saudi Arabia and Israel as the country with the lowest foreign bank share of financial assets. The average of the foreign bank share for the 21 countries was 32 percent (Mihaljek 2010).

system is more state-centric than even India's (a country not covered by the BIS survey), where foreign banks have a 6 percent share of bank assets and domestic private banks control about a fifth of all bank assets.[14] The role of foreign firms in China in the insurance and securities industries is even more limited than in banking.[15]

State domination of China's banking system is reflected not only in the high share of state ownership of banks but also in the almost constant flow of senior bank executives to and from the People's Bank of China (China's central bank) and the China Banking Regulatory Commission. This flow may not only provide an additional channel for the state to influence banking decisions, it also raises questions about the ability of the central bank and the bank regulator to effectively supervise and regulate China's largest state-owned banks.[16] In contrast, in the United States retiring chairmen, vice chairmen, and governors of the Federal Reserve Board, the regulator of the most important US banks, sometimes assume positions in the financial sector, but it appears that in the post–World War II era none has ever assumed the leadership of a top US commercial bank.[17]

However, this study argues that focusing solely or largely on the role of China's banks in the allocation of credit fails to recognize the fundamental transformation that has occurred in the way capital is allocated in China. As already noted, at the outset of the reform process in 1978, almost all investment—95 percent—was financed through the state budget (National Bureau of Statistics of China 1982, 295, 395–96). Thus for all practical purposes there was no market for capital; investment funding was allocated through the planning process. But the share of investment financed through the budget

---

14. James Crabtree, Lionel Barber, and Victor Mallet, "Indian central bank chief pledges era of competition," *Financial Times*, November 19, 2013, p. 1.

15. With one exception, foreign participation in the insurance industry is restricted to joint ventures in which the foreign share is limited to 50 percent. These joint ventures account for only 2 percent of premium income, so roughly speaking the foreign share in the industry is 1 percent. Foreign participation in the securities industry is also restricted to joint ventures in which the cap was originally 33 percent but was raised to 49 percent in 2012. These joint ventures accounted for 2 percent of assets in the industry in 2012. Since few foreign securities firms were immediately able to increase their ownership shares in their joint ventures, roughly speaking the foreign share in the industry in 2012 was 0.7 percent.

16. For example, Shang Fulin was vice governor of the central bank from 1996 to 2000, then moved directly to become chairman of the Agricultural Bank of China. He subsequently served as chairman of the China Securities Regulatory Commission and now serves as chairman and party secretary of the China Banking Regulatory Commission. Guo Shuqing served as vice governor of the central bank from 1998 to 2005 and then moved directly to become chairman of the China Construction Bank. Zhou Xiaochuan, the current central bank governor, in 1998 moved directly from his previous post as vice governor of the People's Bank of China to become head of the China Construction Bank.

17. I am indebted to my colleagues Edwin Truman and David Stockton, who together served more than 50 years at the Federal Reserve Board, for this assessment.

declined precipitously in the first half of the 1980s as the government instituted reform measures, such as allowing firms to retain an increasing share of their profits rather than remitting them in their entirety to the state budget. As early as 1985 the share of investment financed through the state budget had fallen to less than one-fifth, by 1988 it was less than one-tenth, and by 1996 under 3 percent (National Bureau of Statistics of China 1997, 151).

The reduction in the role of budgetary funds as a source of capital was offset in part by an expansion in the role of bank credit, but more important was the expansion of retained earnings of enterprises. In the first half of the 1980s, bank credit financed between 12 and 14 percent of investment. From the second half of the 1980s through the mid-1990s, bank funding accounted for a fairly constant one-fifth of investment finance (National Bureau of Statistics of China 1997, 151). But the share financed from enterprise retained earnings jumped to 55 percent as early as 1984 and averaged over 50 percent from 1985 through 1990 (National Bureau of Statistics of China 1986, 365; 1991, 143).

The same trend can be examined from another angle—the sharp reduction in the government revenue share of GDP. The unified state budget, which includes central, provincial, and local fiscal revenues, dropped from 31 percent of GDP in 1978 to only 11 percent of GDP by 1996.[18] This is mostly explained by a drop in profit remissions by firms to the Ministry of Finance, from RMB57.2 billion in 1978, when these funds accounted for just over half of all government revenue, to only RMB4.9 billion in 1993, which was only 1 percent of government revenue. Profit remission was eliminated after 1993. To offset the decline in profits remitted to the Ministry of Finance, the government in 1985 introduced a corporate income tax levied on state, collective, and private enterprises. But the offset was very partial; in 1996 the corporate income tax accounted for only 13 percent of government revenues (National Bureau of Statistics of China 2001b, 246–48).

The key point to emerge from this analysis is that once reform began China transitioned quickly from a system in which almost all investment funds were allocated by the government bureaucrats who compiled the state investment plan to one in which most investment was financed from the retained earnings of enterprises, with lesser amounts financed by bank credit. Taken in conjunction with the reform of prices analyzed earlier, this means that starting in the mid-1980s retained earnings financed most investment in an environment in which prices increasingly reflected scarcity values as established in markets. The most productive firms had larger retained earnings and therefore were able to grow more quickly by using these earnings to finance expansion. The result was an improvement in the allocation of capital and much faster economic growth than had been achieved when bureaucrats determined the allocation of investment funds.

---

18. These figures are exclusive of what are known as extrabudgetary revenues, which grew in importance between 1978 and 1996.

Despite this transformation, the market for capital and some other factors of production remains distorted. Most importantly, the government still controls the interest rates that banks can pay on deposits and the price of foreign exchange. This control has led to a significant degree of financial repression, particularly in the Hu Jintao-Wen Jiabao era (Lardy 2012). In addition, as noted earlier, the government continues to influence the prices of key energy products, such as oil, gas, and electricity, as well as the price of land for industrial uses. Since liberalization of product markets and to a lesser extent the labor market has outpaced the liberalization of the markets for capital, Yiping Huang has characterized China's market reforms as asymmetric. He estimates that the distortions resulting from the failure of the government to fully liberalize the markets for capital, land, and energy, as well as environmental cost distortions and the ability of employers to avoid making social insurance contributions for migrant workers, amounted to as much as 7 percent of GDP in 2008. The underpricing of capital, as a result of government policies leading to financial repression, was the largest of the five distortions (Huang 2010, 77–79). These distortions should be thought of as a subsidy to producers, the costs of which are borne by owners of the factors of production, frequently households. This is particularly the case for capital, which largely originates from household savings.

But what if the markets determining prices are not competitive? Then prices likely would not reflect scarcity values, and the increased financing of investment from retained earnings rather than government budget allocations might not improve the allocation of capital. It is therefore important to ask whether China's markets are in fact competitive.

Competition

The key characteristic of a market economy is competition. Even if product prices are freely determined by supply and demand, there is a flexible labor market, investment is financed mostly with retained earnings, and the remaining distortions due to asymmetric price liberalization are eliminated, the efficiency gains of a market economy will not be fully realized if there is insufficient competition. The most common reason for insufficient competition is the presence of a monopolistic or oligopolistic market structure—when a single firm or a small number of firms dominate a single product market and thus are in a position to raise prices above the marginal cost of production, in the process earning supranormal profits. In that case a system in which investment is financed primarily from retained earnings will not necessarily lead to an allocation of capital that is more efficient than that achieved under China's pre-1978 system of economic planning.

One of the most common critiques of state capitalism in China is that in many sectors state-owned enterprises have substantial market power, allowing them to dictate prices and earn above-normal profits (US-China Economic and Security Review Commission 2011, 42). Competition, according to this critique, is inhibited either outright by state regulations prohibiting the entry of private firms into these sectors or by a lack of access to bank credit and other sources of finance by potential private competitors, which effectively protects incumbent state-owned firms, particularly in more capital-intensive industries. Even though, as will be shown in chapters 2 and 3, the share of output produced by state firms in most sectors has shrunk dramatically, critics charge that "though fewer in number, today's SOEs are more powerful than ever."[19] Those who argue that China is pursuing a model of state capitalism cite the growing number of Chinese state firms that are included in lists of the largest global companies in support of this "fewer but more powerful" hypothesis (US-China Economic and Security Review Commission 2012, 78–79). Indeed, only one Chinese company was included in the Fortune Global 500 in 1990, but 70 Chinese companies made the list by 2012. All but four of these were state companies, and 42 of them were firms under the administration of the State-owned Assets Supervision and Administration Commission of the State Council.[20]

Two types of evidence undermine the argument that state firms generally have substantial market power, are more powerful than ever, and thus can set prices in order to earn supranormal profits. First, even in sectors closely linked to heavy industry, where one might expect a handful of very large state firms to dominate, the opposite is true. For example, in 2011 there were 880 state-controlled firms in coal mining, 109 in ferrous metal ore mining and processing, 264 in nonferrous metal ores mining and processing, 312 in steel production, and so forth (National Bureau of Statistics of China 2012b, 512).[21] Given the large number of state players in most sectors, it is difficult to imagine that these firms can exercise substantial market power. The exceptions, such as telecommunications, are analyzed later in this chapter.

Even if it were possible for such a large number of state firms to collude to restrict production and raise prices or there were a central government agency or party unit performing this function, in each of these industries there is an even larger number of private firms. In 2011 in the coal mining industry there were 4,420 private firms, in ferrous metal ores 2,536 private firms, in nonferrous metal ores 1,058 private firms, and in steel 4,246 private firms (National Bureau of Statistics of China 2012b, 522). And as will be shown in chapter 3, these private firms control a substantial share of output in each of these indus-

---

19. "The state advances," *Economist*, October 6, 2012, p. 53.

20. Hu Angang, "State enterprises are a bellwether of China's economic rise," *Red Flag Manuscripts* 2012, no. 19. Available at www.qstheory.cn/hqwg/2012/201219/201210/t20121011_185632.htm (accessed on September 18, 2013).

21. As explained in chapter 3, there are relatively few traditional state-owned enterprises remaining in China; most have been corporatized. The data on state-controlled firms include traditional state-owned enterprises and corporatized firms in which the state is the dominant or majority shareholder. See chapter 3 for details.

tries, further undermining the possibility of state firms engaging in monopolistic or oligopolistic pricing practices.

The hypothesis that in general state firms cannot exercise market power is confirmed by a more systematic analysis of the degree of concentration in production in various industries. This analytical approach looks at industrial concentration ratios, typically the share of output controlled by the largest four or eight firms in an industry. Market power is more likely to exist when a small number of firms control a large share of output since this could give rise to collusion in price setting among the big players, with minor producers following the pricing of the market leaders. Alternatively, the potential for a small number of firms to exercise market power can be measured by the Herfindahl-Hirschman index, a measure of concentration that gives more weight to larger firms.

It is important to recognize that early in the reform era the Chinese economy was characterized by an extraordinarily low degree of industrial concentration, even when examined at a highly disaggregated level. In 1985 the eight largest firms contributed more than 70 percent of output in only 6.5 percent of 523 industrial subsectors; nearly three-fourths of Chinese subsectors had eight-firm concentration ratios of 40 percent or less. In contrast, in Russia in 1989 the four largest firms accounted for at least 70 percent of output in nearly half of 406 industrial subsectors (Rawski 2011, 332). Thus the industrial sector in China early in the reform era was significantly less concentrated than most observers would expect.

Even though the state has promoted consolidation among its manufacturing firms in several sectors over the past 30 years, in some critical industries concentration has actually declined since the mid-1980s. In steel, for example, the top eight steel firms produced 49 percent of output in 1985 and 44 percent in 2010.[22]

The same two points—that reform began with a relatively low degree of industrial concentration and that concentration has fallen since—emerge from an Organization for Economic Cooperation and Development (OECD) working paper (Conway et al. 2010, 13) and a formal OECD (2010) study, which both examined industrial concentration in China in 1988 and 2007. Assessed on the basis of the Herfindahl-Hirschman index, the authors of the working paper judged that in 1988 production was highly concentrated in only 15 percent of almost 600 industrial subsectors, a share that fell to a tiny 6 percent in 2007.[23] In 1988 73 percent of the subsectors were judged not concentrated, a share that rose to 81 percent in 2007. The OECD study also disaggregated these figures based on the extent of state ownership. Interestingly, the number

---

22. Data for 1985 are from Rawski (2011, 332) and for 2010 are from BOC International, *2012 Steel Industry Outlook*, February 1, 2012. Available at www.bocigroup.com (accessed on June 6, 2013).

23. Subsectors were rated as highly concentrated if the Herfindahl-Hirschman index was greater than 0.25, concentrated if the index was between 0.15 and 0.25, and not concentrated if the index was less than 0.15.

of subsectors where state firms accounted for more than half of output and where concentration also was judged to be highly concentrated fell from 50 in 1988 to only 9, less than 2 percent of the subsectors, in 2007.

It once was argued that China's economy has been characterized by a considerable degree of provincial economic autarky as a result of local protection combined with weak institutional and physical infrastructure to support interprovincial trade (Young 2000). As a result, this argument went, China did not have an integrated national market but rather about 30 semiautonomous provincial-level markets. Thus the lack of regional economic integration raised the possibility that state firms in some sectors in some localities could exercise market power and raise their prices above competitive levels despite a relatively large number of state and private companies on a national basis. In short, a four- or eight-firm concentration ratio calculated at the provincial level would be substantially higher than the national concentration ratio, suggesting that some firms could exercise substantial power in local autarkic markets.

Empirical evidence, however, does not support this view. Barry Naughton's path-breaking work on domestic trade flows led him to conclude that "interprovincial trade is large, both relative to GDP and relative to foreign trade. The picture of Chinese provinces as relatively autarkic units, separated from each other, though perhaps open to foreign trade, is clearly false" (Naughton 2003, 209). An examination of data on interprovincial flows of railway freight haulage and other substantial evidence of cross-regional competition reaches a similar conclusion (Brandt, Rawski, and Sutton 2008, 575–76).

The second type of evidence supporting the view that state firms lack substantial price-setting power is based on an analysis of firm profit margins rather than indicators of the degree of concentration of production in various industries. Firms with market power presumably would charge higher prices than firms in competitive markets and thus earn higher profit margins than firms in more competitive sectors. The simplest way to test whether state firms as a group have substantial market power is thus to look at reported profits divided by sales revenues for firms with different types of ownership. As shown in figure 1.1, in manufacturing the sales margins of state firms since the mid-1980s have been somewhat more volatile than those of nonstate firms, with a larger decline at the time of the Asian financial crisis of 1997–98 that was then offset by a sharp increase in margins through the mid-2000s. But average profit margins for state and nonstate enterprises from 1985 through 2010 were almost the same, 5.8 percent for state firms and 5.6 percent for nonstate firms. And the profit margins of the two types of firms are virtually indistinguishable in the past few years. Thus there is no evidence either that state firms as a group have long had market power that boosts their profitability relative to firms with other types of ownership or that state firms have become more powerful in recent years.

Of course, if one focuses on a subsector where a few state firms dominate, there is strong evidence of market power leading to supranormal profits for at least a few firms. In the petroleum sector, for example, the average profit

Figure 1.1 Profit margins in Chinese industry by ownership, 1985–2013

total profit as a share of sales revenue

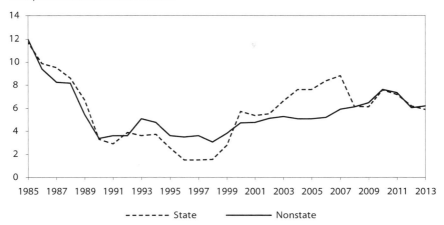

------- State   ———— Nonstate

Note: Total profits are earnings before corporate income tax. The earnings and revenue for nonstate industrial enterprises are calculated as the difference between the total for all industrial enterprises and the total for all state-controlled industrial enterprises. These data are for above-scale firms and thus only include firms with revenue greater than RMB5 million between 1998 and 2011. After 2011, the threshold was raised to RMB20 million. Prior to 1991, gross output value is used as a substitute for sales revenue.

Sources: National Bureau of Statistics of China (1991, 391; 1992, 420–21; 2013c, 478–79); ISI Emerging Markets, CEIC Database.

margin of the listed China National Offshore Oil Corporation (CNOOC) from 2004 through 2012 was an astounding 44 percent, six times the average of state industrial companies in the same period. PetroChina from 2004 through 2007 also had extraordinarily high profit margins, averaging about 30 percent, but the firm's profit margin has eroded steadily since and by 2012 stood at only 7.6 percent, above the 5.8 percent average for state-owned industrial firms but not in the same league as CNOOC.[24] Sinopec's performance is substantially weaker, with average profit margins in 2004–12 of only 6.5 percent. The firm's margins in 2012 were only 3.3 percent, well below the average for state-owned industrial firms.

The finding that only CNOOC enjoys super-elevated profits is somewhat surprising given that there has been very little entry by private firms in the oil sector so that state-owned firms still control more than 90 percent of production of crude oil and about two-thirds of petroleum refining (see table 3.6).

---

24. The slide in PetroChina's profitability coincides with the period when Jiang Jiemin served as chairman. Jiang was detained on corruption charges shortly after he stepped down as chairman in 2013. At least one financial analysis has attributed part of the slide in PetroChina's profitability to an understatement of revenue, funds that were drained off by Jiang and his associates, a charge the company has denied. Simon Rabinovitch, "Probe points to shake-up for PetroChina," *Financial Times*, September 18, 2013, p. 15.

CNOOC earns supranormal profits for at least three reasons. First, CNOOC was created in 1982 as practically a startup firm and thus has a much leaner corporate structure.[25] In contrast, Sinopec was formed in 1983 from the merger of 39 large state-owned companies controlled by the Ministries of Petroleum, Chemicals, and Textiles. The China National Petroleum Corporation (CNPC), the parent of the listed PetroChina, was formed when it replaced the Ministry of Petroleum in 1998.[26] Thus Sinopec and PetroChina each exhibit the major legacy burdens of state-owned enterprises: massive numbers of staff, old technology and equipment, and bureaucratic inertia built up over the decades.[27]

Second, CNOOC is less disadvantaged than the other major state oil companies by state price policy. For example, it is not in the oil refining business, where state control of refined product prices periodically has led to significant financial losses for firms like Sinopec, China's largest oil refiner (Lardy 2012, 107–109). Similarly, price controls erode the profits of PetroChina, China's biggest gas supplier. It imports natural gas at a price determined in the global market, but because domestic gas prices are controlled, it makes a loss of one renminbi on every cubic meter of imports.[28] CNOOC imports gas but sells it to the CNOOC Gas and Power Group at market price, insulating CNOOC from losses in this business.[29]

Third, in contrast with CNOOC, which is heavily concentrated in upstream gas businesses, PetroChina and Sinopec are more integrated oil companies with substantial downstream activities, for example in the chemical industry. But there has been massive entry of private firms in the chemical industry, reflected in a decline in the share of output produced by state firms to under a fifth by 2011. In short, a significant part of the business activity of both PetroChina and Sinopec is in very competitive segments of the petrochemical industry. The combined effect of these three factors is that among the big state oil companies only CNOOC is able to earn monopoly-like profits. CNOOC is successful not only compared with its domestic peers but also internationally.

---

25. CNOOC absorbed a single previously existing company—the China National Oil and Gas Exploration and Development Corporation, which had been a unit of the Ministry of Petroleum Industry (Lieberthal and Oksenberg 1988, 86). ·

26. Sinopec Group and its listed arm, Sinopec Corp., technically are of relatively recent origin since they were not incorporated until 1998 and 2000, respectively. But Sinopec Group grew out of the China Petrochemical Corporation.

27. Julia Grindell and Robert Armstrong, "Lex in depth: CNOOC," *Financial Times*, November 15, 2012, p. 6.

28. "China Natural Gas," *Financial Times*, July 3, 2013, p. 12. The firm's losses on imported natural gas in 2012 were RMB41.9 billion. Without these losses, PetroChina's reported after-tax profits in 2012 would have been 40 percent higher. *PetroChina Limited 2012 Annual Report*, pp. 28, 160. Available at www.petrochina.com.cn (accessed on September 25, 2013).

29. CNOOC Gas and Power Group appears to be a direct subsidiary of the CNOOC Group, the holding company that has a 64.45 percent stake in CNOOC Limited, the formal name of the listed company.

Figure 1.2 Profit margins of state nonfinancial corporations, 2000–2013

total profit as a share of sales revenue

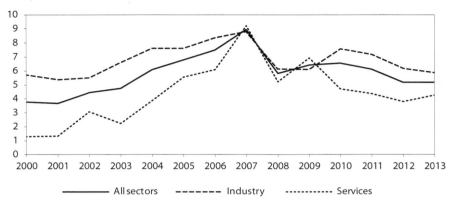

Note: Total profits are earnings before corporate income tax. The earnings and revenue for services are calculated as the difference between the total for all state-owned enterprises and the total for industrial state-owned enterprises. Services includes construction.

Sources: National Bureau of Statistics of China (2013c, 478–79); Ministry of Finance, www.mof.gov.cn (accessed on March 28, 2014); ISI Emerging Markets, CEIC Database.

On the metrics of net income per barrel of petroleum equivalent produced and return on equity, CNOOC ranks a tenth above Chevron. The price of CNOOC stock has risen more than 1,000 percent over the decade, five times more than that of ExxonMobil.[30]

We can expand the analysis of the relative profit margins of state and private firms beyond the industrial sector by looking at the profit margins of all state nonfinancial firms, including firms both in industry and in services. This is important for two reasons. First, state service-sector firms account for a growing share of profits of state nonfinancial firms, rising from 15 percent in 2000 to 31 percent by 2012.[31] Second, some key service sectors, such as telecommunications, are dominated by a handful of state firms that might well have above-average profit margins due to their oligopolistic market structures. Similarly, the state has a complete monopoly in the case of rail transport, and the state-owned China Ocean Shipping Company (COSCO) and China Shipping Group have a near duopoly in ocean shipping. Figure 1.2 shows the profitability of the entire universe of state nonfinancial firms for the period 2000 (the first year for which data are available) through 2013, as well as prof-

---

30. Julia Grindell and Robert Armstrong, "Lex in depth: CNOOC," *Financial Times*, November 15, 2012, p. 6.

31. The share of profits in state service firms is estimated by subtracting profits of state industrial firms from the profits of all state nonfinancial enterprises. The underlying data for the calculation are available at www.stats.gov.cn and www.mof.gov.cn (accessed on July 17, 2014).

itability for state industrial and state services firms. The average profit margin for all state nonfinancial firms in this period was 5.8 percent, less than the 6.8 percent profit margin for state industrial firms over the same period. The disaggregated data for industrial and services firms clearly show that, except for 2007–09, the profitability of state industrial firms is well above that of state service sector firms. Thus the hypothesis that state nonfinancial firms in the service sector as a group have market power that allows them to earn unusually high profits is rejected.

But again a drill-down to a component of services dominated by a few state firms reveals some evidence of market power. The best example is China Mobile. This firm assumed the wireless business of China Telecom, which had been China's monopolist telecommunication company until it was broken up in 1999. China Mobile benefited from its position as the monopolist in the wireless space during a decade of extraordinary rapid growth of wireless services, vaulting it to the position of the world's largest wireless service provider. Although China Telecom regained a wireless license in 2008, China Mobile remains dominant in mobile telephone service with about 800 million subscribers. Like CNOOC, China Mobile has superelevated profit margins—averaging 33 percent in 2004–12. But as in the oil sector, the other large state telecom players are far less profitable. The profit margins of China Unicom and China Telecom in 2004–07 both averaged about 20 percent, but their margins have fallen in recent years to 3.8 percent and 7.0 percent, respectively. China Telecom's profits are dragged down by its mandate to provide wired service to the entire domestic market. But this has been a market with relatively slow growth compared with wireless. So even in an important sector with almost complete state control, only one of the three players has high profit margins.

What about state firms in China's financial sector? Do they exercise market power that allows them to earn supranormal profits? The analysis below focuses on banking. Although nonbank financial institutions in China have expanded in the last decade or so, assets in the banking system are still many times larger than the combined assets of insurance companies, securities firms, asset management companies, and other nonbank financial institutions.[32]

The first thing to note is that concentration in the banking sector has been falling steadily throughout the reform period, suggesting strongly that if the largest banks once had market power it has eroded. China initially had a monobank system in which the People's Bank of China served simultaneously as the central bank and the only commercial bank. At the outset of reform, there also was a network of rural credit cooperatives to serve rural areas, but the assets of this network were dwarfed by the People's Bank. But early in the reform period, government policy led to the emergence of a number of new

---

32. At the end of 2011, assets in the banking system were RMB113.3 trillion, assets of all securities firms totaled RMB1.6 trillion, and the combined assets of the five largest insurance companies (a highly concentrated industry) were RMB5.6 trillion (China Banking Society 2012, 419, 482, 491–99).

banks. In 1979 the government recreated the Agriculture Bank of China, which had been abolished in 1965; separated the Bank of China from the People's Bank; and in 1980 converted the Construction Bank from a payments agency under the Ministry of Finance to a real bank, able to take deposits and make loans. More importantly, in 1984 the State Council created a central bank by designating the People's Bank of China as the central bank and establishing the Industrial and Commercial Bank to take over the deposit taking and lending functions of the People's Bank (Lardy 1998, 62–63). But by the mid-1980s, China still had a highly concentrated banking system, with the four state-owned banks accounting for 99 percent of all bank assets and about 90 percent of the combined assets of banks and rural credit cooperatives (Lardy 1998, 224).[33]

Competition in the banking system early in the reform era was inhibited not only by the high degree of bank concentration, but also by restrictions on the geographies and types of banking services each bank could provide. For this reason, within China the four state-owned banks in the 1980s were invariably referred to as "specialized banks" (专业银行). Lending to support agriculture and rural industrial and commercial enterprises was the exclusive domain of the network of rural credit cooperatives and the Agricultural Bank; state enterprises borrowed mostly from the Industrial and Commercial Bank of China; the Construction Bank was a principal source of funds for new investment projects; and the Bank of China had a monopoly to carry out all types of foreign exchange transactions (Lardy 1998, 64–65).

Competition in banking increased beginning in the mid-1980s as a result of both the creation of a number of new banks and the gradual expansion of the scope of business of the existing specialized banks. The government authorized the creation of about a dozen new national joint stock banks beginning in the mid-1980s and continuing in the 1990s. Perhaps the most famous of these is China Minsheng Bank, authorized in 1995. Its initial 59 shareholders were almost entirely private enterprises, making the bank China's first private shareholding bank. The government began licensing urban credit cooperatives starting in 1986, and by 1994 their numbers had expanded to more than 5,200. Beginning in the mid-1990s in most cities networks of these cooperatives merged to form urban cooperative banks. Later these institutions became known as city commercial banks, the best known of which are Bank of Shanghai and Bank of Beijing. By 2011 China had some 500 banks, including 5 large-scale commercial banks, 3 policy banks, 12 shareholding banks, 144 city commercial banks, 212 rural commercial banks, 190 rural cooperative banks, 40 foreign banks (with 253 branches and subsidiaries) established as legal entities in China, and 95 foreign bank branches, as well as 2,265 rural credit cooperatives (China Banking Society 2012, 517–18).

The transformation of the banking sector since the mid-1980s also is reflected in a dramatic decline in concentration. By 2011 the original four large

33. Data are for 1986.

state-owned banks accounted for only 44 percent of the assets of the banking system (including credit cooperatives), slightly less than half the share they controlled in the mid-1980s. Including the Bank of Communications, which with the original four large banks make up the universe that the Chinese now identify as the five large-scale commercial banks, boosts this ratio to 48 percent (China Banking Society 2012, 419, 423–427). This is exactly equal to the concentration ratio for the top five banks in the United States in 2011.[34] Moreover, bank concentration is rising in the United States since the financial crisis, whereas it has been falling in China for decades. If judged only on the criterion of concentration, within a few years China is likely to have a more competitive banking system than the United States.

Competition in the banking sector also increased as the government eased regulatory barriers. The best example is the erosion of the Bank of China's initial monopoly on all types of businesses involving foreign currency. Banks other than the Bank of China were authorized to conduct foreign exchange business in their branches located in the four special economic zones on China's southeast coast as early as 1985. By the end of 1992 the government had authorized more than 1,000 domestic branch banks and 145 nonbank financial institutions to carry out foreign exchange business. Thus the Bank of China gradually lost its monopolies on offering deposits and loans denominated in foreign currency, the settlement of foreign trade transactions, and other types of foreign exchange transactions. By 1996, Bank of China's share of the foreign trade settlement business had fallen to two-fifths (Lardy 1998, 65).

How does the return on assets in China's banking system, which is heavily state dominated, stack up against the return on assets in other national banking systems? Are returns relatively elevated, suggesting either that banks benefit from the remaining government controls on interest rates that banks can pay on deposits or that declining concentration in the banking industry and the easing of some regulatory barriers have not prevented the exercise of market power in the state-dominated banking system? The short answer is that the average return on assets in China's banking system is very close to returns of banking systems in other Asian countries. The average return on bank assets in China in 2012 was 1.26 percent,[35] above returns in India (1.05 percent) and Singapore (1.21 percent) but below those in Malaysia (1.31 percent), Hong Kong (1.38 percent), Thailand (1.38 percent), and the Philippines (1.74 percent) (IMF 2013a, 17). Returns in China were higher than the 0.97 percent in the United States in 2012, but profitability in US banks was badly depressed by the global financial crisis, and profit recovery was still under way in 2012. By the

---

34. Audrey Redler, "International Comparison of Banking Sectors," European Banking Federation, March 18, 2014. Available at www.ebf-fbe.eu (accessed on June 10, 2013).

35. This is the number reported by the International Monetary Fund and is used in the text since the IMF is the source for the return on assets of banks in other Asian countries. The Chinese regulator reports that the return on bank assets in 2012 was 1.2 percent (China Banking Regulatory Commission 2013, 168).

first quarter of 2013, return on assets of the roughly 7,000 banks supervised by the US Federal Deposit Insurance Corporation had risen to 1.12 percent.[36] In short, it does not appear that returns in the Chinese banking system, which is still heavily state dominated, are now higher than comparator countries. For the five-year period before the global crisis (2002–07), the average return on assets for Chinese banks was 0.78 percent, which was actually well below the returns in banking systems in all the comparator Asian countries just listed (IMF 2013a). This difference was due largely to the protracted banking cleanup process during the 2000s, which gradually addressed the huge volume of nonperforming loans created in China in the 1990s.

In short, it is difficult to make the case that state banks have substantial market power that elevates profitability. Indeed, the opposite seems to be the case. State-owned banks may have had substantial potential market power in the early years of reform, when a handful of these institutions controlled almost all bank assets. However, during this era the central bank tightly controlled both deposit and lending rates, limiting the ability of banks to exercise potential market power. More obviously, state-owned banks were under considerable pressure from the government to support money-losing state-owned enterprises, which led to the insolvency of these banks rather than to excess profits (Lardy 1998, 119). But since then, the number of banks has expanded dramatically, resulting in a reduction by half in the degree of concentration. Moreover, the share of bank assets controlled by the five largest Chinese banks is identical to the five-firm concentration ratio in the United States, a fairly competitive banking system. Finally, return on assets in China's banking system in recent years is about the same as other Asian comparator countries.

Another critique of state firms is that many receive subsidies that allow them to escape the discipline the market normally imposes on persistently money-losing firms—a takeover by another firm via merger and acquisition or exit via bankruptcy. Such protection could undermine the competitive nature of the market and in particular could impose a substantial hurdle for private firms seeking to gain market share in subsectors in which state firms are dominant. State firms, even if less efficient than private firms, could sell their output below cost, confident that subsidies would be forthcoming to cover their losses.

The assertion that pervasive subsidies to state firms undermine the competitive character of markets in China is difficult to evaluate since subsidies can be channeled by various routes, few of them fully transparent. As shown in table 1.2, the share of state industrial firms running in the red rose from about a quarter at the beginning of the 1990s to about two-fifths by the end of the decade. The financial losses of these firms were substantial, averaging almost 1.5 percent of GDP annually over the course of the decade. Harry Broadman estimated the annual subsidies to state industrial and service enterprises in 1990–93 at about 9 to 10 percent of GDP annually. His estimate takes

---

36. Gretchen Morgenson, "Quantity Over Quality in Bank Profits," *New York Times*, June 2, 2013, Business section, p. 1.

Table 1.2 Losses of state industrial firms, 1978–2012

Year	Share of enterprises losing money (percent)	Total losses (percent of GDP)	Total losses (percent of sales revenue)
1978	n.a.	1.1	n.a.
1980	19.2	0.8	n.a.
1985	9.6	0.4	0.5
1986	13.1	0.5	0.8
1987	13.0	0.5	0.7
1988	10.9	0.5	0.8
1989	16.0	1.1	1.6
1990	27.6	2.9	3.0
1991	25.8	1.7	2.6
1992	23.4	1.4	2.7
1993	30.3	1.3	2.0
1994	n.a.	1.0	2.2
1995	33.5	1.1	2.5
1996	33.6	1.1	2.9
1997	38.2	1.1	3.0
1998	40.6	1.4	3.4
1999	39.2	1.1	2.7
2000	34.1	0.7	1.7
2001	36.0	0.7	1.7
2002	36.1	0.6	1.4
2003	35.2	0.5	1.2
2004	37.4	0.5	1.2
2005	35.5	0.6	1.3
2006	31.9	0.5	1.2
2007	25.8	0.3	0.7
2008	27.4	1.1	2.3
2009	26.3	0.5	1.0
2010	21.4	0.3	0.6
2011	20.6	0.5	1.0
2012	24.5	0.6	1.3

n.a. = not available

Sources: Lardy (1998, 35); National Bureau of Statistics of China (2013b, 126); ISI Emerging Markets, CEIC Database.

into account explicit subsidies provided through the state budget to unprofit-able enterprises averaging 2.3 percent of GDP, partly due to policy factors such as sales prices set below cost, most obviously for grain sold in urban areas, implicit fiscal subsidies in the form of interest rate subsidies on loans, as well as quasi-fiscal subsidies in the form of low-cost policy loans (Broadman 1995, 13–15).

But, since the downsizing of the state sector begun under Premier Zhu Rongji in the second half of the 1990s, the share of state-owned industrial enterprises losing money has declined, and their losses have been much smaller, averaging 0.6 percent of GDP in the first decade of the 2000s and slightly less than that in 2010–12 (National Bureau of Statistics of China 2012a, 130). Government subsidies of these losses have dropped dramatically for two reasons. First, explicit subsidies through the budget fell to an annual average of only 0.5 percent of GDP in the 2001–10 decade (Anderson 2012, 9). Second, bank policy lending financed by funds provided by the central bank at low interest rates was phased out.

Moreover, in the past decade or so a large share of state industrial firms' losses appear to be transitory and self-financed rather than chronic, as was the case with a subset of state firms in the 1990s. In short, as market conditions vary in different sectors, firms that lose money in one year may return to profitability the next, while other firms move in the opposite direction. In this respect China's state-owned firms may not be very different from firms in market economies. Jon Anderson examined the universe of 5,000 companies listed on the New York Stock Exchange and NASDAQ for the period 2003–07. This group of firms relative to the size of the US economy is similar to that of state enterprises relative to the size of the Chinese economy. He found that in any given year an average of 28 percent of the US listed firms lost money in an amount that aggregated to an average of about 1 percent of US GDP. This picture was not so different from that of China in the same period when, on average and over the same years, 34 percent of state-owned firms lost money in any given year in an amount that aggregated to 0.5 percent of GDP (Anderson 2012, 10).

If government subsidies to corporations were a sufficient criterion to label a country's economic system as "state capitalist," many market economies would qualify. The US federal government extends subsidies directly through, for example, payments to farmers in a variety of programs that cost US taxpayers about $25 billion annually; indirectly through what are called tax expenditures, in effect tax breaks for special interests such as the oil and gas industry; and also indirectly through high tariffs. The best examples of the latter subsidies are the 25 percent tariff on imported pickup trucks, a tariff that makes pickups the most profitable segment for US auto makers, and tariff rate quotas on sugar imports, which mean that US consumers pay about three times the world price for sugar, amounting to an extra $3.5 billion a year.[37]

US state and local governments also provide subsidies to retain and attract businesses. In what appears to be the first major effort to tally state and local government subsidies, the *New York Times* documented that these annual subsidies total about $80 billion but noted that the incentives are awarded by "thousands of government agencies and officials and many do not know

---

37. "That Sickening Sugar Subsidy," Bloomberg View Editorials, March 13, 2013. Available at www.bloomberg.com (accessed on December 18, 2013). Froma Harrop, "US sugar subsidies a sour deal for taxpayers," *News and Observer*, October 24, 2013. Available at www.newsobserver.com (accessed on December 18, 2013).

the value of all their awards." Thus the cost of these subsidies "is certainly far higher." The investigative reporting showed Texas, at $19 billion annually, awarded the most subsidies of any state and that 48 companies had received more than $100 million in state grants since 2007.[38]

A prominent example of state subsidies to a private company in the United States occurred when the Boeing Corporation announced in 2013 that it would consider producing its critical, next-generation wide-body 777X aircraft in a location other than Washington State, where the firm's first wide-body 747 plane came off the Everett, Washington, assembly line in 1968. The announcement set off a frenzied bidding war in which ultimately 22 states, offering tens of billions of dollars in subsidies, sought to attract a new Boeing assembly facility and the thousands of associated jobs. In the end the firm decided to use its existing Everett facility, in part because the state of Washington offered $8.7 billion in subsidies, reportedly the largest state subsidy ever offered to a single corporation.[39]

Finally, in evaluating the degree of competition in China's domestic market, one should look at two additional factors: imports and the domestic sales of foreign affiliates operating in China. Even a market with a single domestic monopolistic producer could be competitive if either the good or service the monopolist produces is tradable and barriers to imports are low or the barriers to foreign direct investment are modest. If the sole domestic producer tries to raise prices, consumers will increase their purchases of the good or service produced abroad. Or competition can be added to the domestic market if foreign firms become significant local producers and sell a portion of their output on the domestic market. In either case the domestic monopolist that raised its prices would lose market share and potentially eventually fail if it continued to maintain an elevated price.

As already noted, as reform was getting under way, China for all practical purposes was an autarkic economy, with all foreign trade monopolized by a handful of state-owned import and export companies, an average import tariff rate of 56 percent, and myriad import quotas and import licensing requirements. As a result, goods imports were only 5 percent of GDP. But by the mid-1980s this share jumped to 14 percent. As China cut tariffs and reduced other import barriers as part of its negotiations to join the World Trade Organization, the ratio of imports to GDP continued to rise, breaching 20 percent in 2002. Despite the considerable slowing of world trade during and in the wake of the global financial crisis, China's imports continued to grow strongly, reaching

---

38. Louise Story, "As Companies Seek Tax Deals, Governments Pay High Price," *New York Times*, December 1, 2012; Louise Story, "Lines Blur as Texas Gives Industries a Bonanza," *New York Times*, December 2, 2012; Louise Story, "Michigan Town Woos Hollywood but Ends Up with a Bit Part," *New York Times*, December 3, 2012. Available at www.nytimes.com (accessed on December 18, 2013).

39. Steven Greenhouse, "Boeing Workers Approve 8-Year Contract Extension," *New York Times*, January 5, 2014, p. 15. Reid Wilson, "States competing for 777X jobs project," *Washington Post*, November 30, 2013. Available at www.washingtonpost.com (accessed on January 8, 2014).

$1.8 trillion by 2012, up 80 percent over the level of 2009 and equivalent to 22 percent of GDP (National Bureau of Statistics of China 2012a, 20, 63). The ratio of imports to GDP is now considerably higher in China than in the United States and provides substantial additional competition in the domestic market.[40]

A second way that foreign firms add competition to the domestic market is via sales from their foreign affiliates in China. As a result of decades of foreign direct investment, foreign firms have a significant presence in China, reflected in a cumulative-value foreign direct investment of $2.2 trillion by the end of 2012, far and away the largest amount of foreign direct investment in any emerging market. Indeed, globally China's stock of inbound direct investment is second only to that of the United States. The role of foreign firms looms particularly large in the manufacturing sector, where these firms now account for fully one-quarter of all output (National Bureau of Statistics of China 2012a, 131).[41] While the export activities of these foreign firms are well understood, many observers do not recognize the importance of the Chinese domestic market to many of these firms. In 2011, domestic sales of foreign affiliates in China reached RMB15 trillion.[42] This is substantially larger than the value of China's imports, which, when measured in domestic currency, was RMB11.3 trillion in 2011, and equivalent to almost one-quarter of the sales revenue of indigenous firms.

Obviously, Chinese firms that seek to export goods and services into the global economy also are subject to competition from other global players. China's exports in 2012 were $2.05 trillion, subjecting 25 percent of GDP to competition from global firms. Services too are subject to global competition. Thus COSCO, China's largest shipping business and the world's largest bulk shipper, has not been immune to increased pricing pressure as global trade slumped in 2009 and then recovered only very gradually. COSCO Holdings,

---

40. A significant share of China's imports is parts, components, and assemblies that are used to produce export goods. Since these imports do not enter the domestic market, it is sometimes argued that China's relatively high import share both overstates China's degree of openness to international trade and the degree of competition provided by imports in China's domestic market. This argument ignores two important points. First, from the point of view of Chinese firms that either are supplying or seek to supply such parts, components, and assemblies to firms producing for the export market, these imports are the key source of competition in the market. Second, China is hardly the only country that is participating in global production chains; the import content of US manufactured exports in the mid-2000s was 16 percent, for example. (OECD, Statextracts, "STAN Input-Output Import Content of Exports." Available at http://stats. oecd.org [accessed on June 7, 2013]).

41. Measured by sales of each firm's main business.

42. Combined foreign and domestic sales of manufactured goods by foreign affiliates were RMB21,860.50 trillion while exports of manufactured goods by foreign affiliates were RMB7,056.05 billion (National Bureau of Statistics of China 2012a, 129, 131). The difference between these two numbers is domestic sales. Both the sales and export data cover only so-called above-scale firms. See discussion of this concept in chapter 3.

the listed arm of COSCO (Group), incurred sizable losses in 2011 and 2012—RMB10.4 billion and RMB9.56 billion, respectively. In 2013, COSCO Holdings was forced to sell assets back to its parent company in an effort to avoid delisting of the company from the Shanghai Stock Exchange.[43]

Evolving Role of Economic Planning

The corollary to the increasing and now dominant role of competitive markets in the allocation of resources is the vastly diminished importance of China's five-year plans. The First Five-Year Plan (1953–57) was a 240-page document setting forth thousands of targets (State Planning Commission 1956). In industry, the plan set levels of physical output for 1957 for almost 50 products ranging from steam turbines to gunny sacks, as well as an aggregate industrial value target. For products such as cotton yarn, cotton piece goods, and paper products, the plan further disaggregated output targets into quantities to be produced in modern factories and quantities to be produced by individual handicraftsmen and handicraft cooperatives using "local methods."

In agriculture, the First Five-Year Plan set sown area, yield, and output targets for more than a dozen different crops ranging from rice to hemp; seven targets for animal husbandry; the amount of acreage to be planted with forests and shelter belts, the latter disaggregated into ten specific geographic regions; and a single target for the increased output of fisheries. These were not abstract targets. The plan also specified the value of agricultural investment to be undertaken (disaggregated into amounts to be spent by the Ministry of Agriculture, the Ministry of Water Conservancy, the Ministry of Forestry, and the Meteorological Bureau); the amount of new land to be brought under cultivation, as well as a target for the expansion of irrigated area; the number of modern plows, water-pumping stations, and other agricultural machinery to be made available; the number of tons of four types of fertilizer to be supplied; and the number of new observatories, weather stations, and weather posts to be established.

The First Five-Year Plan contained similarly detailed targets for important services, including transport, post, and telecommunications; commerce; education; and health. The plan even had small sections on art and literature, cinema, and libraries and museums. The plan specified the number of new theatrical troupes to be organized and further divided the number between state-sponsored troupes and troupes "organized by the people themselves." Similarly the plan set forth the number of new theaters to be established by 1957 with the number broken down into state-operated (413), joint state-private (75), and private (1,200); the number of new films to be produced (400), the number of foreign films to be dubbed (308), the number of new mobile film projection teams (4,720, which would bring the total to 5,279) to be

---

43. Wang Ying, "New Head to Steer COSCO," *China Daily*, July 3, 2013, p. 13.

established under state cultural departments; and the number of new cultural centers (2,600), libraries (109), and museums (57) to be built.

But the heart of the First Five-Year Plan was the plan for capital investment. The plan called for 694 "above-norm" investment projects and 2,300 "below-norm projects," for which responsibility was divided among central government industrial ministries, other central government ministries, and local authorities. Plans 'for investment in the steel, nonferrous metal, power, coal, petroleum, machine building, chemical, building material, lumber, textile, pharmaceutical, and paper industries were particularly detailed.

In certain respects, the First Five-Year Plan was the apex of China's attempt to steer economic growth via detailed plans. Before the ink was dry on the Second Five-Year Plan (1958–1962), Mao Zedong launched the Great Leap Forward, a catastrophic attempt to accelerate China's growth from the already rapid 8.9 percent per annum pace of the First Plan. The Great Leap displaced a reasonably well-developed Second Plan, leading to a mass starvation that killed upward of 40 million and produced the worst five-year economic performance of the post-1949 period—national income shrank at an average annual rate of 3.1 percent (National Bureau of Statistics of China 1983, 23). The disruptive effects of the Great Leap were so severe that when the Second Plan officially ended in 1962 formal planning efforts were suspended until the government launched the Third Five-Year Plan in 1966. Unfortunately, that coincided with the onset of the Cultural Revolution, which lasted until 1976, when Deng Xiaoping made a gradual comeback and provided traction to the Fifth Five-Year Plan, "which set the economy on a more constructive trajectory" (Roach 2014, 85).

The Sixth Five-Year Plan (1981–85), the first to escape the pernicious after-effects of the Cultural Revolution, was in many respects similar to the first (State Planning Commission 1984). Running at well over 250 pages in the English language version, it set a huge number of targets for output (again in detailed physical terms and more aggregated value terms) in agriculture, industry, and services. The chapters on science and technology and education were more detailed than the First Plan. Again, the core of the document was the investment plan. Perhaps not quite as detailed as the First Plan, its organization is similar—in particular, its plans for expansion of productive capacity are in the same series of industries as the First Plan—but it includes plans for new industries such as electronics and computers.

The current Twelfth Five-Year Program (2011–15) differs from the first and sixth in several respects (National Development and Reform Commission 2011). First, as with the Chinese title of the Eleventh Plan, the characters for "plan" (计划) have been dropped from the title in favor of "program outline" (规划纲要). This change of terminology is consistent with the evolution of the name of the State Planning Commission, which was responsible for drawing up five-year plans since its formal establishment in 1952. In 1998 it was renamed the State Development and Planning Commission, and in 2003 it morphed into the National Development and Reform Commission. According to China's official news agency, the "objective reason" for the change in terminology from plan to program "is because over the years the market has developed so that it already has become the main engine determining economic growth; after the development and transformation of the various economic bureaus, planning actually is no longer able to exercise sufficient controlling power over the great majority of economic activity and principal output."[44]

A second difference between the Twelfth Five-Year Program and the first and sixth plans is that it sets far fewer targets. There is not a single output target for an industrial product in the Twelfth Program. In agriculture, there is a single target—to maintain annual aggregate grain production at a level of 540 million tons or more in 2011–15 rather than the highly disaggregated crop targets of the First Plan. And unlike the First Plan, the current program sets forth no arrangements for the investment and supplies of inputs judged necessary to achieve the grain output target.

Third, the targets in the Twelfth Program are more aggregate in nature: for example, 7 percent annual growth of real GDP; a 4 percentage point increase in the share of GDP originating in the service sector, clearly a reflection of the rebalancing agenda of the leadership; and a 4 percentage point increase in the share of the population living in urban areas. Four major targets in science and education include a 3.3 percentage point increase in the share of the relevant age cohort completing nine years of compulsory education and an increase of 1.6 in the number of patents filed per 10,000 residents. There are also a number of targets under the heading of resources and the environment, including no decline in the amount of agricultural sown area, a 3.1 percentage point increase in the nonfossil fuel share of energy consumption, a 17 percentage point reduction in carbon dioxide emissions per unit of GDP, and absolute targets for reduction of emissions of sulfur dioxide and three other chemical pollutants. Quite a number of targets focus on living standards and welfare. These include the growth of per capita disposable income in urban areas and the growth of per capita cash income in rural areas, the maximum rate of unemployment in urban areas, and a one-year increase in average life expectancy. Long lists of physical output targets have vanished.

Fourth, even these aggregate targets are mainly labeled as "forecasts" (预期性) rather than "mandatory" (约束性).[45] This is a far cry from the output targets in the First Plan, when national targets for important industrial products were disaggregated all the way down to the plant level and managers were rewarded or punished depending on whether the targets were met.

---

44. "The transformation from plan to program is a breath of fresh air," October 9, 2005. Available at http://news.xinhuanet.com/comments/2005-10/09content_3595992.htm (accessed on October 2, 2013).

45. Of the 28 aggregate targets in the Twelfth Program, 16 are binding and 12 are forecasts. The larger number of binding targets is due to the large number of emission and pollution reduction targets (carbon dioxide, organic pollutants, sulfur dioxide, ammonia nitrogen, and nitrogen oxide), each of which is mandatory and specified separately.

Only in investment does the Twelfth Program carry over the level of detail characteristic of the First Plan. And even in the investment domain, the targets for increases in capacity are focused on a few high-priority areas rather than a large number of basic industrial products. In infrastructure, for example, the plan specifies beginning construction on nuclear and hydro-electric power plants with a capacity of 40 and 120 gigawatts, respectively, to complete 200,000 kilometers of electric power transmission lines of 330 kilovolts or more capacity, and to bring the total operational network of the fast rail system to 45,000 kilometers.[46] Unlike the First Plan, there are no investment plans for increasing production capacity for steel and a large number of other basic industrial products.

China has transitioned from an economy where allocation of both financial and human resources was directed in large part by economic plans drawn up by government bureaucrats to one in which markets are dominant. The introduction of labor markets and the reform of the price formation process were essential to creating the basis for a market economy. Initially, a system of lifetime job assignment, wage rigidity, and extraordinary limits on geographic mobility impeded the ability of workers to seek employment that best used their skills. But early in the reform process, this system began to give way to market-driven job recruitment, flexible wages, and increasing geographic mobility.

Similarly, at the outset of reform, arbitrarily fixed, distorted prices meant that there was little or no connection between profitability and economic or social returns. Some firms were highly profitable because they benefited from underpriced inputs or overpriced output; others were loss making because their inputs were overpriced or their output was underpriced. Thus the initial price structure was entirely unsuited to a more decentralized investment decision-making environment in which firms financed investment largely with retained earnings. But this environment shifted as the scope of prices determined in competitive markets expanded and profitability more accurately signaled real economic returns. As will be analyzed in chapter 4, there is substantial room to further improve the allocation of capital through the elimination of a few important remaining price distortions and additional reforms in the financial sector. But the fundamental change already occurred in the first decade or so of reform.

---

46. High-speed rail is a subset of the fast rail target, but a number was not specified in the Twelfth Program. High-speed rail requires dedicated rail lines for trains that operate at speeds of either 250 km/h or 350 km/h.

2

Reform of State-Owned Enterprises

While major economic reform initiatives from the late 1970s through at least the mid-1980s focused primarily on agriculture, China's government also launched various experiments in the 1980s to reform state-owned firms, particularly industrial firms (Lin, Cai, and Li 1996, 211–19). These reforms aimed to expand enterprise autonomy with regard to production, marketing, and investment decisions, in part by allowing firms to retain a portion of their profits rather than handing them over in their entirety to the Ministry of Finance, as had previously been the case. These reforms were paired with experiments in enterprise finance and price setting. Fixed asset investment was no longer financed almost entirely by budgetary grants, but rather through retained earnings and bank loans. What came to be called a dual-track pricing system replaced a unitary system of state fixed prices. The State Price Commission continued to set the prices of a broad range of raw materials, intermediate inputs, and final goods, but these prices applied only to planned units of output while above-plan output could be sold at prices determined by the market (Wu and Zhao 1987). This approach meant that scarcity-based prices increasingly influenced firm production decisions at the margin, leading to a more efficient allocation of resources. This reform became increasingly important in the mid-1980s, when the State Planning Commission discontinued ratcheting up annual output requirements, allowing firms to channel virtually all incremental output to the market (Naughton 2007, 93).

These initial reforms did little to improve the economic performance of state-owned industrial firms. For a number of reasons, profits of state-owned firms declined steadily in the 1980s and well into the 1990s. First, relaxation of the government's monopoly over wide swaths of industry led large numbers of startup, mostly private firms to enter profitable segments of the industrial sector (a phenomenon analyzed in chapter 3). The new firms increased competition, eroding the profits of the incumbent state-owned firms (Naughton 2007, 94).

Second, rural reforms depended initially on reducing and ultimately largely eliminating the high tax implicit in government-set procurement prices for agricultural products. This led to rapid increases in prices that farmers received for grain, cotton, and other important agricultural products, eroding profits of state firms, especially in the food processing, textile, and garment industries (Lardy 1983, 88–92). These branches of industry were disproportionately dependent on inputs from the agricultural sector and thus had unusually high levels of profitability as reform was getting under way (Lardy 1983, 123–27; 1998, 48).

Third, employment in the state sector expanded substantially in the first phase of reform. Between 1977 and 1993, employment in the state sector broadly defined expanded by 50 percent. In state-owned industry, where the share of output had declined to half of output by 1992 compared with its four-fifths share in 1978, employment also had increased by half, to 45 million. In short, it appears that state-owned firms continued to bear a major responsibility for absorbing new entrants into the urban labor force, meaning that the significant levels of excess staffing seen in the prereform era continued after 1978. At least 20 percent of the employees of state-owned firms at the end of 1993 were surplus labor, according to an official from the Ministry of Labor (Hu Xiaoyi 1996, 125).

Fourth, state-owned firms devoted a growing share of their revenues to providing benefits to their workers, everything from health care and pensions to subsidized housing. For example, workers in state-owned firms who had entered the work force in the 1950s began to retire in large numbers in the 1980s, pushing the ratio of retirees to employees from less than 4 percent in 1978 to 18 percent by 1993. Given the pay-as-you-go nature of China's pension system, the premiums paid by firms rose steadily (Hu Xiaoyi 1996, 125–26).

Even before these four developments, which put downward pressure on the profitability of state enterprises, about a fifth of all state-owned firms were posting financial losses in the early 1980s. Though this share dipped to as low as one-tenth for a few years in the mid-1980s, it rose to an average of one-quarter in 1990–92 and then 30 percent by 1993. More worrying, the magnitude of financial losses of state-owned firms soared, reaching a peak of 3 percent of GDP in 1990 (see table 1.2).

Other indicators confirmed the increasingly precarious financial condition of state-owned firms. The average debt to equity ratio of state firms rose steadily, exceeding 100 percent in 1989 and reaching 300 percent by 1994. Eighty-five percent of the liabilities of these enterprises was bank debt (Lardy 1998, 41, 243). By 1994 state-owned firms were so heavily indebted and their profitability so low that their total annual profits covered only a little more than half of the interest payable on their bank debt.[1] This suggests that many state-owned firms continuously expanded their bank borrowing to cover operating losses and/or to finance capital investment that generated returns insufficient to amortize the loans.

Grasping the Large, Releasing the Small

The limited success of the early efforts to raise productivity and profitability in state-owned firms by increasing enterprise autonomy led to a second stage of economic reform following the Third Plenum of the 14th Party Congress in November 1993. This plenum "marked a major turning point on China's road to a market economy" (Qian and Wu 2003, 36). It called for the creation of market-supporting institutions, such as fiscal federalism, emphasized the separation of state-owned enterprises from the government, and, most importantly, for the first time broached the privatization of smaller state-owned firms. The Central Committee gave this latter initiative a further boost in the fall of 1995 when it explicitly endorsed the idea of "grasping the large and releasing the small" (Garnaut et al. 2005, 3). The number of state-owned industrial enterprises fell from 127,600 in 1996 to 61,300 in 1999. There were only 34,280 by the end of 2003 as money-losing firms went bankrupt, were merged with profitable firms, or were privatized (National Bureau of Statistics of China 2000, 407; 2004, 514). Privatization of small state-owned firms typically took the form of sale of shares to employees, where the sale price of the firm frequently was equal to the value of outstanding bank loans plus other debt. These firms thus were transformed from state-owned companies into stock cooperative companies (股份合作企业). After the 1994 Company Law made it possible, many later converted to limited liability companies, typically after managers bought a controlling number of shares from workers (Lardy 1998, 53–54).

Simultaneous with this initiative to reduce the number of small, loss-making state-owned companies, the government launched a reform of large state-owned companies. This "grasping the large" component of economic reform focused not on privatization but rather corporatization. It involved reorganizing traditional state-owned companies into joint stock companies or limited liability companies. Even before the new law introduced these forms of legal organization in China, local experiments in corporate reform had been launched in Shenzhen in south China.

Corporatization was designed to give managers more authority to ensure

---

1. Estimated based on the statement of an economist at the Central Party School that as of the end of 1994 state banks would have to write off RMB1.215 trillion in loans to state-owned enterprises (SOEs) to reduce firm indebtedness to a level where firm profits would cover interest payments (Lardy 1998, 38). In 1995, loans outstanding to state-owned firms stood at RMB3.36 trillion (Lardy 1998, 83). Assuming loans to SOEs grew at the same 24 percent increase in all bank loans, SOE loans at end-1994 would have been RMB2.710 trillion. Thus the necessary writeoff can be estimated as 45 percent of loans outstanding to SOEs at the end of 1994.

the alignment of interests of managers and government owners, and to allow diversification of ownership, sometimes through a public listing (Naughton 2007, 315). Managers of corporatized state-owned enterprises are accountable to the firm's board of directors, and if the firm is listed on the Shanghai stock exchange, regulations require one-third of the board members to be independent. When these firms are listed, the state typically retains control, because only a minority of the firm's shares are sold. For this reason the National Bureau of Statistics of China classifies corporatized state-owned companies, in which the state remains the majority or dominant shareholder, as state-controlled shareholding companies. For details, see box 2.1. Over 10,000 traditional state-owned industrial enterprises, about a fifth of the total, were corporatized as early as 1999. They accounted for almost two-fifths of industrial output, indicating that corporatized firms on average were much larger than the remaining traditional state-owned industrial enterprises. While the number of state-controlled industrial shareholding companies remains at about 10,000, by 2011 these firms accounted for three-fifths of all state companies and 70 percent of the industrial output produced by traditional state-owned companies and state-controlled shareholding companies combined (National Bureau of Statistics of China 2012b, 501, 512–13).[2]

The corporatization initiative extended beyond the industrial sector. In 1996 there were 442,000 traditional state-owned corporations, three-quarters of them outside of the industrial sector. By 2003 this number was reduced to 370,000 and by 2012 to only 160,000 (National Bureau of Statistics of China 2013c, 29). This significant reduction reflected the transformation of about 100,000 of these companies into state-controlled limited liability and shareholding limited companies, the bankruptcy and exit of small, loss-making industrial firms, and the widespread privatization of traditional state-owned enterprises in some components of the service sector. These latter transformations are detailed in chapter 3 on the rise of the private sector.

While data limitations preclude measuring these reforms' effects on the service sector, it is clear in the case of state-owned industrial enterprises that the reforms, plus the opening to foreign competition during China's negotiation to join the World Trade Organization, sparked a decade-long, substantial improvement in their financial performance. The share of state industrial enterprises losing money declined from a peak of two-fifths in 1998 to only a quarter by 2007, and the losses of these firms fell from 1.4 percent to only 0.3 percent of GDP (see table 1.2). And, as will be shown in chapter 3, the return on assets of state firms quintupled to about 5 percent in 2007 compared with 1996–97, substantially closing the gap with the superior financial performance of private companies. But, as also analyzed in chapter 3, the financial performance of state industrial firms declined in absolute terms after 2007 and fell dramatically compared with that of private firms.

---

2. The share is rising because the number of traditional state-owned industrial enterprises shrank to only 6,707 by 2011. The reduction from about 115,000 in 1996 is due to mergers, exits, and takeovers by private companies.

Box 2.1 Definitions and terminology

Ownership of Firms and Measurement of Output

In China there are now two types of state-owned firms. The first, formally known as enterprises owned by the whole people (全民所有制企业), are usually simply referred to as "state-owned enterprises" (国有企业). The second are state-controlled shareholding companies (国有控股企业), frequently confusingly translated in English-language Chinese sources as state holding companies. State-controlled shareholding companies are independent legal entities, usually registered as limited liability companies or shareholding limited companies, in which the state is the majority or dominant shareholder. State-controlled enterprises also exist in two other registration categories: state joint ownership enterprises (firms owned jointly by two state-owned enterprises) and joint state-collective ownership enterprises (firms owned jointly by a state-owned enterprise and a collectively owned enterprise). But in 2011 there was only a minuscule number of firms of these two latter types, and together they accounted for only one-tenth of 1 percent of national industrial output (National Bureau of Statistics of China 2012b, 501). State-controlled shareholding companies may be publicly listed, but most are not. State firms may be under the control of the central government, via an industrial ministry or by the State-owned Assets Supervision and Administration Commission (SASAC), or under the control of a provincial or local government, via an industrial bureau of the provincial government, a provincial-level SASAC, or a municipal government.

The National Bureau of Statistics of China in September 1998 for the first time publicly set forth the concept of state-controlled ownership and the methodology for identifying state control in Regulations for the Statistical Division of the Economy. Appendix 3 of this document is titled "Measures for the Statistical Classification of the Portion of the Economy That Is State-controlled." In November 2006 the National Bureau of Statistics in the document "Measures for the Statistical Classification of the Public and Nonpublic Portions of the Economy," extended the control concept beyond the state sector by adding the categories private-controlled, collective-controlled, Hong Kong–Macau–Taiwan-controlled, and foreign-controlled.[1]

By 2012 there were 278,479 state firms, of which 159,644 were traditional state-owned companies. The balance were state-controlled shareholding companies.

(box continues next page)

---

1. The documents cited in this paragraph are available at www.stats.gov.cn (accessed on August 20, 2013).

Emergence of SASAC

Although "grasping the large and releasing the small" substantially increased the role of the private sector in many segments of the economy, there are several domains in which state firms—whether traditional ones or limited liability firms and shareholding limited companies in which the state is the majority or dominant shareholder—remain dominant. State firms continue to maintain a monopoly or near monopoly position in basic telecommunication services, financial services, oil and gas extraction, tobacco, and public utilities such as water and electric power. Moreover, while the number of state firms has declined dramatically, the remaining ones are much larger and, according to the critics of state capitalism, have increased their market power dramatically. Particularly notable are the large profits generated by these firms relative to private firms. James McGregor (2012, 23), who has characterized China as an example of "authoritarian capitalism," notes that in 2009 the total profits of two large state companies, China Mobile and China Petroleum & Chemical Corporation (Sinopec), exceeded the combined profits of China's 500 largest private enterprises.

James McGregor's argument that state-owned firms returned to prominence in the decade of leadership of President Hu Jintao and Premier Wen Jiabao (2003–12) has also been advanced by the US-China Economic and Security Review Commission (2011, 40–50; 2012, 47–79), a number of leading academic specialists, and numerous columnists.[3] Several developments during the Hu Jintao–Wen Jiabao era appear to be consistent with their hypothesis of the rising importance of state-owned firms in China. In March 2003, China created the State-owned Assets Supervision and Administration Commission (SASAC), a high-level government agency that was charged with transforming large state-owned companies into "national champions." In early 2006, the Chinese State Council promulgated the National Medium and Long-Term Plan for the Development of Science and Technology (2006–20), which called for strengthening basic research and reducing the country's reliance on foreign technology. The broad plan was followed in 2007 by aggressive industrial policies that appeared to give large state-owned companies an edge over both foreign and indigenous private firms and included government procurement policies with strong domestic content requirements designed to promote indigenous innovation. The government also launched a Strategic Emerging Industries initiative in October 2010.

Two of the developments that appear to support the resurgence hypothesis came early in the Hu-Wen era: a substantially enhanced role for the National Development and Reform Commission (NDRC) and the creation of SASAC, which was the first economic initiative after Wen assumed office. The State Development and Planning Commission was renamed the NDRC in 2003 and took over the functions of the State Economic and Trade Commission and some of the functions of the State Council Office for Economic Restructuring, substantially enhancing its role. Shortly thereafter, the NDRC regained the authority to approve all major investment projects, in part to improve the efficiency of investment.[4] These developments allowed it to dominate economic policymaking from almost the beginning of the Hu-Wen era.[5] In a further

---

3. Minxin Pei, a professor of government at Claremont College, argues, "Evidence of the demise of economic reform is easy to spot. The Chinese state has reasserted its control over the economy." "Remembering Deng in our era of crony capitalism," *Financial Times*, January 23, 2012. Available at www.ft.com (accessed on January 24, 2012). Gideon Rachman writes that "the key target that liberalisers have in their sights is the network of mammoth state-owned enterprises, whose role has actually expanded over the past decade." "How China plans to prove the skeptics wrong," *Financial Times*, November 5, 2013, p. 9.

4. State Council, "Decision concerning reform of the investment system," August 12, 2005. Available at www.gov.cn (accessed on March 24, 2014).

5. Peter Martin, "The Humbling of the NDRC: China's National Development and Reform Commission Searches for a New Role Amid Restructuring," *China Brief* 14, no. 5. Available at www. Jamestown.org (accessed on March 24, 2014).

reshuffling of the bureaucracy in 2008, the NDRC absorbed the National Grain Bureau and the National Energy Bureau, in effect making the NDRC "a Super-Ministry, one half-step above everyone else in the government, the general headquarters of the economy." It had "a high propensity to intervene in market operations and outcomes" (Naughton 2014).

The new government entity, SASAC, took charge of about 200 of the most important nonfinancial state enterprises owned and controlled at the central level.[6] The creation of SASAC led James McGregor (2012, 13) to charge that "state-owned firms, which had faded into the background during Deng Xiaoping's reforms . . . returned to prominence under the Hu Jintao and Wen Jiabao administration as anointed 'national champions' to lead China's international ambitions and serve as guarantors of Party supremacy." Similarly, Rosalea Yao (2012, 1) argues that "the average SOE is much larger and financially stronger than it was a few years ago, and so a tougher competitor to private firms."

SASAC firms include the three national oil companies—China National Petroleum Corporation (CNPC), Sinopec, and the China National Offshore Oil Corporation (CNOOC); the large state telecommunication companies—China Mobile, China Unicom, and China Telecom; most of the large state power-generating companies such as China Guodian Corporation and China Huadian Corporation; Shenhua Group, China's largest state-owned coal producer; the major state power distribution companies, State Grid Corporation and China Southern Power Grid Company; as well as the major state airlines—Air China, China Southern, and China Eastern.

The Boston Consulting Group calls SASAC "the world's largest controlling shareholder."[7] The US-China Economic and Security Review Commission (2012, 48) characterizes SASAC as "the world's largest and most powerful holding company." The commission (2011, 44–45) points out that three SASAC-controlled state corporations ranked in the top 10 in the 2010 Fortune Global 500 list of the largest corporations ranked by revenue. Only two American corporations made the top 10.

Certainly the scope of businesses controlled by SASAC is large—far greater than suggested by the small number of firms it directly controls. While SASAC originally controlled about 200 entities, through mergers designed to build even larger, more powerful companies, this number fell to only 113 by early 2014. This small universe of enterprises exerts a large influence on China's economy because most SASAC entities have many subsidiaries, each with multiple factories. This is particularly true of group corporations and holding companies, which account for a substantial share of SASAC entities.[8] For ex-

---

6. Provincial-level SASACs were established at about the same time in many provinces to manage the development of companies owned by provincial and local governments.

7. Boston Consulting Group, "SASAC: China's Megashareholder," December 2007. Available at www.bcgperspectives.com (accessed on November 20, 2013).

8. Groups in China are organized under the "Provisional Rules on Business Group Registration"

ample, China Guodian Corporation, one of the five largest nationwide power-generating groups, is a sprawling conglomerate with over 100,000 employees. It owns 16 regional and provincial branch companies, 13 extra-large subsidiary companies, 2 research and development institutes, and nearly 200 power enterprises spread over 31 provinces. Its subsidiary companies include five listed companies, four of which are A-share companies listed on the Shanghai Stock Exchange and one a so-called H-share company listed on the Hong Kong Stock Exchange.[9] Similarly, Sinopec Corporation has more than 100 subsidiaries and branches. Numerous other corporations under central SASAC control similarly sprawling business empires. As a result the universe of central SASAC entities in 2010 included 23,738 firms or one-fifth of the number of state-owned firms of all types (China's State-Owned Assets Supervision and Administration Commission 2011, 739).[10]

Moreover, many of the group companies SASAC controls also have expanded their activities far beyond what might be regarded as their core businesses. China Guodian, for example, is the majority shareholder in city commercial banks in Shizuishan City in Ningxia Province and in Shijiazhuang, the capital of Hebei Province. It also has founded an insurance company and has invested in securities, trust, and fund management businesses (China's State-Owned Assets Supervision and Administration Commission 2011, 432). Large numbers of SASAC-controlled firms have also either loaned funds to or invested directly in property development companies, especially in periods when the government has sought to limit direct bank lending to property developers.

The Chinese Communist Party plays an important role in many SASAC entities, a factor that proponents of the notion that state capitalism has taken hold cite as evidence that China is not a market economy but rather one managed by the party-state. The Organization Department of the party appoints the top three executives (party secretary, chief executive officer, and chairman of the board; frequently the first two positions are held by a single individual) in 53 of the most important state-owned enterprises under the purview of SASAC, leading James McGregor (2012, vii) to argue that "this places control of the national champion SOEs that dominate all key sectors

---

promulgated in 1998 and must have two layers, a parent company and at least five controlled subsidiaries. Many groups have two additional levels—uncontrolled subsidiaries and other firms that collaborate with either the parent company or its controlled subsidiaries (Lin and Milhaupt 2013, 715).

9. China Guodian Corporation. Available at www.cgdc.com.cn/corporate.jhtml (accessed on May 2, 2013).

10. The 23,738 number is based on the *hu* (户) measurement concept, which includes group companies plus subsidiary firms three levels down from the group level. In 2010 there were 261,944 enterprise legal person units (企业法人单位) that were either traditional state-owned companies or state-controlled shareholding companies (National Bureau of Statistics of China 2012b, 27). This is roughly twice as many as the 124,455 state enterprises reported in the SASAC Yearbook, because it includes subsidiary firms more than three levels down from the group level (China's State-Owned Assets Supervision and Administration Commission 2011, 737).

of the economy directly in the hands of top Party bosses who deploy them to boost the economy and buttress the Party's monopoly on political power." The intimate link between the party and these top state-owned firms perhaps is best symbolized by the red phones on the desks of these firms' CEOs, which provide a direct, encrypted link between the firms and Zhongnanhai, the location of the Chinese Communist Party headquarters in Beijing. About 300 of these phones, known as "red machines," link top party and government officials as well as the heads of the largest state-owned companies, providing "the party apparatus a hotline into multiple arms of the state, including the government-owned companies that China promotes around the world these days as independent commercial entities" (Richard McGregor 2010, 8, 10). The party also appoints the top leadership in a much larger number of firms that are state-owned but controlled at the provincial and local level.

Moreover, the revolving door of leaders in this top group of state firms raises questions about the degree of competition among state-owned firms in the same business. For example, in 2004 the party reshuffled the top bosses at China's three telecom firms (Richard McGregor 2010, 83–84). Wang Xiaochu, the executive director of China Mobile, was appointed general manager of China Telecom; Wang Jianzhou, the chairman of China Unicom, became the chairman of China Mobile; and Chang Xiaobing, the vice general manager of China Telecom, became Chairman of China Unicom. Similarly, in 2010 the party reshuffled the leadership of China's three major national state-owned oil companies. The party secretary and general manager of the China National Offshore Oil Corporation (CNOOC) moved to the same positions at Sinopec, while a senior executive at China National Petroleum Corporation (CNPC) was appointed as chairman and party secretary at CNOOC (James McGregor 2012, 72). These rotations suggest a cozy relationship among state-owned firms in key sectors of the economy, presumably undermining whatever competition might exist in the oligopolistic market structures in these industries.

The state also issues regulations that are widely interpreted as providing SASAC-managed firms with substantial economic benefits. While mergers and acquisitions of foreign and Chinese private companies are reviewed for compliance with China's Anti-Monopoly Law, which went into effect in August 2008, "state-owned enterprises have had a free pass on M&As as the government mandates mergers of state-owned enterprise competitors within and across target sectors to develop economies of scale and cultivate state-owned enterprise national champions" (James McGregor 2012, 25). State-owned firms are further protected in many cases by strict restrictions on entry by potential competitors. The state has not allowed, for example, the creation of any mobile phone companies other than China Mobile, Unicom, and China Telecom, which in effect enjoy an oligopoly on mobile telephony services. Equally important, while SASAC-controlled group companies in many cases are the dominant owners of their many listed subsidiary companies on the Shanghai stock exchange, until 2007 these firms paid no dividends to the Ministry of Finance. Moreover, the dividends they now pay are surprisingly modest. The amounts collected in the phase-in year of 2007 were de minimis, only RMB14 billion (Lardy 2012, 72). This rose gradually to RMB97 billion by 2012, still well under 10 percent of the central SASAC firms' profits and very low compared with the United States, where industrial firms typically pay dividends ranging from two-fifths to just over half of their earnings (Lardy 2012, 72).

Finally, most of the dividends paid by SASAC-affiliated companies do not go directly to the state budget administered by the Ministry of Finance but into a separate state capital management budget. Yet almost all of the funds administered through this mechanism are reinvested in the firms SASAC controls. For example, in 2012 only RMB5 billion was transferred from the state capital management budget to the national government budget administered by the Ministry of Finance to be used for social programs to raise people's living standards. RMB5 billion represents 0.04 percent of national fiscal expenditures of almost RMB12 trillion in 2012. Instead, almost all of the dividends paid into the state capital management budget were reinvested within the universe of central SASAC and other centrally controlled firms to support mergers, reorganizations, and restructurings, or were injected into the largest power-generating companies in order to bolster their capital (Ministry of Finance 2013). In short, dividend income allows SASAC to bolster the performance of its own firms. Finally, it is asserted that state-owned banks are required to make loans on favorable terms to state-owned companies, including those controlled by SASAC, and that in some cases they are required to forgive these loans (US-China Economic and Security Review Commission 2011, 46).

The view that the state was resurgent in the past decade is further buttressed by the active use of industrial policy, much of it drafted in whole or in part by the NDRC. In sharp contrast with the preceding period when, under the leadership of President Jiang Zemin and Premier Zhu Rongji, China instituted a far-reaching restructuring of state-owned companies and brought China into the World Trade Organization, in the Hu-Wen decade fundamental economic reform slowed to a crawl. Instead, the Hu-Wen regime aggressively promoted a series of industrial policies, many of which seemed designed to promote state-owned firms at the expense of both foreign firms and indigenous private companies.

The 2006 Plan for the Development of Science and Technology (2006–20) identified 11 key industries that were to receive priority in technological development (State Council 2006a). The plan appears to have stimulated a subsequent initiative linking government procurement to indigenous innovation as well as the strategic emerging industries policy, which identified 37 subsectors in seven industries for priority development (James McGregor 2010).

Later the same year the State Council promulgated a guiding opinion on the adjustment of state capital and the reorganization of the operations of state-owned enterprises drafted by central SASAC (State Council Management Office 2006). The document was relatively balanced, calling for an acceleration of the process of corporatization of state-owned enterprises, improving the coordination of government leadership and market adjustment, and guarding against the loss of state assets. It further called for maintaining state ownership as the main element of the economy, concentrating state assets in important sectors and what it called critical realms, and strengthening the controlling power and leading role of the state economy. But it also called for state encouragement and support of individual and private businesses and the full development of the market as a tool for allocating resources.

Less than two weeks after the State Council acted, Li Rongrong, the chairman of SASAC, gave an interview with reporters of the government's official news agency that was posted on the central government's website and is frequently cited by those who see a resurgence of state control during the period. His language went far beyond the document approved by the State Council. Li said that to carry out the guiding opinion it would be necessary for the state to "guarantee absolute controlling power" over enterprises in seven strategic sectors: military industry, power generation and distribution, petroleum and petrochemicals, telecommunications, coal, civil aviation, and shipping. Chairman Li also identified nine so-called pillar industries—manufacture of equipment, automobiles, information technology, construction, iron and steel, nonferrous metals, chemical industry, prospecting and design, and technology—in which the state was to maintain "comparatively strong control."[11]

The Ministry of Finance in 2007 promulgated a series of documents that required all government procurements to give priority to products embodying indigenous innovation. Within two years the government had launched an accreditation process to determine which products qualified as "indigenous innovation products." This work was subsequently embodied in lengthy product catalogues issued mostly by provincial governments. To qualify, a product's intellectual property, trademarks, and brands must be originally registered in China and embody technology that meets or exceeds international standards (US-China Economic and Security Review Commission 2010, 48). This program, "not surprisingly, was seen by foreign multinationals and their governments as a blatant blueprint for massive technology theft" (James McGregor 2012, 5).

The State Council officially launched the Strategic Emerging Industries policy in October 2010. This initiative identified seven next generation technologies and products, disaggregated into 37 subindustries, that "government officials hope will become the backbone of China's next phase of industrial modernization and technological development."[12] These industries are to be

---

11. China's State-owned Assets Supervision and Administration Commission, "The state economy must guarantee absolute controlling power over seven sectors," December 18, 2006. Available at www.gov.cn (accessed on October 1, 2012).

12. US-China Business Council, *China's Strategic Emerging Industries: Policy, Implementation, Challenges, & Recommendations*, March 2013. Available at www.uschina.org (accessed on September 23, 2013).

promoted through tax rebates and financial incentives to help companies conduct research and development and commercialize new technologies in industries such as next generation information technology, biotechnology, and new materials.

Did the Hu-Wen Reforms Succeed?

The combination of the creation of SASAC early in the Hu-Wen decade, the enhanced role of the NDRC, and the industrial policies outlined above undermined the previously widespread view in the West that China was in a long but steady transition to a market economy in which state monopolies would be limited to public utilities.

Despite the multiple advantages state firms allegedly enjoy as a result of state industrial policy, it does not appear that SASAC firms in financial terms have performed substantially better than other enterprises or relative to the economy as a whole. Profits of central SASAC firms more than quintupled between 2002, just prior to its founding, and 2012, seemingly supporting the view that SASAC firms earn rapidly increasing, outsized profits (table 2.1, column 2). This strong growth led some to believe that "a remarkable turnaround has been achieved in China's state-owned sector" (Oi and Han 2011, 20). But that assessment appears to have been premature. SASAC-controlled firms enjoyed the most dramatic growth in profits in the early years after SASAC's founding; profit growth slowed after 2007. The relatively weak performance of SASAC firms after 2007 is confirmed in column 3, showing the profits of central SASAC firms as a share of profits of all nonfinancial enterprises. This share rose through 2007 but since has fallen significantly to a level slightly below that of 2003. Profits of central SASAC firms as a share of GDP follow a similar path. In the first few years after SASAC's creation, profits of central SASAC firms as a share of GDP rose. But after 2007 the growth of SASAC firms' profits failed to keep up with China's GDP growth, and by 2012 SASAC firms' profits as a share of GDP had declined by a quarter compared with the 2007 peak. As will be shown in chapter 3, this decline in the relative profitability of SASAC-controlled firms since 2007 also holds for the larger universe of state-controlled firms—including central-level firms still under the control of various government ministries and state-owned firms controlled by provincial-level SASACs—and contrasts sharply with the increasingly superior financial performance of private companies, which account for a rapidly rising share of the profits of all nonfinancial enterprises.

Moreover, on the all-important measure of return on assets (pretax profits divided by assets) SASAC firms do not appear particularly efficient. As shown in the final column of the table, the return on assets of SASAC firms has fallen since 2007, and by 2013 they earned only 3.7 percent on their assets, a rate of return far below that achieved by China's private firms.[13] Equally impor-

---

13. Details on the return on assets of private industrial and service sector firms are in chapter 3.

Table 2.1 Profits of central SASAC firms, 2002–13

	All nonfinancial enterprises	Central SASAC firms		
Year	Billions of renminbi	Billions of renminbi	Percent of total profits of nonfinancial enterprises	Percent of GDP	Return on assets
2002	2,350	231	9.8	1.9	n.a.
2003	2,695	296	11.0	2.2	n.a.
2004	3,674	590	16.1	3.7	n.a.
2005	4,123	641	15.6	3.5	6.0
2006	4,783	765	16.0	3.5	6.3
2007	6,112	997	16.3	3.8	6.7
2008	7,417	696	9.4	2.2	3.9
2009	7,252	815	11.2	2.4	3.9
2010	8,226	1,143	13.9	2.8	4.7
2011	9,236	1,266	13.7	2.7	4.5
2012	10,824	1,300	12.0	2.5	4.1
2013	12,345	1,300	10.5	2.4	3.7

n.a. = not available; SASAC = State-owned Assets Supervision and Administration Commission

Notes: Total profits are earnings before corporate income tax. For the years 2002 through 2011, profits of all nonfinancial enterprises were calculated by adding corporate income tax payments to enterprise disposable income. Total profit for nonfinancial enterprises are estimated for 2012 and 2013 based on enterprise income tax receipts.

Sources: National Bureau of Statistics of China (2013c, 80–81, 329); SASAC, www.sasac.gov.cn (accessed on February 28, 2014); ISI Emerging Markets, CEIC Database; Wind Information System, Wind Economic Database.

tant, a return of 3.7 percent is well below any reasonable measure of the cost of capital. This strongly suggests that SASAC firms have grown their profits through an investment-heavy growth strategy rather than improvements in operating efficiency.

The relatively weak performance of SASAC firms since 2007 on the traditional measures of profitability and return on assets does not appear to be the result of the managers and directors of these firms pursuing noneconomic objectives. Since SASAC's establishment in 2003, managers of its traditional state-owned enterprises and managers and board members of its wholly state-owned limited liability companies and state-controlled limited liability companies, as well as members of the party committees in these firms, have been subject to both annual and three-year performance assessments that determine their bonuses. The annual assessments place substantial weight on the growth earnings before corporate income tax (EBT) and economic value added (net operating profits less capital costs) with modest positive adjustments to scores for conforming to various international standards and modest negative adjustments for any regulatory violations or errors in financial accounting. Three-year assessments take into account the annual reviews during the period, longer-term metrics such as the increase in the equity value of the firm, as well as (where relevant) negative adjustments for failure to meet pollution reduction targets.[14] The metrics for both the annual and triennial assessments would look familiar to the CEO and top managers of any publicly traded US company.

Critics charge that China's government has aggressively deployed industrial policies favoring large state-owned companies at the expense of both foreign and private domestic firms in order to create national champions that are larger, more powerful, and more profitable. Yet the evidence suggests that these policies have not enjoyed the success that the critics claim. The firms managed by central SASAC have indeed grown enormously in size as a result of both internal growth and mergers. But the massive increase in the average size of SASAC firms has not led to any visible long-run improvement in financial performance (Batson 2014). While the central SASAC entities did increase their share of profits of all nonfinancial corporations through 2007, this share has fallen sharply since. Similarly, SASAC firms' profits as a share of GDP rose through 2007 but since have fallen to a level a third less than in 2007. Most importantly, the return on assets of these SASAC firms has fallen steadily since 2006 to a level well below the cost of capital. These data point toward neither SASAC firms' efficient use of China's capital nor a recipe for producing national champions.

Similarly, while the NDRC may have accumulated substantial economic power in the Hu-Wen decade, it apparently has not been able to harness this

---

14. State-owned Assets Supervision and Administration Commission, "Temporary Regulations governing the performance evaluation of central state-owned enterprises," December 29, 2012. Available at www.sasac.gov.cn (accessed on February 4, 2014).

power to achieve the goals assigned to it: "to guarantee a rational scale of investment, to optimize the structure of investment, and raise the efficiency of investment."[15] As will be shown in the next chapter, a prime indicator of investment efficiency, return on assets, slumped badly for all state-owned industrial firms from the middle of the 2000s onward, while the returns on investment of private firms, which escaped the purview of the NDRC, rose considerably, at least through 2011. Two key factors undermine the view that 2003–13 marked the ascendency of state control of resources and a resurgence of the role of state firms: the higher share of national investment undertaken by private firms and the rising efficiency of these firms' investments, which together were a major source of economic growth in the Hu-Wen era.

15. State Council, "Decision concerning reform of the investment system," August 12, 2005. Available at www.gov.cn (accessed on March 24, 2014).

3

Rise of the Private Sector

The central theme of this chapter is that most of both the current academic literature and popular commentary on China's economy have substantially underestimated the contribution of the private sector to China's economic growth since 1978 while exaggerating the role of the state and state-owned firms. As already noted, state-owned firms remain dominant in a number of key sectors despite the far-reaching reforms of the 1990s. But, as this chapter will show, overall private businesses grew very rapidly throughout the reform era despite government policies that initially constrained their development. The private sector is now the major driver of China's economic growth, employment, and exports and in recent years has even begun to contribute to the increase in China's outbound foreign direct investment. Moreover, available evidence fails to support the frequently expressed view that China's 2009–10 stimulus program, adopted in response to the global financial crisis, directed credit disproportionately to state-owned companies, thus squeezing out the private sector. To the contrary, on a number of metrics private businesses continued to outperform state-owned enterprises by a wide margin both during and after the financial crisis, in part because of their improved access to bank credit.

This chapter traces the rise of private companies and the decline of state companies in agriculture, in industry and construction, and in services. After reviewing changes in the ownership structure of the economy, the second half of the chapter shows how the growth of private firms far surpassed the growth of state companies after 1978, and it examines whether the party-state increasingly controls the economy not through direct ownership of firms, as in the past, but rather by recruiting private entrepreneurs to party membership, thereby exercising control of the economy indirectly.

Changing Structure of Ownership

Agriculture

Documenting the rise of private economic activity in the reform era is easiest in agriculture. On the eve of reform, agricultural production was totally dominated by collective units called people's communes. Commune leaders and bureaucrats in government supply and marketing agencies in rural areas "were deeply involved with all aspects of pre- and post-harvest decisions" (Huang, Otsuka, and Rozelle 2008, 483). Outside of tiny private plots there was no private use or control of agricultural land. Collectives were compelled to deliver a large share of their output to state-owned procurement agencies at prices fixed by the State Price Commission; the balance of agricultural output produced on collective land was distributed in kind to commune members based on individual labor contributions as measured through a system of work points. Private local marketing activity and state-organized interprovincial marketing of agricultural products were heavily restricted during the Cultural Revolution (1966–76), reflecting both the general political bias against private commercial activity and the official government policy of local food grain self-sufficiency (Lardy 1985, 43–45).

These statist arrangements had a profoundly adverse effect on the growth of agricultural output, farm income, and levels of food consumption in both rural and urban China. On the eve of reform in 1978 average per capita consumption of grain and edible vegetable oils was slightly below and a third below the respective levels of 1957, just prior to the Great Leap Forward when farmers were organized into communes. Per capita rural income growth between 1957 and 1978 was only 1 percent per annum in real terms (Lardy 1984, 850–52). Socialist agriculture led to stagnation in productivity and incomes primarily because "neither the organization of production nor the systems of pricing and marketing institutions provided suitable incentives" (Huang, Otsuka, and Rozelle 2008, 477).

After 1978 the statist production and market arrangements of the pre-reform era were gradually transformed, giving rise to private farming. While official policy at the outset of reform still called for collective farming arrangements, as early as 1978 Wan Li, who had become first party secretary of Anhui Province in 1977, began to promote the decentralization of production tasks to small groups or even to individual families. This decentralization, or as it was called "contracting to households" (包产到户), quickly restored production incentives and greatly boosted agricultural production in the localities in Anhui Province where it was adopted. In the fall of 1980 Wan Li, who by then simultaneously held three powerful positions—vice premier, director of the State Agricultural Commission, and the member of the Party Secretariat in charge of agriculture—oversaw the drafting of an official government directive allowing contracting down to the household level throughout China. By October 1981 over half of rural production teams, the lowest level in the commune structure, had adopted some form of household contracting, and by the end of 1982 this share rose to 98 percent (Vogel 2011, 436–37, 442).

Thus in the early 1980s collective production arrangements effectively were disbanded throughout rural China, replaced by the household responsibility system in which farm land was assigned to individual families. Initially land assignments were for relatively short periods, typically one to three years. But to encourage private investment in land improvement, by the mid-1980s the government extended the length of land leases to 15 years. Nonetheless, these land use rights were somewhat insecure since local authorities could reassign land within the contract period, discouraging investments to improve land productivity.

The government subsequently instituted additional reforms to secure farmers' land use rights. These steps included extending the contract period for land leases to 30 years in 1993, an initiative that was codified in the Land Management Law in 1998. This was followed up with campaigns to issue written land contracts. Government-directed efforts to improve land use rights continued. In 2007 the Property Law declared that farmers' 30-year land use rights are private property rights. Subleasing of land use rights within the remaining portion of the 30-year lease term is increasingly common, and longer-term subleases have become more widespread in recent years. This subleasing has allowed farmers to work outside of agriculture without losing access to farm land. It has also made possible the emergence of private companies that are able to lease large amounts of contiguous land to operate larger-scale agricultural production units (Prosterman et al. 2009).

Post-1978 changes in marketing arrangements were equally important. As economic reform got under way, the state relied increasingly on price incentives rather than compulsory delivery quotas to acquire grain and other agricultural products required to feed China's urban population. Free markets began to reopen in large numbers in rural areas, and by the early 1980s free markets were springing up in urban areas as well. The share of agricultural output that farmers sold directly through these markets rose from less than 10 percent in 1978 to almost 20 percent by the mid-1980s (National Bureau of Statistics of China 1983, 386; 1986, 472). Subsequently, further reforms, including the abolition of rationing of grain and edible vegetable oil in urban areas in 1993, led to a drastic reduction in the role of government parastatals in marketing so that "today a large majority of sales of grains, oilseeds, and fiber crops and virtually all of horticultural and livestock products flow to small private traders," a development that has led to increasing specialization and productivity since the mid-1990s (State Council 1993; Huang, Otsuka, and Rozelle 2008, 484).

The more market-oriented production arrangements adopted starting in 1978 led to a dramatic surge in agricultural production, food consumption, and farm income. In the first five years of the new arrangements, "per capita grain consumption rose 19 percent, vegetable oil consumption more than doubled, and pork consumption rose 60 percent" (Lardy 1984, 857). Similarly, between 1978 and 1985 rural per capita income growth soared by an average of almost 15 percent per year in real terms, a huge multiple of the sluggish growth between 1957 and 1978 (National Bureau of Statistics of China 1986, 555).

Only one small segment of agriculture was untouched by the transformations in agricultural production and marketing discussed above—state farms, the origins of which date back to the 1950s. But this is a very small, rather static universe. There were about 2,000 state farms in the mid-1960s, a number that was basically unchanged through the early 2000s. By 2011 the number of state farms had dropped slightly, to around 1,800. Similarly, the cultivated area of these farms has changed little over the decades, but the number of workers declined gradually from 5.1 million in 1978 to 3.3 million in 2011. The main point is that state farms are a minuscule portion of Chinese agriculture, accounting in 2011 for about 1 percent of the agricultural labor force and 3 percent of the value of farm output (National Bureau of Statistics of China 1986, 173; 2001b, 395; 2012b, 125, 463, 495).

Although the ultimate ownership of rural land still lies in the hands of village communities rather than individual farm families, farmers' land use rights have been improved dramatically since 1978. Given the transformation of production and marketing arrangements, agriculture (outside of state farms) should be regarded as private and within the sphere of the marketized portion of China's economy.

Industry, Construction, and Services

Analyzing the transformation of the structure of ownership in China in industry, construction, and services is more complex than in agriculture for several reasons. Most importantly, these sectors cannot always be easily separated into private and state domains. China has always had hybrid forms of ownership, including collectives, cooperatives, and joint ownership enterprises, that do not always fall neatly into either the private or state category. And, as mentioned in chapter 2, in the 1990s the government introduced additional corporate forms of ownership such as limited liability companies and shareholding limited companies.[1] Without detailed information on the contributors of capital and the distribution of share ownership in these corporatized firms, it is difficult to determine whether the majority or dominant owner of these new corporate types is private, state, or some other type of legal person. Some early analysis of reforms in industry was done based on a division of firms into two broad categories, state and nonstate, where the nonstate sector includes most or all of the firms with hybrid ownership arrangements (Jefferson and Rawski 1994). However, since state units were sometimes the underlying owner of these hybrid firms, particularly collectives, this approach of using the nonstate

---

1. In some analyses the Chinese term for shareholding limited companies (股份有限公司) is translated as joint stock companies.

sector as a proxy for the private sector tends to overstate the transformation of the ownership structure of Chinese firms. This is particularly true in the first decade or two of economic reform, when hybrid forms of ownership were far more important than in the past decade or so. Thus, with few exceptions, this study avoids using nonstate as a substitute measure for private.

The second reason tracing the changing structure of ownership outside of agriculture is difficult is that traditionally the National Bureau of Statistics and other government agencies have organized and presented economic data based on the legal registration status of individual firms. This creates problems, as there are both state and private firms included within the most important registration categories. For example, as noted in chapter 2, many traditional state-owned enterprises have been transformed into limited liability companies or shareholding limited companies in which the state is the sole, majority, or dominant owner. But within the categories of limited liability and shareholding limited companies, there are also firms in which the state has a very limited or even no ownership stake whatsoever. Thus data on the output, assets, profits, and employment of limited liability companies and shareholding limited companies cannot be attributed to state or private ownership without more detailed information. Fortunately, it has become more common in recent years for various Chinese bureaucracies to separate data into universes of firms in which the majority or dominant shareholder is state, private, collective, or foreign. This disaggregation allows us to peer inside the universe of firms registered as limited liability companies, shareholding limited companies, and other registration categories to determine the underlying nature of the controlling owner or shareholder. The following discussion examines alternative ways of measuring the size of the private sector in industry and services taking into account these various lacunae in the definitions employed in official data.

The first and most frequent approach to measuring the size of the private sector in industry and services in China is to rely on data that is based on the official registration status of firms. All domestic firms in China must be registered.[2] Industrial enterprises, for example, fall into one of seven broad categories, depending on their legal basis and ownership structure. Within most of these categories there is a further breakdown of firm type depending on additional characteristics, such as the magnitude of the firm's registered capital, number of shareholders, and so forth. This scheme is summarized in table 3.1.

Registered private firms, one of the seven broad firm types, are further delineated into subcategories, shown in table 3.2. These include private sole proprietorship enterprises, private partnership enterprises, private limited liability companies, and private shareholding limited companies. Firms of the first two types are enterprises owned by a single individual or two or more persons in a partnership, and in both cases the owners have unlimited liability for the debts

---

2. Even individual industrial and commercial households (个体工商户), referred to in this study as "individual businesses" or "family businesses" and technically not considered to be firms (企业), must register.

Table 3.1   Enterprises classification system

Enterprise type	Asset ownership	Legal basis
State-owned enterprise (国有企业)	Owned by state	Law on Industrial Enterprises Owned by the Whole People (1988); Law on the State-Owned Assets of Enterprises (2009)
Collective enterprise (集体企业)	Ownership shared by employees and other economic entities	Provisional Regulations on Urban and Township Collective Enterprises (1992)
Share cooperative enterprise (股份合作企业)	Shareholders are employees of enterprise; initial startup using some public funds	Provisional Regulations on Urban and Township Collective Enterprises (1992)
Joint enterprise (联营企业)	Jointly invested by two or more enterprise legal persons or public institutions of the same or different forms of ownership	Provisional Regulations on Urban and Township Collective Enterprises (1992)
Limited liability corporation (有限责任公司)	Ownership based on capital contributions	Company Law (1994, revised 2006)
Shareholding limited corporation (股份有限公司)	Ownership based on shareholdings	Company Law (1994, revised 2006)
Private enterprise (私营企业)	Enterprise established by a natural person or majority owned by a natural person	Provisional Regulations on Private Enterprises (1988); Law on Wholly Individually Owned Enterprises (2000); Law on Partnership Enterprises (1997, revised 2007); Company Law (1994, revised 2006)

Source: National Bureau of Statistics of China (2001a).

Table 3.2 Private enterprise and household business classification system

Enterprise type	Asset ownership	Minimum capital requirement	Tax status	Liability	Law
Private sole proprietorship enterprise (私营独资企业)	owned solely by one natural person	n.a.	individual	unlimited	Provisional Regulations on Private Enterprises (1988), Law on Wholly Individually Owned Enterprises (2000)
Private partnership enterprise (私营合伙企业)	shares are owned by two or more natural persons	n.a.	individual	unlimited	Provisional Regulations on Private Enterprises (1988), Law on Partnership Enterprises (1997, revised 2006)
Private limited liability company (私营有限责任公司)	ownership based on capital contributions	RMB30,000; RMB100,000 (individual)	corporation	limited to respective capital contributions	Provisional Regulations on Private Enterprises (1988), Company Law (1994, revised 2006)
Private shareholding limited company (私营股份有限公司)	ownership based on shareholdings	RMB5 million	corporation	limited to respective share holdings	Company Law (1994, revised 2006)
Individual business (个体户)	owned solely by one natural person	n.a.	individual	unlimited	Provisions on Individual Commercial Businesses (1987, revised 2011)

n.a. = not applicable

Sources: State Council (2000; 2006b; 2011); National Bureau of Statistics of China (2001a).

of the company. The third and fourth types of private firms are limited liability companies organized under the Chinese Company Law. In private limited liability companies the capital comes from a single person or jointly from two or more persons. In private limited shareholding companies the capital is contributed by a single individual or jointly by 5 or more individuals.

The Chinese statistical authorities in the late 1990s started publishing output and other data on registered private firms in the industrial sector and for some components of the service sector. Thus there is information on the number of such firms, their output, level of investment, magnitude of their assets, and so forth. In some cases these data extend back to 1996. They show that the number of registered private enterprises expanded from 443,000 in 1996, when they accounted for less than a fifth of all enterprises, to 5,918,000 in 2012, when they accounted for more than seven-tenths of all firms (National Bureau of Statistics of China 1998; 2013c, 28–29). In the industrial sector the number of registered private firms soared from 14,600 in 1999 to 273,000 by 2010, and the share of industrial output produced by these firms rose from 4.4 percent to 30.5 percent over the same period. Similarly, employment in registered private firms soared, exceeding 94 million by 2010, of which 33 million were employed in industry (National Bureau of Statistics of China 2001b, 401; 2011a, 125, 499).

However, there are three major weaknesses in these official data on output and employment based on firm registration status that result in a substantial understatement of the importance of private firms in the industrial sector and the economy more generally. Failure to take these weaknesses into account has led a number of previous studies to underestimate the importance of the private sector.

First, the National Bureau of Statistics began in 1988 to compile and annually publish data on the output of privately registered industrial firms only for firms that have annual sales revenue above a fixed threshold, referred to as "above-scale" (规模以上) firms. When China's statistical authorities adopted this practice, the cutoff point was RMB5 million; in 2011 they raised it to RMB20 million.[3] As a result, the output of hundreds of thousands of small firms, which are disproportionately private, is not included in this annually published data. Fortunately, statistical authorities carried out two national economic censuses that included these "below-scale" firms. The 2004 national economic census revealed, for example, that there were 947,000 registered private industrial firms, almost eight times the 120,000 above-scale registered private industrial firms (National Bureau of Statistics of China 2005b). While the National Bureau of Statistics does not regularly report the output of these below-scale private firms, the 2004 economic census did. Including the output of below-scale pri-

---

3. As a result of the increase in the threshold, the number of above-scale registered private industrial firms fell between 2010 and 2011 from 273,259 to 180,612, and the number of employees in these firms fell from 33.1 million to 29.6 million (National Bureau of Statistics of China 2012b, 501).

vate firms boosted the total value of industrial output of the private industrial sector by three-fifths that year. Thus in that year above-scale registered private firms accounted for 16.5 percent of industrial output produced by all above-scale firms, but expanding both the numerator and the denominator to include output of below-scale registered private firms and all below-scale firms, respectively, boosts the private registered firms' share of output to 22.4 percent of total industrial output (National Bureau of Statistics of China 2005a, 488; 2006, 505).

The second reason annual data based on the official registration status of firms fail to capture the extent of private economic activity in China, particularly in industry, is that many firms in which the majority or dominant owner or shareholder is private (i.e., privately controlled firms) are registered in categories other than private. This may arise for several reasons. As discussed further below, in the 1980s some private firms registered as collective firms for political reasons. In other cases private firms are registered in categories other than private because their owners may wish to gain the advantage, for example, of limited liability, which was not possible for solely owned private registered firms until 2006. In other cases the ownership structure of firms evolves over time, but some of these firms do not reregister after such a change has occurred or do so only with a long lag (Dougherty, Herd, and He 2007, 312).

Another example of why the registration system fails to reflect the true extent of private economic activity is that all firms in which a foreign company contributes 25 percent or more of a firm's capital are classified separately, with a further subclassification based on whether the firm's legal status is a joint venture, a wholly foreign-owned firm, and so forth. This approach was adopted to allow the government to track the success of China's programs to attract foreign investment, such as the law on joint ventures promulgated in 1979 and the establishment of special economic zones on the southeast coast of China beginning in 1980. While perhaps useful for this purpose, many of these firms, particularly wholly foreign-owned firms in which the foreign owner is a private corporation, in most economies would normally be regarded and classified as private firms. This issue is further analyzed below.

An alternative approach to relying on a firm's formal registration status to track the changing structure of ownership in China's economy is to look at the ownership structure of firms and determine whether the majority or dominant owner is private or state.[4] This is possible because, as explained in box 2.1, in 1998 the National Bureau of Statistics of China introduced the concept of control and a year later began systematic publication of data on the industrial output of firms that were registered in categories other than state owned but were in fact majority or dominantly owned by the state. While the government has not published such annual data on the output of privately controlled industrial companies, the two economic censuses have provided

---

4. There are also a small number of limited liability companies and shareholding limited companies in which collective units are the majority or dominant owners.

detailed ownership data for industrial firms that can be used to measure the output of firms in which the majority or dominant share holder is private.

The earliest comprehensive published effort to measure the output of privately controlled industrial firms was undertaken by economists at the Organization for Economic Cooperation and Development (OECD) in collaboration with the National Bureau of Statistics of China. Using a comprehensive firm-level data set covering a quarter-million industrial companies, they found that privately registered and privately controlled domestic industrial firms in 2003 accounted for a combined 33.1 percent of value added in industry, or roughly 2.5 times the 12.8 percent private share reflected in official output data based solely on firm registration status (Dougherty, Herd, and He 2007, 315; National Bureau of Statistics of China 2005a, 488). The substantial understatement in the official data arises primarily because in 2003 privately controlled firms accounted for about a third of the value added of firms that were registered as collective enterprises and over half of the value added of firms registered as other limited liability corporations.[5] The OECD applied the same methodology to a comparable data set for 1998 and found that privately registered and privately controlled industrial firms together accounted for 15.3 percent of value added in industry, indicating that the share of output of this group of firms doubled in the five years leading up to 2003 (Dougherty, Herd, and He 2007, 315).

The same approach of classifying firms based on whether the majority or dominant owner is private or state can be applied to firms with foreign funding. The Chinese enterprise registration system does not classify firms with foreign funding as private, state, or any of the other categories shown in table 3.1.[6] Rather, the registration system treats firms with foreign funding amounting to 25 percent or more of the firm's capital separately. In Chinese statistics there are two categories of firms with foreign funding: those with funding from Hong Kong, Taiwan, or Macao, and those with funding from abroad.[7] There are four variants within each broad category, depending on the details of the ownership structure.

Should any of these firms with foreign funding be considered private? In the early days of foreign-funded firms the answer to this question was basically no. Through the mid-1980s virtually all foreign direct investment in China was in the form of joint ventures. Although the domestic partner in some cases, particularly for smaller joint ventures, was a private Chinese company, the joint venture category was dominated by arrangements in which a state-owned enterprise was the domestic partner of the foreign firm. Very frequently the

---

5. The line for limited liability corporations shown in table 3.1 is further divided into state sole-funded corporations and other limited liability corporations. In 2004 the former category included only 2,083 corporations, or 2 percent of the total (National Bureau of Statistics of China 2006, 505).

6. If the foreign ownership share is less than 25 percent, the firm is classified into one of the ownership categories shown in table 3.1.

7. In the text I sometimes refer to this combined universe of firms as "foreign funded."

Chinese state firm was the majority shareholder in the joint venture. Thus for the purposes of assessing the overall ownership structure within the Chinese economy, firms with foreign funding through the mid-1980s should be considered predominantly state owned.

Over time this pattern changed. In 1986 the Chinese National People's Congress adopted a law governing foreign direct investment in the form of wholly foreign-owned companies, in which there was no domestic ownership, by either a state or a private firm.[8] Subsequently, an increasing share of foreign direct investment in China took the form of wholly foreign-owned firms. As early as 1989, 30 percent of all incoming foreign direct investment was in this form, up from only 1 percent in 1985 (National Bureau of Statistics of China 1990, 653). A decade later, the share had risen to two-fifths, and by 2010 just over three-quarters of $106 billion in foreign direct investment entered China in the form of wholly foreign-owned companies while less than one-quarter was in the form of joint ventures (National Bureau of Statistics of China 2000, 605; 2011a, 244).[9] In addition, in many cases foreign partners in firms that were originally established as joint ventures with state firms subsequently bought out their partners and converted their registration status to wholly foreign-owned firms.[10] The owners of these wholly foreign-owned firms are private and thus should be regarded as private firms.

While foreign direct investment accounts for a very small share of capital formation in China, in some sectors foreign-funded firms make a very large contribution to output. In the manufacturing sector, for example, foreign-funded firms accounted for over one-quarter of the value of output in 2010, with about 15 percentage points of this produced by wholly foreign-owned companies. Since manufacturing accounts for two-fifths of China's GDP, the contribution of wholly foreign-owned firms to the private sector should not be overlooked. As early as 2003 two-thirds of the output of joint venture firms was produced by firms in which the majority or dominant shareholder was private; only a third of the output was produced by firms in which the majority or dominant shareholder was a state or collective unit (Dougherty, Herd, and He 2007, 315).

A third major weakness of the official data is that they exclude a broad range of economic activity carried out by what in China are referred to as "family" or "individual businesses" (个体户).[11] These businesses are not classi-

---

8. Law of the People's Republic of China on Wholly Foreign-Funded Enterprises. The law was revised in 2000, removing some restrictions on wholly foreign-funded firms, further encouraging investment in that form of ownership. It should be noted that a few foreign investors established wholly foreign-owned enterprises prior to the promulgation of the 1986 law.

9. The data cited in the text exclude foreign direct investment in China's financial sector.

10. These ownership transformations are not reflected in the data just cited, which cover only new investments.

11. The formal name for these businesses, "individual industrial and commercial households," clearly indicates that this category of economic activity excludes family-based agriculture. See note 2 in this chapter.

Table 3.3   Individual businesses and registered private enterprises in China, 2002–12 (millions)

Year	Individual businesses		Private enterprises	
	Businesses	Employees	Enterprises	Employees
2002	23.8	47.4	2.6	32.5
2003	23.5	43.0	3.3	43.0
2004	23.5	45.9	4.0	50.2
2005	24.6	49.0	4.7	58.2
2006	26.0	51.6	5.4	65.9
2007	27.4	55.0	6.0	72.5
2008	29.2	57.8	6.6	79.0
2009	32.0	66.3	7.4	86.1
2010	34.5	70.1	8.5	94.2
2011	37.6	79.5	9.7	103.5
2012	40.6	86.3	10.9	113.0

Sources: All-China Federation of Industry and Commerce (2011, 2; 2012, 30, 34; 2013, 26, 30).

fied as enterprises but are shown in the last line of table 3.2. Workers in these businesses are classified as self-employed. Their numbers have grown enormously over time. In urban areas in 1978, the number of self-employed was a minuscule 150,000, less than one-tenth of 1 percent of urban employment (National Bureau of Statistics of China 1986, 92). This reflected the systematic repression of private economic activity during the Cultural Revolution (1966–76). By 2011 self-employed workers in urban areas numbered 52.3 million and accounted for 15 percent of the urban workforce. In the same year there were an additional 27.2 million individuals self-employed in nonfarming activities in rural areas, up from 15 million in 1990, the first year for which data on self-employed workers in rural areas have been published (National Bureau of Statistics of China 2012b, 126–27; 1997, 97).[12]

While official data on registered private firms exclude the output and employment of individual businesses, other data sources provide a more comprehensive picture of private firms and individual businesses, including those outside the industrial sector. Table 3.3 shows the expansion since 2002. By 2012 these businesses employed 200 million, two and a half times the level of 2002. The sectoral breakdown in 2009 is shown in tables 3.4 and 3.5,

---

12. However, the rise from 1990 to 2010 was not linear. Reported self-employment in rural areas peaked at 39 million in 1998. The decline from this peak presumably reflects several factors. First, the rapid development of the export processing and urban construction sectors led to a large increase in the number of rural residents who migrated to urban areas to seek employment. While some of these migrant workers had previously been employed in agriculture, others presumably had been employed in township and village enterprises. Second, some household businesses in rural areas presumably converted to registered private enterprises once they reached the limit of seven nonfamily employees.

respectively. The most striking thing to emerge from both tables is that private firms and individual businesses are concentrated in the service sector and that, within services, wholesale and retail activity dominates, as measured by the share of firms and share of employees in private and individual businesses. Manufacturing accounts for almost a quarter of private firms, but fewer than 10 percent of all employees in individual businesses. Given the restriction that individual businesses until 2011 could not have more than seven nonfamily employees, it is not surprising that their role in manufacturing, where economies of scale are usually significant, is so limited.

Figure 3.1, which summarizes the discussion above, shows the complexity of answering the seemingly simple question "How large was the private industrial sector in China in 2003 and 2007?" The answer depends on how one defines private. On the narrowest definition, based solely on firm registration status, above-scale registered private firms accounted for only one-eighth of China's industrial output in 2003. But taking into account the output of both private registered firms with revenue less than RMB5 million and domestic firms registered in categories other than private but in which the majority or dominant shareholder was private brings the private share to almost two-fifths of all industrial production. Adding in the output of firms with foreign investment, where the majority or dominant shareholder is private, pushes the total up to almost three-fifths. The data for 2007 show a similar pattern, but the private share is somewhat higher for each definition of private, reaching over three-fifths on the broadest definition. In both years the narrowest definition clearly understates the contribution of the private sector to industrial output, but the broadest probably overstates it because there must be some firms where the extent of the government's de facto control exceeds its ownership share.

In the following analysis of the importance of the private sector in generating output, employment, and exports, the definition of private is the sum of registered private firms and individual businesses. It would be useful to be able to base the analysis on the concept of privately controlled firms, following the lead of the OECD. However, the large firm-level data set required to measure the extent of private control of firms with various registration statuses is available only for years in which China's statistical authorities conduct an economic census, typically every five years, and even these data become available with a substantial lag.[13] Moreover, the OECD has published its findings for only two years, 1998 and 2003, and thus cannot shed light on developments in the decade since. Finally, the large firm-level data set that the OECD used to determine control only covered firms in the industrial sector, and not ownership transformation in services. As a result, this analysis initially relies on a narrower definition of private, but the reader should keep in mind that

---

13. Summary data from the 2003 census and the 2008 census were released at the end of December 2005 and the end of December 2009, respectively. The more detailed microdata from each economic census were available with an even longer time lag.

Table 3.4   Private enterprises by sector, 2009 (thousands)

Total	7,402
Primary	164
Farming, forestry, animal husbandry	164
Secondary	2,206
Manufacturing	1,745
Mining	60
Construction	367
Electricity, heat production, and supply	35
Tertiary	5,032
Wholesale and retail trade	2,632
Leasing and commercial services	717
Scientific research and polytechnical services	379
Information transmission, software, and information technology service	274
Real estate	249
Resident services and other services	243
Transport, storage, and postal services	195
Accommodation and catering trade	137
Culture, sports, and entertainment	86
Other	48
Water conservancy, environment, and utility management	30
Finance	24
Health, social welfare, and social services	10
Education	9

Source: All-China Federation of Industry and Commerce and China Nonstate (Private) Economy Research Association (2011, 738).

the result understates private businesses' role in China. (Later in the chapter, in the section explaining the growth of the private sector, I do examine official data series on investment, lending, and other variables that are based on a broader definition of private.)

Industry and Construction

The rise of private firms and the decline in the role of state firms is easiest to measure in industry and construction. Until 2013 industry and construction combined accounted for a larger share of China's GDP than either agriculture or services, so understanding the changing ownership arrangements in industry and construction is crucial to any evaluation of the evolving relative roles of state and private firms in the Chinese economy. As shown in figure 3.2, the share of industrial output produced by state firms (including both traditional state-owned enterprises and enterprises in other registration categories where the state is the majority or dominant shareholder) fell from 78 percent in 1978 to 26 percent by 2011 (National Bureau of Statistics of China 1990, 416; 2012b, 501, 513).

Table 3.5   Employees of individual businesses by sector, 2009
(thousands)

Total	31,974
Primary	427
Farming, forestry, animal husbandry	427
Secondary	2,776
Manufacturing	2,640
Mining	53
Construction	67
Electricity, heat production, and supply	16
Tertiary	28,801
Wholesale and retail trade	19,903
Resident services and other services	3,245
Accommodation and catering trade	2,813
Transport, storage, and postal services	1,596
Leasing and commercial services	374
Other	289
Information transmission, software, and information technology service	210
Culture, sports, and entertainment	196
Health, social welfare, and social services	87
Real estate	45
Scientific research and polytechnical services	26
Education	9
Water conservancy, environment, and utility management	7
Finance	1

Source: All-China Federation of Industry and Commerce and China Nonstate (Private) Economy Research Association (2011, 740).

But this series understates the decline of state industry because, as already noted, data on the value of industrial output are available on an annual basis after 1998 only for above-scale firms. The abrupt jump in state-owned firms' share of industrial output in 1998, reflected in figure 3.2, is entirely a statistical artifact driven by the deletion of below-scale firms, which were overwhelmingly private firms or collective enterprises.[14] For 2004, China's statistical authorities published data including below-scale firms. Thus, while the figure shows that state firms in 2004 accounted for 35 percent of above-scale firms' industrial output, taking into account the additional RMB3.5 trillion in output produced by below-scale firms drops the state share to 30 percent. A little over half of the output of below-scale firms was produced in private enterprises.

---

14. From 1998 through 2006 the output value of above-scale industrial firms included the output value of all state firms and the output value of nonstate firms with sales revenue of RMB5 million or more. For the four years 2007–10, it includes the output value of all firms with sales revenue of RMB5 million or more. Beginning in 2011 it includes the output value of all firms with sales revenue of RMB20 million or more.

Figure 3.1 Alternative measures of the private share of value-added industrial output, 2003 and 2007

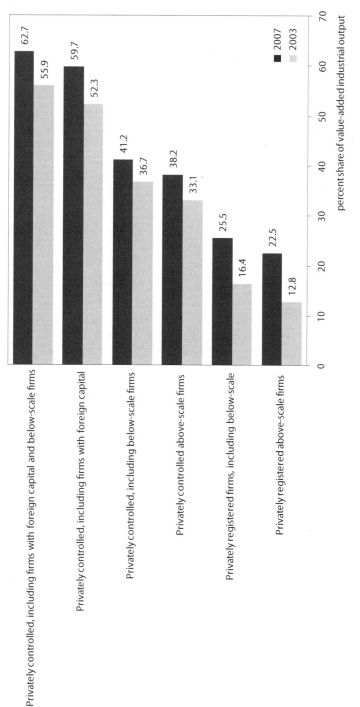

percent share of value-added industrial output

Privately controlled, including firms with foreign capital and below-scale firms — 2007: 62.7, 2003: 55.9

Privately controlled, including firms with foreign capital — 2007: 59.7, 2003: 52.3

Privately controlled, including below-scale firms — 2007: 41.2, 2003: 36.7

Privately controlled above-scale firms — 2007: 38.2, 2003: 33.1

Privately registered firms, including below-scale — 2007: 25.5, 2003: 16.4

Privately registered above-scale firms — 2007: 22.5, 2003: 12.8

Sources: Author's calculations based on data from the National Bureau of Statistics of China, Industrial Survey Firm-Level Database (2007); Dougherty, Herd, and He (2007, 315).

Figure 3.2 Gross industrial output of state enterprises, 1978–2011

percent of total gross industrial output

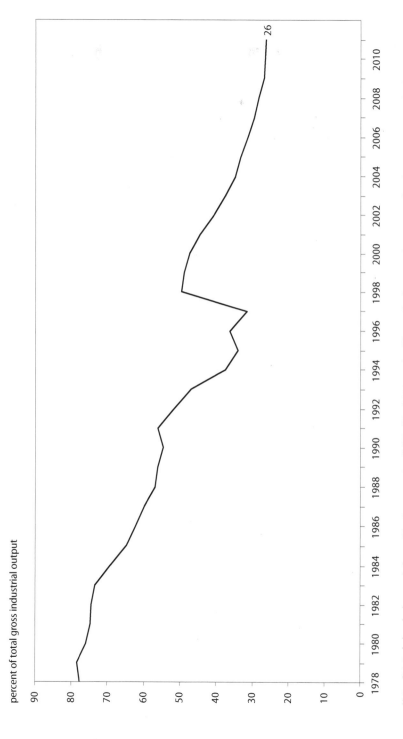

Notes: Data include only above-scale firms, with sales greater than RMB5 million (1998–2011) and firms with sales greater than RMB20 million (beginning in 2011). This data series appears to have been discontinued.

Sources: National Bureau of Statistics of China (2012b, 518); National Bureau of Statistics of China, www.stats.gov.cn (accessed on February 28, 2014).

Thus in 2004 private firms' share of all industrial output was 22.4 percent, well above the 16.5 percent share of above-scale private firms' output. In short, the official data underlying figure 3.2 accurately reflect the long-term decline in the role of state firms in China's industrial sector, but after 1998 their share of output is overstated. If the relative importance of below-scale firms in 2011 was the same as in 2008, state firms' share would be 24 percent, rather than the 26 percent shown in the figure.[15] Roughly speaking, it is therefore fair to say that between 1978 and 2011 the share of industrial output produced by state firms fell from about three-quarters to one-quarter.

The retreat of state firms in Chinese industry has been across almost all product lines. By 2011 there were only 6 of 40 branches of industry where state firms produced more than 50 percent of output (table 3.6). Two of the six, electric power and water, are natural monopolies in which state ownership is common in many market economies. In OECD countries, for example, state-owned utilities account for almost 30 percent of the value of all state-owned companies (Christiansen 2011, 15). Moreover, in 24 branches of industry the state share of output was less than 15 percent. Even these data overstate the role of state firms since the output data exclude firms with sales of less than RMB20 million, a universe that comprises predominantly private firms.[16] Especially worth noting is the significant erosion of state-controlled firms' role even in some of the nine key "pillar" industries discussed in chapter 2. In the coal industry, the state's share of output by 2011 had slipped to barely over 50 percent, down significantly from the 66 percent share it held in 2006, when Li Rongrong declared that it was necessary for the state to guarantee absolute controlling power in this industry. In steel, another so-called pillar industry deemed as requiring strong state control, the share of output by state-controlled firms slid from 43 percent in 2006 to 37 percent in 2011 (National Bureau of Statistics of China 2007, 501, 512; 2012b, 502–503, 512–13).

While China's three national oil companies continue to control over nine-tenths of oil and gas extraction, the one-time dominance of these firms in some downstream activities has been significantly eroded. The best example is natural gas, where state firms by 2011 controlled less than half of gas distribution. As early as 2002 the distribution of natural gas in China's cities was opened to private players, including foreign companies. There are now more than 60 companies in the city gas business. Some are state-owned, including China's largest gas company, Beijing Enterprise Holdings Limited. Others are

---

15. Data for the gross value of total industrial output and the gross value of industrial output of above-scale firms are available for 2008 since statistical authorities conducted an industrial census that year.

16. When the threshold for above-scale changed in 2011, the number of state above-scale firms fell by 3,200 between 2010 and 2011, while the number of private above-scale firms dropped by about 90,000 (see note 14). These numbers suggest that the data in table 3.6 overstate the role of state firms in industry.

Table 3.6   State share of industrial output by subsectors, 2011

Sector	Percent of total
Manufacture of tobacco	99.3
Production and supply of electric power and heat power	93.0
Extraction of petroleum and natural gas	92.1
Production and supply of water	69.4
Processing of petroleum, coking, processing of nuclear fuel	68.6
Mining and washing of coal	53.6
Production and supply of gas	44.4
Manufacture of transport equipment	44.0
Smelting and pressing of ferrous metals	36.9
Smelting and pressing of nonferrous metals	28.8
Mining and processing of nonferrous metal ores	28.7
National average	**26.2**
Manufacture of special purpose machinery	20.5
Manufacture of raw chemical materials and chemical products	18.7
Mining and processing of ferrous metal ores	16.7
Manufacture of beverages	16.5
Manufacture of general purpose machinery	12.5
Mining and processing of nonmetal ores	12.3
Manufacture of rubber	12.1
Manufacture of medicines	11.8
Printing, reproduction of recording media	11.5
Manufacture of nonmetallic mineral products	10.6
Manufacture of measuring instruments and machinery for cultural activity and office work	10.3
Manufacture of electrical machinery and equipment	8.9
Manufacture of artwork and other manufacturing	8.9
Manufacture of communication equipment, computers, and other electronic equipment	8.3
Manufacture of chemical fibers	8.2
Manufacture of paper and paper products	6.9
Manufacture of foods	5.8
Manufacture of metal products	5.8
Processing of food from agricultural products	5.4
Recycling and disposal of waste	3.8
Manufacture of plastics	2.7
Manufacture of textile	2.4
Processing of timber, manufacture of wood, bamboo, rattan, palm, and straw products	2.3
Manufacture of furniture	1.7
Manufacture of textile wearing apparel, footware, and caps	1.4
Manufacture of articles for culture, education, and sport activities	1.2
Manufacture of leather, fur, feather, and related products	0.3
Mining of other ores	0

Source: National Bureau of Statistics of China (2012b, 502–13).

private. These include ENN, China's largest private gas company, which is listed in Hong Kong and majority owned by Wang Yusuo and his wife. China Gas, the second largest private gas company, is a Hong Kong listed company majority owned by Liu Minghui, another private entrepreneur.[17] China Gas has concessions to supply piped gas in 160 Chinese cities and also owns a number of long-distance natural gas pipelines and a network of compressed natural gas refilling stations for vehicles. The growing role of private gas companies is strongly reflected in their share of investment in the industry, which by 2012 had risen to 40 percent, with an additional 6 percent coming from foreign private-controlled companies (National Bureau of Statistics of China 2013c, 170–71).

The three national oil companies have retreated from another downstream activity, refining. Their once virtual monopoly has gradually eroded so that by 2011 they accounted for less than 70 percent of refined petroleum, with the balance roughly split between private and foreign firms (National Bureau of Statistics of China 2012b, 502–503, 512–13, 532–33).

The state has also ceded considerable space to private firms in water supply, a utility that is state owned in many market economies. In 1999 state companies accounted for 90 percent of the value of output of the sector (National Bureau of Statistics of China 2000, 414, 424). As shown in table 3.6, by 2011 this share had fallen to under 70 percent. Foreign companies, which were allowed to enter the sector in 2002, currently account for about a fifth of output and registered private domestic companies another 6 percent. The single biggest foreign player is the French firm Veoli. It has full service water concessions in the Pudong business district in Shanghai, in several districts in the city of Tianjin, and in other cities, where it provides water to 27 million inhabitants.

The long-term retreat of state firms in Chinese industry did not slow during the global financial crisis and its aftermath, a period many studies have characterized as marking their resurgence. The average annual increase in industrial value added in the four years after 2008 across firms of all ownership types was 12.7 percent. But the universe of state and state-controlled firms continued to underperform, expanding by an annual average of only 9.2 percent, while registered private firms grew at an average rate of 18.2 percent (National Bureau of Statistics of China 2010c; 2011b; 2012c; 2013a).[18]

---

17. While China Gas is usually considered a privately controlled company, Sinopec owns a 6 percent stake in the firm, and an arm of the Beijing municipal government, Beijing Enterprise Holdings Limited, holds a stake just under that of the firm's founder Liu Minghui. Foreign shareholders in China Gas include Korea's SK Group and Fortune Oil PLC, a UK company.

18. The release of industrial value-added data is asymmetric in the sense that the reported growth rate for state firms is based on a measure of output that is inclusive of both traditional state-owned companies and companies of all registration types where the state is the majority or dominant owner, while the reported growth rate for private firms is based strictly on the output of private registered firms.

There has been a similar long-term decline in the importance of state firms in the construction industry, which accounted for 7 percent of GDP in 2011 (National Bureau of Statistics of China 2013c, 54). In 1980 state firms employed three-quarters of all workers in the industry and were responsible for just over three-quarters of the value of construction. Collective construction enterprises accounted for the remainder of both employment and the value of construction (National Bureau of Statistics of China 2012b, 567). There was no private construction industry in the early years of the reform era. By 2010 the share of output of state construction firms had shrunk to less than a third.[19] The role of collective enterprises in the construction industry basically collapsed; by 2010 they accounted for less than 4 percent of the output value of the construction industry. In the same year foreign firms accounted for only 1 percent of output value (National Bureau of Statistics of China 2012b, 567). Thus privately controlled domestic firms now dominate the industry: in 2010 they accounted for about three-quarters of the employment and two-thirds of the value of output.

Services

Measuring the changing contributions of state and private firms to output and employment in the service sector is a more difficult task. For one, the data are much less detailed than those for industry. Although the National Bureau of Statistics publishes annual data on aggregate service output, there is no systematic breakdown of ownership types of service firms. Thus, disaggregation is problematic. One is forced to look at each of the 14 components of China's service sector. For a few, good data are available. For others, there is useful qualitative information. But for some components the empirical basis for analysis is much more limited. Of course, any discussion of services has to begin by recognizing that state-owned and state-controlled firms completely dominate several key components of the sector: finance, which includes banking, insurance, securities, and asset management; basic telecommunications; and some forms of transportation (airlines, rail, and ocean shipping), which frequently but not always are privately run in a market economy. One should also recognize that state units still dominate other services—educa-

---

19. Data on the number of state-owned firms, the number of workers, and the value of output of these firms in the construction industry published by the National Bureau of Statistics cover only traditional state-owned companies. These state-owned construction enterprises in 2010 employed 5,769,000 workers and accounted for 18.9 percent of the output in the sector (National Bureau of Statistics of China 2012b, 567). The combined employment of state-owned construction enterprises and state-controlled construction companies in 2010 was 8,959,000 workers, according to "An Analysis of Statistics on the Development of the Construction Industry," *Zhongguo jianshe bao* (*China Construction Newspaper*), May 28, 2011. Available at www.chinajsb.cn (accessed on January 30, 2013). Assuming that labor productivity in the two types of state firms is the same, state-owned enterprises and state-controlled companies together account for 29 percent of construction output.

tion, health, social security, and social welfare—that are mostly government run even in market economies. In short, unlike in agriculture, industry, and construction, in large swaths of China's service sector there has been no ownership transformation.

Wholesale and retail trade is the single largest component of the service sector, accounting in 2011 for just over one-fifth of value added in services or 5 percent of GDP (National Bureau of Statistics of China 2012b, 44, 49). In 1978 wholesale and retail trade was overwhelmingly controlled by state and collective enterprises. In retailing, for example, the private sector (entirely individual businesses at that time) was almost invisible. In 1978 only about 10 percent of all retail units were private, and they accounted for only a tiny 3 percent of retail employment and a minuscule 0.1 percent of retail sales. The shares of state retail establishments, employment, and sales were 34 percent, 58 percent, and 90 percent, respectively (National Bureau of Statistics of China 1986, 414, 445–46). The balance of retailing activity was controlled by collective enterprises, which typically meant some degree of local government ownership and control.

By 2008 four-fifths of all retailers were privately controlled, and they accounted for half of retail sales and a little more than half of profits in the retail sector.[20] In addition, foreign retailers, a group that includes the likes of Wal-Mart, Tesco, Carrefour, and Metro, accounted for almost 10 percent of retail sales. Since these firms are wholly owned by foreign private firms, they certainly should be regarded as private. State retailers in 2008 accounted for 3.5 percent, 22 percent, and 22 percent, respectively, of retail units, employment, and sales (National Bureau of Statistics of China 2010a). In short, in three decades the share of retail sales by state firms fell from nine-tenths to two-tenths.

The transformation of ownership in wholesaling has not been as dramatic, presumably because wholesale businesses on average are much larger and raising the capital required to finance the larger inventories of these firms was a greater challenge for private firms. In 1978 state and collective units accounted for 98 percent of wholesale transactions. The share of wholesale turnover accounted for by individual businesses was only 0.1 percent (National Bureau of Statistics of China 1985, 465). By 2008 state-owned and state-controlled and collectively owned and collectively controlled wholesaling units together accounted for only two-fifths of sales, while privately controlled firms

---

20. The end point of the analysis is 2008, the year of the last economic census. Annual data on retailing published by the National Bureau of Statistics have two shortcomings. First, the annual data cover only above-scale retail units, which leave out many private small-scale retailers. Second, the data are based entirely on registration status so they do not identify, for example, employment in and sales by limited liability companies in which the majority or dominant owner is private. For example, four-fifths of private retail units in 2008 were privately controlled. Of these 80 percent, 75 percentage points were registered private companies and 5 percentage points were firms of other types of ownership registration in which the dominant owner was private.

accounted for 45 percent. Adding wholesaling activity controlled by private foreign firms boosts the private total to just over 50 percent of sales (National Bureau of Statistics of China 2010a).

The ownership transformation in the catering industry is similar to that in retailing, presumably because there are no significant regulatory barriers to entry and the capital required to open a restaurant is similarly modest. On the eve of reform state and collective enterprises dominated. Almost a third of catering firms were private, but they must have been very small on average since they accounted for only 7 percent of employment in the industry (National Bureau of Statistics of China 1986, 414).[21] China's 2008 economic census shows an industry in which the structure of ownership has been totally transformed, with four-fifths of employment and almost two-thirds of revenue generated by private catering firms (National Bureau of Statistics of China 2010a).

It is likely that the share of employment and sales by state firms in retailing, wholesaling, and catering has continued to decline since 2008, but measurement of this decline will have to await the results of China's 2013 economic census.[22]

In summary, in the contestable sectors of the economy where there are relatively low barriers to entry, privately registered and privately controlled companies have largely displaced state companies. This displacement includes most of manufacturing and mining as well as construction, retailing, wholesaling, and catering (Anderson 2012). In sectors where there are barriers to entry due to natural monopoly, high capital requirements, or government regulation, the dominant position state firms enjoyed in 1978 has in most cases eroded only slightly. The best examples of the latter in industry are tobacco manufacturing, electric power, and oil and gas extraction, where state firms in 2011 still accounted for 99, 93, and 92 percent of output, respectively (table 3.6).

The state exercises complete control of the tobacco industry through the aptly named State Tobacco Monopoly Administration, which directly controls the China National Tobacco Corporation (CNTC), which in turn controls cigarette companies accounting for 96 percent of the assets in the industry. The state is unwilling to cede control of the tobacco industry for fiscal reasons—CNTC is China's fourth largest company in terms of net profit (Li 2012, 3–7).

The state monopolizes the oil and gas extraction industry, presumably for strategic reasons, a pattern observed in a number of market economies as well. Obvious examples are the state-controlled firms Pemex in Mexico and Petrobras in Brazil. Electric power generation and distribution is a natural monopoly. In many market economies this is a privately run, state-regulated industry, but China has chosen direct state ownership instead.

---

21. Unlike retailing, catering revenue disaggregated by ownership is not available for the late 1970s.

22. Based on the lag last time, publication of preliminary results of the 2013 census is likely to occur at the end of 2014.

In services the state firms still exercise virtual monopoly control of financial services, large swaths of transportation services, and basic telecommunication services, which in many but not all market economies are provided by private companies. Of course, the state dominates education, health, and other social services that in many other countries also are provided by governments. The state also plays an outsized role in journalism and publishing, broadcasting and movies, culture and art, and sports, a pattern typical in one-party, authoritarian political systems.[23]

Role of Private Firms in Generating Employment and Exports

Despite the predominance of state firms in production in certain sectors, state firms as a group have not been a significant source of growth of employment in the reform era. Indeed, employment in state firms has fallen in absolute terms for more than a decade and now accounts for only 13 percent of urban employment. Conversely, the importance of private and individual businesses in generating employment is difficult to overstate. The analysis that follows looks first at urban and then rural employment.

In 1978 employment in individual businesses in urban areas had been reduced to only 150,000, down from 1.71 million in 1965, just before the Cultural Revolution began (National Bureau of Statistics of China 1986, 92). As shown in table 3.7, employment in individual businesses in urban China subsequently grew rapidly, reaching 4.5 million by 1985 and 56 million by 2012. Registered private businesses in urban areas were not important until after the legal framework for them was established in 1988. Employment in these businesses then expanded rapidly, reaching 76 million by 2012. By 2012 individual businesses and registered private firms thus employed over 132 million individuals, almost four and a half times the number employed in 2000 and accounting for over one-third of urban employment.

But due to limitations in the methodology used by the Ministry of Human Resources and Social Security and the National Bureau of Statistics to compile employment data, 132 million is an understatement of employment in urban private businesses. The first limitation is that official annual data on urban private employment are compiled strictly on the basis of the registration status of firms. The data do not include those employed in firms registered as limited liability companies, shareholding limited companies, collectives, and other registration categories in which the majority or dominant owner is private. While the statistical authorities, as noted above, have started to provide certain types of data based on the nature of the majority or dominant owner, annual

---

23. One measure of state domination in these fields is the share of investment undertaken by state and state-controlled units. This investment ranges from a high of 71 percent in journalism and publishing to a low of 59 percent in culture and art (National Bureau of Statistics of China 2012b, 176–79).

Table 3.7 Urban registered private enterprise and individual business employment, 1978–2012

Year	Total employment (thousands)	Private enterprises (thousands)	Individual businesses (thousands)	Private enterprises and individual businesses as percent of total employment
1978	95,140	n.a.	150	0.2
1979	99,990	n.a.	320	0.3
1980	105,250	n.a.	810	0.8
1985	128,080	n.a.	4,500	3.5
1990	170,410	570	6,140	3.9
2000	231,510	12,679	21,361	14.7
2001	241,230	15,268	21,312	15.2
2002	251,590	19,987	22,688	17.0
2003	262,300	25,452	23,770	18.8
2004	272,930	29,937	25,212	20.2
2005	283,890	34,584	27,777	22.0
2006	296,300	39,543	30,125	23.5
2007	309,530	45,810	33,100	25.5
2008	321,030	51,240	36,090	27.2
2009	333,220	55,443	42,445	29.4
2010	346,870	60,709	44,675	30.4
2011	359,140	69,120	52,270	33.8
2012	371,020	75,570	56,430	35.6

n.a. = not applicable

Sources: National Bureau of Statistics of China (2013c, 121); ISI Emerging Markets, CEIC Database.

data on this basis have not yet been published except in the case of state firms. In 2011 almost 75 million urban workers were employed in registration categories other than state, private, and individual (National Bureau of Statistics of China 2012b, 125). We estimate private employment in firms of other types based on the 2007 Industrial Survey Firm-Level Database, which enumerated employment in industrial firms of every registration category where the majority or dominant owner is private. Assuming the share of employment in each of these categories in 2011 is the same as that for 2007, I estimate private employment in registration categories other than private or individual businesses accounts for an additional 51 million workers.[24] This brings the estimated total urban private employment in 2011 to 183 million, raising the

24. This assumption probably leads to a downward-biased estimate of private employment in firm registration categories other than private or individual businesses because the share of firms in each of these categories where the majority or dominant owner is private has been gradually increasing.

private share of urban employment by 14 percentage points to equal half of urban employment.

The second limitation of official employment data is that they do not provide any information on the registration status of firms accounting for a large share of urban employment. For example, in 2011, reported total urban employment was 359 million, yet the statistical authorities have provided no information on the registration status of firms employing 97 million of these workers (National Bureau of Statistics of China 2012b, 125). This large gap arises because the National Bureau of Statistics estimates total urban employment based on the most recent national population census and an annual labor force sample survey, whereas data on employment by registration status are based on reporting by enterprise units.[25] But the employment data reported by these enterprise units do not include informal urban workers—mostly migrant workers but also some urban residents who work in these units but do not have stable labor contracts, do not make contributions to various social insurance funds, and do not receive social benefits (Cai and Chan 2009). The latter group includes student interns, part-time student employees, and temporary and seasonal workers. It seems likely that the majority of these 97 million are employed in firms in which the majority or dominant owner is private.[26]

This analysis supports the conclusion that almost all of the growth of urban employment in China since 1978 is due to the expansion of private firms, including privately owned foreign firms. Private urban employment expanded from 150,000 in 1978, or 0.2 percent of urban employment, to an estimated 253 million in 2011 (table 3.8). In 2011 employment in privately controlled firms accounted for two-thirds of China's urban labor force. More impressively, the increase in private urban employment, almost entirely the result of the formation of new privately owned or privately controlled businesses,

---

25. Data on self-employment and employment by private enterprises published by the National Bureau of Statistics of China are provided by the State Administration for Industry and Commerce.

26. This assumption is based on data on the distribution of employment of migrant workers across various industries as reported in "Report on the 2012 National Migrant Worker Investigation Survey," May 27, 2013, available at www.stats.gov.cn (accessed on May 28, 2013). In 2011, one-quarter were employed in wholesaling and retailing, hotels and catering, and household services—all sectors where private firms or households are dominant. About one-third were employed in manufacturing, presumably almost entirely in wholly foreign-owned enterprises (and thus private) that rely heavily on female migrant workers to produce export goods. Just under a fifth were employed in construction, where the role of the state is somewhat larger. The smallest share, less than 7 percent, was employed in transport, storage, and post, a sector that the state still heavily dominates. But this domination is due to the state's sole ownership of the national rail system and majority ownership of the largest airlines and international shipping companies. It is likely that migrant workers were employed in trucking and logistics businesses, where private ownership is more important. Based on this analysis, I assume that just over 80 percent of the 97 million urban workers employed in firms where the registration status is not provided were employed in private firms.

Table 3.8 Urban employment in privately controlled firms, 2011

Enterprise type	Thousands of employees
Registered urban private enterprises	68,959[a]
Urban individual businesses	52,270
Registered enterprises other than private where the majority or dominant owner is private	51,312
Unclassified enterprises that are majority private	80,000
Total	252,541

a. This number is very slightly less than the 69.12 million shown in table 3.7 because of a tiny number of registered private enterprises in which the majority or dominant owner is not private.

Sources: Author's calculations based on data from the National Bureau of Statistics, Industrial Survey Firm-Level Database (2007); National Bureau of Statistics of China (2012b, 125).

accounts for 95 percent of the growth of the urban labor force since 1978.[27] Government employment also expanded by an estimated 15 million over the same period.[28] The corollary of these changes is that the absolute numbers of employees in state and collective firms in urban areas today is slightly less than in 1978.[29] But, given the large expansion of the urban labor force, the employment share of state and collective firms fell from 99.8 percent in 1978 to about 18 percent by 2011.

The growth of employment in rural China is also almost entirely attributable to the private sector. As noted in chapter 1, agricultural activities were essentially privatized in the early 1980s. Given large increases in labor productivity in agriculture, farm employment is now slightly less than it was in 1978.[30] But by 2011 there was a more than offsetting growth of 60 million workers in registered private enterprises and individual business in rural areas (National Bureau of Statistics of China 2012b, 125).

There is one potential counterindicator to the finding that expanding employment of private firms accounts for virtually all of the growth of China's labor force since 1978: As late as 2010 China's 27.4 million township and village enterprises still employed 160 million workers that were classified as

---

27. The total urban labor force increased by 264 million from 95.14 million in 1978 to 359.14 million in 2011 (National Bureau of Statistics of China 2012b, 126).

28. This is a crude estimate based on the data in table 4.2, which shows that employment in the government and party bureaucracy expanded by roughly 5 million, or 11 percent, between 1999 and 2011. I assume the same pace of increase in the 1980s and 1990s.

29. The sum of the increase in employment in private firms, 252.39 million, and the increase in government employment, 15 million, is 267.4 million, which exceeds the 264 million increase in the total labor force. Thus employment in state enterprises, including traditional state-owned firms and firms of other registration types where the state is the majority or dominant owner, must have declined slightly.

30. Employment in what the statistical authorities classify as primary industry fell from 284 million in 1978 to 266 million in 2012 (National Bureau of Statistics of China 1990, 114; 2012, 125). Primary industry includes forestry, animal husbandry, and fisheries as well as agriculture.

rural (National Bureau of Statistics of China 2011a, 109). The collective origins of most of these firms might give the impression that local governments are still playing a role in generating nonagricultural jobs in the countryside. But from the mid-1980s onward, a growing share of employment in township and village enterprises was in firms that were either individual businesses or registered private firms. After the mid-1980s employment in collective township and village enterprises grew slowly, peaking in 1995 and then falling in the ensuing decade (Naughton 2007, 286–87). By 2010, 95 percent of these 27.4 million rural production units were registered as either private enterprises or individual businesses. These private and individual businesses employed almost 120 million workers, about three-quarters of the total number of workers in township and village enterprises (Zhang Tianzuo 2011, 137).

In addition, there were about 1.2 million township and village enterprises registered as share cooperative enterprises, limited liability companies, shareholding limited companies, or foreign enterprises; these enterprises employed 38 million workers. It is likely that the share of these firms that are majority privately owned is quite a bit higher than the share of these firms in urban industry and that most of their employees should be included in any estimate of private employment.[31] Collective township and village enterprises, the universe that is most likely to continue to have significant local government ownership and control, accounted for only 0.4 percent of all township and village enterprises and employed only 4 million workers in 2011. Including both those employed in township and village enterprises that are registered as individual or private businesses and an estimated 25 million employed by firms in other registration categories that are privately owned raises private sector employment in private township and village enterprises to 145 million in 2010. Thus farm employment appears to have shrunk, and private nonagricultural firms account for virtually all the growth of employment in rural China since 1978.

The growing role of the private sector in generating China's exports is also worth noting. As reflected in figure 3.3, state-owned companies accounted for two-thirds of China's total exports as recently as 1995. But their share fell continuously starting in the second half of the 1990s. By 2012 state firms accounted for only 11 percent of China's by then much larger volume of exports. Initially, as the role of state-owned firms in exporting receded, foreign firms expanded their share of China's exports, allowing China's total exports to continue to grow robustly. But the foreign firm share of total exports peaked in

---

31. For example, in 2007 almost 70 percent of the employees in above-scale industrial enterprises registered as limited liability companies worked in firms where the majority or dominant owner was private. This share is likely to be considerably higher in township and village enterprises registered as limited liability companies because that universe includes many firms that in the industrial sector would be classified as below-scale and thus much more likely to be privately owned. Moreover, average employment in township and village enterprises was less than six workers, a scale so small that almost all the registration categories comprise firms in which the sole or dominant owner is private (Zhang Tianzuo 2011, 137).

Figure 3.3 Sources of Chinese exports by ownership status, 1995–2013

percent share of total exports

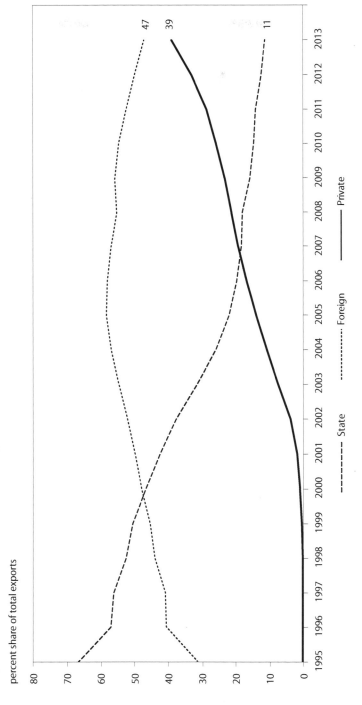

Notes: Prior to 2013, exports by privately owned firms are estimated as the difference between total exports and the sum of exports by state, foreign, and collective firms. Collective enterprise exports are not shown. In 2013, collective enterprise exports were only 3 percent of total exports.

Sources: General Customs Administration, www.customs.gov.cn; ISI Emerging Markets, CEIC Database.

2005, and China has since become increasingly dependent on private domestic firms to sustain its role as a major exporting economy. Private firms' share of exports has grown so much that since 2009 the expansion of the value of private firms' exports has exceeded that of foreign firms.[32]

Since 95 percent of China's exports are manufactured goods, the rise of private firms as important exporters reflects their displacement of state firms in most branches of manufacturing, as detailed earlier. The rise of private firms in exporting also explains the evolution of China's export structure. The share of processed exports, which involve the assembly of imported parts and components largely carried out by foreign firms, is declining, resulting in an increase in the value-added component of China's exports. The rise of the private sector has led China to move up the value chain in both industrial production and exports.[33]

While it is little noticed, private firms are also becoming a factor in China's growing outbound foreign direct investment. Large-scale investments abroad by giant state-owned companies, such as the China National Offshore Oil Corporation (CNOOC), capture inordinate attention in the western press. CNOOC's failed $18.5 billion bid to take over US oil company Unocal in 2005 and the firm's successful acquisition of Canadian energy firm Nexen in 2013 for $15.1 billion are just two examples. But China's private firms are also investing abroad. The earliest notable example of an outbound investment into the United States was Lenovo's acquisition of the personal computer business of IBM in 2005. More recent examples include Wanda Group, controlled by one of China's richest entrepreneurs. It paid $2.6 billion in 2012 to acquire AMC Entertainment, which operates the second largest movie theater chain in the United States. Privately controlled Wanxiang, China's largest auto parts company, entered the US market in 1994 and now has manufacturing operations in 14 states employing 6,000 workers. In 2013 in a widely publicized transaction Wanxiang America, the Chicago-based arm of Wanxiang, acquired the US firm A123 Systems, a Massachusetts-based maker of electric car batteries, for $257 million.[34] In China's largest acquisition in the United States to date, Shuanghui International, a private company, acquired Smithfield Foods in 2013 for $7.1 billion. Overall, private Chinese companies accounted for almost two-fifths of cumulative Chinese direct investment in the United States from 2000 through the second quarter of 2012.[35] Private Chinese firms

---

32. For example, in 2013, exports of private firms increased by $144.3 billion, while exports of foreign firms rose only $21.5 billion. Exports of state firms in 2013 fell by $7.3 billion.

33. Louis Kuijs, "Is China upgrading its industrial structure?" May 21, 2013, RBS Emerging Markets Asia Top View/China.

34. Zhang Yuwei, "US Approves Wanxiang's $257 million purchase," *China Daily*, January 30, 2013, p. 1.

35. Rhodium Group, China Investment Monitor. Available at http://rhgroup.net/interactive/china-investment-monitor (accessed on October 5, 2012).

are also actively investing in Europe, where they accounted for almost 30 percent of a cumulative $15 billion in Chinese investment from 2000 through 2011 (Hanemann and Rosen 2012, 46). However, in the aggregate, state firms still dominate China's global outward foreign direct investment, in large part because investments in natural resources and raw materials (almost all outside the United States and Europe) loom very large in these outflows and state firms most frequently generate them.

Explaining the Growth of the Private Sector

So far, this chapter has made the case for the continued overall rise in the role of the private sector in China and established why the nature of the data have led some analysts to underestimate its role. But what explains the private sector's steady displacement of state firms in manufacturing and its significant inroads in some other parts of the economy? The balance of the chapter argues that the evolution of state policy toward the private sector and the greater efficiency of private firms explain the shift. In the early years of reform the policy environment for private nonagricultural business was basically hostile, but very gradually this changed, facilitating the emergence of an increasingly robust private sector. But the higher efficiency of private businesses compared with state firms was also critical to their displacement of state firms as major sources of output across broad swaths of the economy as well as their ability to generate almost all the growth of employment since 1978. Greater efficiency of private firms is reflected in a much higher return on assets, meaning that they have a higher level of retained earnings relative to their assets than state companies do. Higher retained earnings allow private firms to expand their assets more rapidly, which, when combined with higher returns, leads to much more rapid growth than state firms enjoy.

Evolution of State Policy toward the Private Sector

As already noted, government regulations issued early in the reform era did allow the emergence of individual businesses in urban and rural areas. For example, the National People's Congress in March 1978 adopted a constitutional amendment allowing "individual laborers" to operate "within the limits permitted by law" (Tsai 2007, 50). The limits included a provision that these family businesses could not employ more than seven nonfamily members. The State Council followed up in 1981 with detailed regulations governing individual businesses in urban areas and issued similar regulations for rural areas three years later.

However, in the 1980s and the early part of the 1990s the environment for private firms was generally inhospitable. This was not surprising in a country where the ruling party for decades had emphasized that private entrepreneurs were exploiters of the working class. The government did not promulgate the Provisional Regulations on Private Enterprises until 1988, a full decade into the economic reform era.[36] These regulations lifted an important constraint on the development of the private sector because they provided a legal framework for private firms with eight or more employees. However, the regulations provided only for private sole proprietorship enterprises, which meant that an entrepreneur's personal wealth could not be legally separated from the assets of his or her business. The absence of limited liability in sole proprietorships naturally tended to restrict the size of these firms; provisions for limited liability companies and shareholding limited companies did not come into effect until 1994. Moreover, in the 1980s private firms were generally regarded as illegitimate and were vulnerable to special local government levies, which many private firms tried to avoid by registering as shareholding cooperatives or collectives. But this required them to pay a management fee to the local government and subjected them to the requirement to contribute to the local government's accumulation fund (Nee and Opper 2012, 110–11).

Even into the mid-1990s there was substantial policy discrimination against private firms. For example, as explained in chapter 2, the authorities saw the Company Law of 1994 as a key method for transforming traditional state-owned enterprises into corporations. The law established high minimum capital requirements, designed in part to prevent private enterprises from becoming companies and thus enjoying limited liability. The state set the minimum capital requirement for most production enterprises to register as a limited liability company at RMB500,000 and at RMB10,000,000 to register as a shareholding limited company. For comparison, the average worker annual wage was then RMB4,500, and bank savings, the most readily available source of funds for an entrepreneur, averaged only RMB1,800 per capita (National Bureau of Statistics of China 1995, 113, 257).

Despite the apparently very high hurdle posed by these minimum capital requirements, private firms quickly adopted the same legal structures as transformed state companies—that is, limited liability companies and joint stock companies—and they frequently did so by short-term borrowing to meet the legal minimum capital requirement and repaying after registration. The incentive for entrepreneurs to take advantage of these new legal forms of ownership was more than limited liability. "[P]rivate businesses registered as sole proprietorships are easily identifiable by the company's name, but firms registered as an LLC or JSC could be anything from wholly state-owned to wholly privately-owned companies" (Nee and Opper 2012, 114). Bureaucrats could not easily identify private limited liability and joint stock companies and thus private firms were protected from discrimination. (Unfortunately, this protection has also made tracking the growth of the private sector more difficult for the analyst.)

After the Company Law took effect, there was a massive change in the recorded ownership structure of Chinese firms. First, the number of collec-

---

36. State Council, "Provisional Regulations on Private Enterprises," June 25, 1988. Available at www.ynfzb.cn/Finance/ChuangYeGS/201107140960.shtml (accessed on October 15, 2013).

tive enterprises declined rapidly, as these firms reregistered to reflect their true private ownership, a process sometimes referred to as "taking off the red hat." The number of collective enterprises (not just in industry but across all sectors) fell from 1.5 million in 1996, when they accounted for just under three-fifths of all firms, to only 265,000 in 2004, when they accounted for only 4 percent of all firms. Over the same period the number of private firms soared from 443,000 to 3.6 million, reflecting both the creation of private firms and the reregistration of collective firms as private (National Bureau of Statistics of China 1998; State Council Leading Small Group Office on the Second National Economic Census and the National Bureau of Statistics of China 2009).[37]

Second, the ownership arrangements within the universe of registered private firms were also transformed. Before 1994 all registered private firms were sole proprietorship enterprises or private partnership enterprises, but only three years later, 48 percent of private firms were registered as limited liability companies, a share that rose to 65 percent by 2004 (Nee and Opper 2012, 116).

The government took other steps to promote the legitimacy of the private sector. In March 1999 the Ninth People's Congress approved a constitutional amendment identifying the nonstate economy as "an essential component" of a mixed economy, a clear improvement from its previous designation as "an important component" of a state-dominated economy (OECD 2000, 52). Two years later Party General Secretary Jiang Zemin, in a speech marking the 80th anniversary of the founding of the Chinese Communist Party, in effect invited private entrepreneurs to join the party. In a followup a year later, the party clarified that it would no longer discriminate against private entrepreneurs but would embrace them because of their contributions to China's economic development (Nee and Opper 2012, 64).

The state also sought to expand the scope of businesses open to private firms by gradually reducing restrictions on entry in various sectors and taking other steps that made the expansion of private activities possible. The State Council launched this initiative in 2005 with a directive that came to be known as the 36 Articles (State Council 2005). It specifically called for encouraging private investment in a number of sectors previously reserved exclusively for state firms including electric power, telecommunications, railroads, civil aviation, and petroleum. And it encouraged all financial institutions to raise the share of their loans to nonstate enterprises. City commercial banks, city credit cooperatives, and policy banks were specifically advised to provide more credit and a broader range of financial products and services to farmers, household businesses, medium and small-scale enterprises, and nonstate enterprises. The banking regulator, the China Banking Regulatory Commission, followed up a

---

37. These data are based on the number of enterprise legal persons.

few months later with specific guidelines on increasing loans to and providing enhanced financial services to small enterprises.[38]

Revisions of the Company Law in 2006 improved the situation for private firms in two respects and led to a further increase in the share of private firms that were organized as limited liability companies. First, the minimum capital requirements to register as a limited liability company or shareholding limited company were reduced to RMB30,000 and RMB5,000,000, respectively, one-tenth and one-half their previous levels. Second, the revision allowed single-person limited liability firms for the first time. Previously, a single owner of a registered private company that sought the advantage of the limited liability legal structure had to circumvent the provisions of the 1994 law by the use of dummy shareholders so he or she could qualify as a private limited liability company.

Progress in opening up various sectors to private investment, however, was slow. For example, following the promulgation of the 36 Articles in 2005, entrepreneurs were able to establish private airline companies such as Spring, Juneyao, Okay, and East Star. But the new entrants were handicapped by state control on ticket prices, which limited their ability to gain market share, and the government initially would not grant them plum routes, such as Shanghai-Beijing, which were monopolized by incumbent state airlines such as Air China, Shanghai Airlines, and China Eastern.[39] Moreover, approval of new private airlines was suspended after July 2007 and did not resume until May 2013.[40]

Partly as a result of the slow progress of private firms in overcoming regulatory obstacles, even in sectors that formally had been opened for private investment, the State Council issued follow-on guidelines in May 2010 further liberalizing investment by nonstate firms.[41] Since this document also had 36 articles, it is widely known as the "New 36 Articles." In this document the State Council called for thorough implementation of the 36 articles of 2005 and newly opened a number of sectors for private investment. These included certain types of infrastructure, public housing, certain types of financial services, and the fields of culture, tourism, and sports.

In a further liberalizing step, in 2011 the government lifted the restriction on the maximum number of nonfamily members that can be employed in individual businesses, so the growth of these firms over time may be less con-

---

38. China Banking Regulatory Commission, "Guiding Opinions on Expanding the Small Enterprise Loan Business of Banks," July 15, 2005. Available at www.cbrc.gov.cn (accessed on October 17, 2006).

39. Wang Xu, "Slowly, Private Firms Chisel an Investment Wall," *Caing*, April 20, 2010. Available at http://english.caing.com (accessed on June 25, 2010).

40. Simon Rabinovitch, "Frills airline reflects challenge to Chinese carriers," *Financial Times*, June 17, 2013, p. 7.

41. State Council, "Several Opinions on Encouraging and Guiding the Healthy Development of Non-state Investment," May 7, 2010. Available at www.gov.cn (accessed on June 25, 2010).

strained and they may provide even more employment opportunities (Lardy 2012, 34).

The government in recent years also has used tax policy to promote the growth of more than 6 million small and microenterprises, which are overwhelmingly registered private companies, and individual businesses. In 2008 the government introduced a corporate income tax rate of only 20 percent, rather than the standard 25 percent for small, microprofit enterprises.[42] In 2010 the government extended this initiative by introducing an even lower rate of 10 percent for firms with annual taxable income of RMB30,000 or less. In 2011 this low rate was applied to firms with income up to RMB60,000, and in 2014 the level was raised further to RMB100,000.[43] In addition, beginning in August 2013 the government exempted both small and microenterprises as well as individual businesses with annual sales revenue below RMB240,000 from both value-added taxes and business taxes.[44] Finally, beginning in 2014, 2.3 million service sector enterprises began to pay a 3 percent value-added tax instead of a 5 percent business tax on their top-line revenue. These initiatives have reduced taxes for some 10 million small and microenterprises and individual businesses (State Council 2014).[45]

---

42. The criteria for microprofit enterprises have been set by the tax authorities and used only to determine tax obligations of firms. In industry, for example, a microprofit enterprise must have before-tax earnings of no more than RMB300,000, no more than 100 employees, and assets of no more than RMB30 million. These criteria are set forth at www.chinatax.gov.cn (accessed on May 28, 2014).

43. "Tax cuts for small firms," *China Daily*, April 10, 2014, p. 13. Individual businesses are not subject to the corporate income tax but do pay value-added taxes and business taxes. In addition, owners of individual businesses are subject to personal income tax on the income they derive from their businesses. The rates that these entrepreneurs pay differ from the rates imposed on wage income.

44. The definition of microenterprises (微型企业) was introduced when the Ministry of Industry and Information Technology, the National Bureau of Statistics, the National Development and Reform Commission, and the Ministry of Finance jointly issued a new regulation on the classification of enterprises by size, replacing the previous 2003 regulation. "Notice concerning the Regulations on the Standards for Classification of Medium and Small Enterprises," June 18, 2011. Available at www.gov.cn (accessed on August 13, 2013). Prior to the change, industrial firms were classified as small (小型企业) if they had sales revenue of less than RMB30 million, fewer than 300 workers, or assets less than RMB40 million. After the change, industrial firms were classified as microsized if they had less than RMB3 million in sales or fewer than 20 employees and as small if they had sales between RMB3 million and RMB20 million and between 20 and 300 workers. This reclassification, which lowered the upper limit on small-size firms and created the new microcategory, facilitated the government's efforts to prioritize the development of small and microenterprises.

45. The measurement of the number of enterprises used here is *hu*, meaning that branches of firms are included in the count. The 10 million includes a small amount of double counting since it is the sum of the number of firms benefiting from a reduction in the corporate income tax, the elimination of the value-added tax and the business tax, and the switch to a 3 percent value-added tax in place of a 5 percent business tax. Some of the 1.2 million firms eligible for the reduced corporate income tax rate also benefited from one of other three tax initiatives.

Financing the Private Sector

While the political, legal, and regulatory environment for private economic activity in China gradually improved, many news analyses, commentators, investment banks, and academics have focused on the lack of access to bank credit, as well as to debt and equity finance, as major constraints on the development of private firms. The *Economist* argued in 2012 that "state giants soak up capital and talent that might have been used better by private companies" while the *New York Times* the same year said that small and medium businesses "now receive as little as 3 percent of bank lending even as they account for at least half the country's economic activity."[46] Analysts at Roubini Global Economics charge that "banks exist to provide funding for the government and its state-owned enterprises" (Wolfe and Aarsnes 2011), and western investment bankers with lengthy experience in China argue that "Chinese banks overwhelmingly lend to SOEs and always have" (Walter and Howie 2011, 4). James McGregor charges that China's largest state-owned banks "serve as ATMs for the SOEs" (2012, 7). David Pilling, the Asia editor of the *Financial Times*, wrote in November 2013 that China's state-owned enterprises, "far from shrinking have grown, recipients of massive injections of state funds designed to keep economic growth growing."[47] Two months later the *Financial Times* opined in an editorial that "the more vibrant segments of the private sector . . . are typically starved of cash. Meanwhile, the larger state-owned enterprises, as well as local governments, enjoy easy access to loans. . . ."[48] Deutsche Bank Securities in a November 2013 report argued that the "discrepancy between private enterprises that account for nearly 70 percent of GDP but get only 20 percent of the credit is the greatest constraint on growth."[49]

Retained Earnings

Before turning to an analysis of actual flows of bank credit, access to debt and equity markets, and bankers' acceptances and trust loans, which are important components of China's growing shadow banking system, it is important to recognize that it is retained earnings that have financed the vast majority of investment in China in the reform era and not borrowing from banks, issuing debt, selling equity, or acquiring funds from the shadow banking system. According to a survey by the World Bank, the ability of Chinese firms to finance

---

46. "The rise of state capitalism," *Economist*, January 21, 2012, p. 11. Keith Bradsher, "China Pushes Deposit Insurance in Bank Overhaul," *New York Times*, December 13, 2012, p. B9.

47. David Pilling, "The ghost at China's third plenum: demographics," *Financial Times*, November 11, 2013, p. 9.

48. "China's dangerous credit addiction," *Financial Times*, January 16, 2014, p. 8.

49. Peter Hooper, Gilles Moec, Michael Spencer, and Torsten Slok, "China's final stage of reform," November 8, 2013, Deutsche Bank Research Global Economic Perspectives.

investment from retained earnings is substantially higher than in other upper-middle-income countries.[50] The heavy reliance on internal finance as a source of investment is a significant change from the pre-reform era, when traditional state-owned enterprises dominated the economy and were required to turn over almost all of their profits to the Ministry of Finance. These funds were then used to finance investment through the state budget according to priorities established by the State Planning Commission. In 1978 more than three-fifths of investment in state-owned units was financed through the state budget. But one of the most important reforms undertaken after 1978 was to allow firms to retain most of their after-tax profits. By 1997 less than 3 percent of industrial investment was financed through the state budget (Naughton 2007, 304).

The important and growing role of retained earnings as a source of investment funds in the 1990s and 2000s is reflected in figure 3.4. From 1992 through 1999 retained earnings financed about 40 to 50 percent of the investment of all nonfinancial corporations. But from 2000 through 2008, this ratio rose to an average of 71 percent. Even when credit growth exploded during the 2009 global financial crisis and its immediate aftermath, an average of 56 percent of all investment was financed from retained earnings. In short, retained earnings since 2000 have consistently been a far more important source of investment finance than the sum of the funds firms borrow from both banks and nonbank financial intermediaries, raise through the sale of stock on the Shanghai, Hong Kong, and other global equity markets, and raise through the sale of bonds and other debt instruments both at home and abroad. Thus the relative financial performance of state versus private firms may go a long way toward explaining the differential growth performance, analyzed earlier in this chapter, of these two types of firms.

Many studies have addressed the relative productivity performance of state and private firms in China's industrial sector. Regardless of whether ownership is defined by registration status or the nature of the majority or dominant owner, these studies have universally found that total factor productivity is substantially higher for private firms.[51] The OECD found that productivity in the universe of registered private firms and privately controlled firms in 1998–2003 was more than twice that of traditional state-owned enterprises and more than half again as high as state firms that had converted their ownership structures to become limited liability companies or shareholding limited companies (OECD 2005, 86). Similarly, a study for the much longer 1978–2004 period found that total factor productivity growth in the state sector was only 1.7 percent per annum, only two-fifths the 4.3 percent per annum pace of the nonstate sector (Brandt, Hsieh, and Zhu 2008, 694).

50. World Bank, "Enterprise Surveys: China Country Profile 2012," July 2013. Available at www.enterprisesurveys.org (accessed on September 10, 2013).

51. In contrast, because state firms typically have far more capital per worker they usually have higher output per worker than private firms. But this does not translate into higher profits per unit of capital or to higher total factor productivity.

Figure 3.4 Retained corporate earnings as a share of corporate investment, 1992–2011

percent

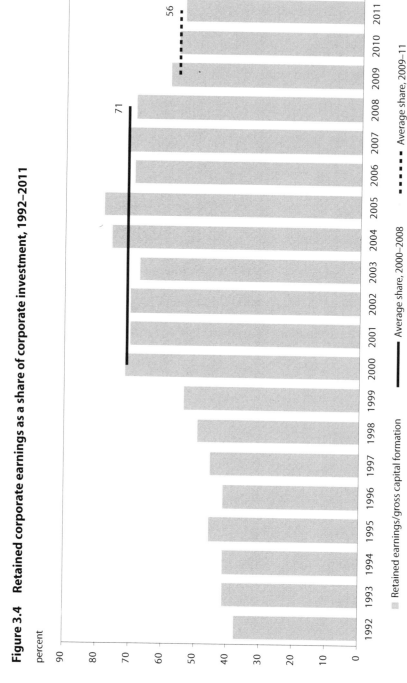

Note: Retained earnings are the disposable income of nonfinancial corporations reported in the flow of funds.

Sources: National Bureau of Statistics of China (2013c, 80–81); ISI Emerging Markets, CEIC Database.

Faster growth of factor productivity in private firms has translated into much stronger financial performance. The OECD study found that private firms were able to maintain their earnings at a relatively high share of value added and that their return on assets and return on equity increased substantially between 1999 and 2003. In 2003 private companies' average return on both assets and equity was about half again as high as state firms' returns (OECD 2005, 87, 99). The World Bank also found a significantly higher return on equity by nonstate firms during the period 1998–2009. By 2009 the gap was huge, with nonstate firms' returns on equity at 20 percent, running 9.9 percentage points ahead of state firms (World Bank 2012, 111). Similarly, David Dollar and Shang-Jin Wei (2007), based on a survey of a random sample of 12,400 firms conducted in 2002–03, found that private firms' average return to capital was half again as high as that of wholly state-owned firms and also well above returns of majority and minority state-owned firms.

Data for the industrial sector going back to the mid-1990s, shown in figure 3.5, demonstrate that registered private enterprises consistently have earned a higher return on assets than the combined universe of state-owned enterprises and state-controlled firms.[52] The reforms of the state-owned industrial sector analyzed in chapter 2 and the increased competition as a result of China's entry into the World Trade Organization did lead to a very substantial improvement in the efficiency of these firms for a decade after 1998. The return on assets in state firms rose from a mediocre level of less than 1 percent in 1997–98 to a peak of 6.8 percent in 2007. But even at this peak, registered private firms were much more efficient, recording a return on assets of 9.5 percent. Since then, with the exception of 2010, performance at state firms has fallen, hitting 4.9 percent in 2012. In contrast, except in 2009 and 2012, returns at registered private firms have continued to rise. Thus the margin in favor of privately registered firms has widened dramatically since the mid-2000s. By 2012 the gap was almost three to one.

There are no time-series data that would allow the calculation of return on assets of state and private firms in the service sector. But data in the 2008

---

52. Ideally, I should compare the relative productivity performance of the combined universe of state and state-controlled industrial firms with that of the combined universe of private and privately-controlled industrial firms. But, as discussed, time-series data on the profits and assets of privately-controlled industrial firms are not available. But there are two reasons to believe that the productivity performance of registered private firms is a reasonable measure of the larger universe of private firms, including those of other registration types where the majority or dominant owner is private. First, as shown in figure 3.1, the output of registered private firms accounted for two-fifths and three-fifths of the output of the larger universe of registered private and privately controlled firms (in both cases including below-scale firms) in 2003 and 2007, respectively. Second, and more important, in 2007, a year for which complete data are available, the gap between the return on assets in the narrow universe of registered private industrial firms, 9.5 percent, and the universe of industrial firms in other registration categories that are privately controlled, 8.3 percent, is relatively small. The return for the entire universe of domestic private firms was 8.9 percent. Thus using returns of registered private firms as a proxy for all private firms overstates returns by 0.6 percentage points or only 7 percent (= 9.5/8.9).

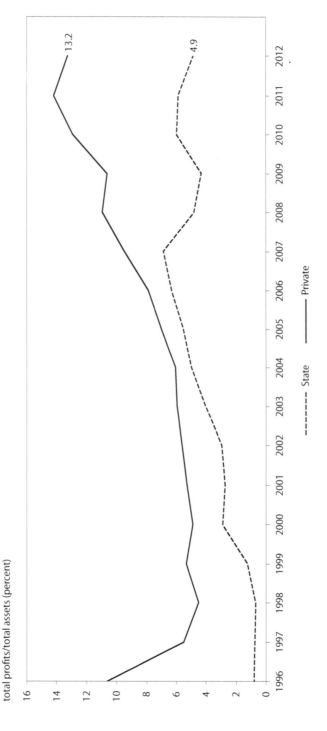

Figure 3.5   Return on assets of state and private industrial enterprises, 1996–2012

total profits/total assets (percent)

13.2

4.9

------ State   —— Private

1996 1997 1998 1999 2000 2001 2002 2003 2004 2005 2006 2007 2008 2009 2010 2011 2012

0   2   4   6   8   10   12   14   16

Note: Total profits are earnings before corporate income tax.

Sources: National Bureau of Statistics of China (2013c, 475–93); National Bureau of Statistics of China, www.stats.gov.cn (accessed on February 28, 2014).

economic census support two points: that the return on assets of state enterprises in the service sector is substantially below the returns that state industrial firms earn and that the performance of state firms in services is far inferior to service firms with other forms of ownership.[53]

Disaggregating the state industrial and service sector provides further insight. The average return on assets of state firms is flattered by the extraordinarily high returns earned by CNOOC, China Mobile, the China National Tobacco Corporation, and a few other large state firms that earn supranormal profits and thus have extraordinarily high return on assets. CNOOC, as noted in chapter 1, enjoyed profit margins in 2004–12 averaging 44 percent and generated an average return on assets of 24.5 percent. The profit margins of China Mobile in 2004–12 averaged 33 percent, translating into a return on assets that averaged 19 percent. The China National Tobacco Corporation in 2012 earned a return on assets of 14 percent (National Bureau of Statistics of China 2012b, 512–15).[54] In the universe of registered private firms, there does not appear to be a small number of firms that make a comparable outsized contribution to profits. Consequently, the average return on assets for private registered firms is probably fairly close to the median return, but the median return in the universe of state firms is likely below the average, both in services and in industry. The significance of this will be analyzed in the next chapter.

The superior financial performance of private industrial firms—whether that universe is defined by who actually controls the firm (as in the case of the OECD study) or by the registration status of firms (as in the case of the World Bank study) or the mixed comparison of state-owned and state-controlled versus registered private (as in the case of the Chinese data on the industrial sector reflected in figure 3.5)—must explain a large share of their relatively rapid growth. Private firms were able to rely much more on retained earnings to finance their expansion, partially overcoming the handicap of the more limited access of private firms to bank credit and other external sources of finance. However, as will be shown below, private-firm access to credit also has improved, contributing further to their superior growth performance.

Bank Credit

The People's Bank of China has published four data series reflecting the flow of credit to the private sector. These series are available for different periods, and each has specific strengths and weaknesses. No single published series

---

53. The data, covering 10 of the 14 subsectors of services, show that the return on assets of state and state-controlled firms was 3.4 percent, while returns in nonstate services enterprises were 6.6 percent. The omitted subsectors are real estate; transport, storage, and post; public management, social welfare, and social organizations; and finance (National Bureau of Statistics of China 2010a).

54. The data are for 2011 for 117 state-owned tobacco companies, all of which are under the purview of the China National Tobacco Corporation.

provides a comprehensive measure of the flow of credit to the private sector during the entire reform era.

The first three data series are partially shown in table 3.9. Data from the first series, in the first set of columns, were cited by the *Economist* in its 2012 survey of state capitalism and by several academic studies in support of the view that the private sector in China has had little access to credit in the reform era.[55] This judgment is flawed for two reasons. First, the data in the first series cover credit flows only to what might be called the narrowly defined private sector—that is, registered private companies and individual businesses. They do not include lending to the large number of limited liability companies in which the majority or dominant owner is private, which, as will be shown, is substantial. Second, the first series includes only short-term credit.[56]

The second data series (middle columns of the table), which begins only in 2002, has the same coverage as the first but includes medium and long-term loans. In 2002–09, the years for which data in both the first and the second series have been released, the data reveal that when medium and long-term loans are included the share of credit going to the private sector is four to ten times larger than the data in the first series. This sizable gap underscores why it is a mistake to look only at short-term loans to measure the flow of credit to the private sector.

The third set of columns shows business loans from financial institutions to households, including working capital loans to farm households.[57] This series excludes lending to registered private businesses. Farm households are not classified as individual businesses, so their borrowing is not included in the data in the first two series. But business loans to farm households should be included in any attempt to measure credit flows to China's private sector for two reasons. First, farming in China is now almost entirely private. Second, loans to farm households may indirectly provide credit to the individual non-agricultural businesses that employed over 80 million rural workers in 2010.[58]

---

55. The *Economist* writes, "In 2009 private firms accounted for only 2 percent of China's official outstanding loans" (January 21, 2012, special report, p. 15). Kellee Tsai (2002, 2) uses this data series to assert, "As of the end of 2000, less than 1 percent of loans from the entire national banking system had gone to the private sector." Ligang Song (2005, 117) cites data from the same series in support of the view that private enterprises and individual businesses received only 0.62 percent of loans from all banks at the end of 1999.

56. In China, short-term loans are loans with a maturity of up to and including one year.

57. Loans by financial institutions to households are divided into business loans and consumer loans. The former category is discussed in the text. Consumer loans include car loans, student loans, credit card loans, and, most importantly, home mortgage loans. At year-end 2011, total loans by financial institutions to households stood at RMB13,607 billion, 21 percent of all loans outstanding from the financial system. About two-thirds of these loans were consumer loans; the balance were business loans. See table A.4 for data on consumption loans to households in recent years.

58. In 2010 there were 25 million workers employed in individual businesses in rural areas and 61 million workers in township and village enterprises in which the actual owner was an individual (National Bureau of Statistics of China 2011a, 109; Zhang 2011, 137).

Table 3.9 Loans by financial institutions to private businesses, 1980–2013

Year	Short-term loans to private and individual businesses		Loans to private and individual businesses		Loans to household businesses	
	Millions of renminbi	Percent of total loans	Millions of renminbi	Percent of total loans	Millions of renminbi	Percent of total loans
1980	23	0.01	n.a.	n.a.	n.a.	n.a.
1985	1,065	0.17	n.a.	n.a.	n.a.	n.a.
1990	4,020	0.23	n.a.	n.a.	n.a.	n.a.
1995	19,620	0.39	n.a.	n.a.	n.a.	n.a.
2000	65,460	0.66	n.a.	n.a.	n.a.	n.a.
2002	105,877	0.81	1,033,300	7.39	n.a.	n.a.
2003	146,159	0.92	1,514,700	8.92	n.a.	n.a.
2004	208,149	1.17	1,456,000	7.72	829,807	4.40
2005	218,075	1.12	1,698,500	8.21	965,229	4.67
2006	266,757	1.18	2,122,100	8.91	1,423,716	5.97
2007	350,766	1.34	3,752,500	13.51	1,792,326	6.45
2008	422,382	1.39	4,173,900	13.04	1,984,763	6.20
2009	712,101	1.78	5,104,600	11.99	2,645,325	6.22
2010	n.a.	n.a.	7,073,700	13.89	3,747,845	7.36
2011	n.a.	n.a.	9,091,800	15.62	4,729,472	8.13
2012	n.a.	n.a.	11,017,500	16.37	5,694,939	8.46
2013	n.a.	n.a.	n.a.	n.a.	6,878,276	9.76

n.a. = not available

Note: Financial institutions include the three policy banks, state commercial banks, shareholding commercial banks, urban commercial banks, rural commercial banks, rural cooperative banks, urban credit cooperatives, rural credit cooperatives, trust and investment companies, foreign banks, the postal savings bank, finance companies, and leasing companies.

Sources: China Banking Society (1990, 152–53; 1996, 429; 2006, 389; 2008, 402); ISI Emerging Markets, CEIC Database; People's Bank of China, www.pbc.gov.cn (accessed on Foebruary 28, 2014); All-China Federation of Industry and Commerce (2011, 76; 2012, 66; 2013, 68).

When a farm household has access to working capital loans to finance the purchase of seed, fuel, and other agricultural inputs, that may free up sufficient family funds to allow a member of the household or a relative to establish or expand an individual business. Business loans to households as a share of all loans outstanding almost doubled between the end of 2004 and the end of 2013, when it reached 9.8 percent.

A more disaggregated analysis of the data in the third series shows that the expansion of medium- and long-term credit accounts for a large share of the growth of credit going to households. These loans to households grew especially rapidly, from just under RMB70 billion in 2004 to RMB2,070 billion by year-end 2012.[59] Thus the medium- and long-term component rose from less than 10 percent to close to 40 percent of loans to household businesses.

The data in table 3.9 confirm that flows of credit to private activity in the early years of the reform era were minuscule. This is hardly surprising given the official antipathy at the time toward private nonagricultural business. There were no private firms and the number of individual businesses was negligible, not only in manufacturing but even in services. As discussed above, individual businesses began to emerge early in the reform era, but these were mostly financed by household savings, borrowing from family and friends, and other informal sources of finance such as rotating credit associations rather than by credit from the formal financial system (Tsai 2002, 3). Banks everywhere are extremely reluctant to extend credit to small startup family-owned firms with little or no collateral. As already noted, a provisional legal structure allowing for the creation of private businesses was not promulgated until 1988 and even then allowed only for private sole proprietorship firms. Not until the Company Law came into effect in 1994 did the private sector begin to grow rapidly, and the rapid growth of short-term credit to private firms starting in the mid-1990s reflects the growth of this sector. Short-term credit loans to the private sector grew further in the 2000s so that by 2009 its share of total loans reached 1.8 percent, almost three times its share in 2000.[60]

The second series reflects extremely rapid growth of credit to private and individual businesses. Their borrowing grew by more than 25 percent annually between 2002 and 2012, more than doubling their share of bank loans. Loans to individual businesses and registered private businesses by year-end 2012 exceeded RMB11 trillion and accounted for 16 percent of all loans by banks and other financial institutions.

The increased flow of loans to the private sector reflected in all three data series was facilitated not only by the evolution of government policy but also

---

59. People's Bank of China, "Financial circulation is healthy and stable; control targets are basically realized," January 13, 2005, available at www.pbc.gov.cn (accessed on January 13, 2005); People's Bank of China, "Sources and Uses of Credit Funds of Financial Institutions (by sectors)," January 21, 2013, available at www.pbc.gov.cn (accessed on March 4, 2013).

60. Short-term loans to private and individual businesses as a share of all short-term loans rose from 1.0 percent in 2000 to 4.9 percent in 2009.

by institutional changes in the financial sector. Initially, virtually all loans to the private sector came from state-owned banks, not surprising given their complete domination of the financial sector at that time. But in the 1980s and the first part of the 1990s, these institutions actually were not well suited to lending to individual businesses and small private firms. State-owned banks then lent money predominantly to large state-owned enterprises, in part because these firms had substantial assets that could serve as collateral and in part because loans to state-owned enterprises were either implicitly or explicitly guaranteed by the state. Indeed, a large share of the lending of state-owned banks was "policy lending" (政策贷款) undertaken at the direction of the state planning agency. The central bank provided the funds for these policy loans directly to the state-owned banks, giving rise to the phrase "relending" (再贷款) to characterize policy loans (Lardy 1998, 83–92). Almost all of these loans went to state-owned enterprises. Lending to small private companies required skills in credit analysis that most state banks lacked.

This situation began to change with the creation of urban credit cooperatives, which China's central bank formally authorized in the mid-1980s. The rise of urban credit cooperatives may seem somewhat surprising given that China's four major state-owned banks had a vast network of offices that blanketed every Chinese city. In 1994, for example, state-owned banks operated almost 150,000 branches, sub-branches, and other offices of various types, mostly located in cities (China Banking Society 1995, 578). Urban credit cooperatives, however, were able to compete with the existing network of state bank offices by offering better services to depositors, mostly individuals and nonstate enterprises. And on the lending side, they found a good market among collective and private firms, whose needs were not being met by existing state-owned banks (Lardy 1998, 71–72).

The number of urban credit cooperatives and their lending activity grew rapidly in the first half of the 1990s so that by the end of 1995 their total credit outstanding reached RMB193 billion (China Banking Society 1996, 428). While these cooperatives initially lent primarily to urban collective firms, they became the principal source of formal credit for small private companies as well. The data for 1995 show that urban credit cooperatives supplied 80 percent of the formal credit flowing to private businesses, while the state banks' share had fallen to less than 20 percent (China Banking Society 1996, 428). After 1995 urban credit cooperatives were merged to form what were originally called urban cooperative banks and, starting in 1998, city commercial banks.[61] These banks' share of the assets of the financial system grew steadily in the 2000s, and they channeled a growing volume of lending to private businesses.

Legal developments also facilitated an increasing flow of bank loans to small enterprises, predominantly private, and family businesses. Ambiguities in the 1995 Security Law (sometimes also translated as the Collateral Law) made banks reluctant to accept movable assets as collateral. As a result, in

---

61. The "Regulations on Urban Cooperative Banks" were promulgated in 1995.

Figure 3.7   Stock of enterprise loans by ownership, 2009 and 2012

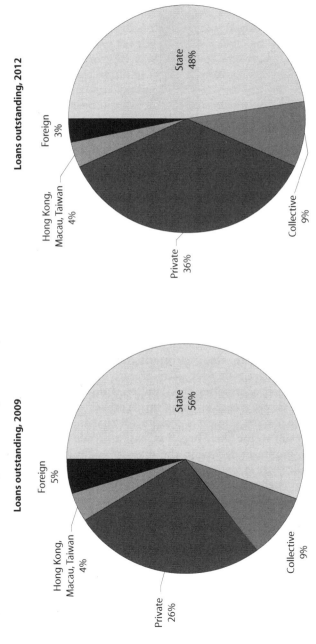

Loans outstanding, 2012

State
48%

Foreign
3%

Hong Kong,
Macau, Taiwan
4%

Private
36%

Collective
9%

Loans outstanding, 2009

State
56%

Foreign
5%

Hong Kong,
Macau, Taiwan
4%

Private
26%

Collective
9%

Sources: China Banking Society (2011, 322; 2012, 369; 2013, 367–68).

showing that state firms were generally much less profitable than nonstate firms and that as a result, from 1990 through 1994 these firms were able to finance only about 20 percent of their investment from retained earnings; the balance came from funds borrowed from the banking system (World Bank 1995, 3–4).

Almost a decade later, at the end of November 2004, lending to state companies accounted for 43.5 percent of all loans outstanding to enterprises, while the share to nonstate firms was 56.5 percent.[64] But lending in China by 2004 had already expanded beyond enterprise loans to include a substantial volume of loans to households, so by late 2004, loans to state companies accounted for less than 43.5 percent of all loans. The situation eight years later, at the end of 2012, is reflected in figure 3.7, which shows that just under 50 percent of all loans outstanding from almost all financial institutions to enterprises were to state-owned and state-controlled companies.[65] But taking into account the further expansion of bank lending to households, especially mortgage loans, by 2012 loans to enterprises amounted to only 61 percent of all loans. So loans to state-owned and state-controlled enterprises accounted for only 29 percent of all loans from the financial system in 2012. There clearly has been a long-term systematic decline in the share of lending to the universe of state-owned enterprises and state-controlled companies, from over six-tenths in 1995 to just over four-tenths in 2004 and then to only three-tenths by 2012.

In summary, all four types of lending data demonstrate that private businesses, whether narrowly or broadly defined, have gained substantially greater access to bank credit during the reform era and that these gains have been particularly large since the mid-1990s. Thus the idea that the economic and credit environment was much more favorable for private firms when Zhao Ziyang was premier in the 1980s is not supported by the aggregate data on bank credit (Huang 2008, 22, 128; Haggard and Huang 2008, 368). Moreover, the popular idea that the voracious credit appetite of state-owned and state-controlled companies has in recent years squeezed out the private sector is

---

64. Zhao Xuefang, "Chinese Finance: The Chinese Central Bank's Macroeconomic Adjustment Policy as Seen in the Data," February 28, 2005. Available at http://finance.sina.com.cn (accessed on January 15, 2012). This article is a question and answer interview with Jiang Wanjin, the deputy director of the Survey and Statistics Department of the People's Bank of China, who should be regarded as an authoritative source. Since the division of lending to enterprises into the universes of state and nonstate sums to 100 percent, there is no doubt the lending to state firms includes both traditional state-owned companies and limited liability and shareholding limited corporations in which the state is the majority or dominant owner.

65. The data underlying figures 3.6 and 3.7 include loans from large, medium, and small Chinese banks, urban credit cooperatives, rural credit cooperatives, and foreign banks but exclude loans made by finance companies, trust companies, leasing companies, automobile finance companies, and rural banks. The omitted institutions in 2010 accounted for 8 percent of loans from all financial institutions. Thus the universe of institutions covered is roughly comparable to the scope of the 1995 data on all financial institutions.

fundamentally misleading. Chinese private firms now enjoy better access to credit than in any previous period in the reform era.

In addition to access to bank credit, there is the question of price. Those who argue that the flow of a disproportionately large share of loans to state firms is a central characteristic of state capitalism also frequently assert that state firms are able to borrow on much more favorable terms than private companies. In its special report on state capitalism, the *Economist* asserted that private firms pay on average three times the level of interest paid by state firms.[66] Direct evidence on this question is quite limited and often flawed. All too frequently, average bank lending rates are compared with usurious rates charged by underground banks, pawnshops, and guarantee companies, presumably paid by private rather than state borrowers. The problem in comparisons of this type, of course, is that a large part of this observed interest rate differential may reflect credit risk rather than discrimination on the basis of ownership. Where direct evidence is cited, for example in the case of the *Economist*, the interest rates were calculated on a fundamentally flawed methodology, as discussed in appendix B of this study.

Two surveys show that private registered firms that have gotten access to bank credit appear, on average, to pay interest rates that are roughly in line with the average rates paid by state-owned companies or the average rate that banks charge on all loans. A joint survey of more than 100 Chinese financial institutions by the People's Bank of China and the International Finance Corporation in 2004–05 showed that the average interest rate charged to state-owned companies, 5.67 percent, was only slightly below the average of 5.96 percent charged to privately owned companies (IFC 2007, 57). A survey of over 5,000 registered private firms in 2011 reveals that little has changed. The survey found that the median interest rate paid by private firms on their bank loans was 7.8 percent, only slightly above the 7.5 percent average bank lending rate.[67] Private firms, however, did pay somewhat more, 8 percent, for borrowings from small-scale financial institutions: rural banks, rural credit cooperatives, and microfinance companies. However, twice as many private firms borrowed from banks than from small-scale financial institutions, and the average size of a bank loan was RMB16.4 million, dwarfing the average loan

---

66. "The rise of state capitalism," *Economist*, January 21, 2012, p. 15.

67. The survey of private enterprises has been undertaken by the Chinese Communist Party United Front Work Department, the All-China Federation of Industry and Commerce, and the State Administration of Industry and Commerce, in cooperation with a number of other academic and research units, on an almost biannual basis starting in 1993. The 10th survey, undertaken in 2011, targeted a 0.55 percent sample of the universe of registered private firms and collected valid data on 92.2 percent of the firms. Data from the survey, including information on the interest rate paid by private-firm borrowers from banks, are available in All-China Federation of Industry and Commerce and China Nonstate (Private) Economy Research Association (2013, 42). The weighted average bank loan rate in 2011 is calculated as the average of the ordinary weighted average lending rate in March, June, September, and December reported by the People's Bank of China Monetary Policy Analysis Small Group (2011a, 67; 2011b, 7; 2011c, 6; 2012, 5).

size of RMB2.19 million from small-scale financial institutions (All-China Federation of Industry and Commerce and China Nonstate (Private) Economy Research Association 2013, 41–42).

Those who are skeptical that China's banks would lend so much on such relatively favorable terms to private firms should keep in mind that, at least in industry, registered private firms are on average a much better credit risk than state-owned and state-controlled companies.[68] Frequently used measures of creditworthiness in market economies include debt servicing capacity and the interest coverage ratio. The latter measure, the ratio of a firm's earnings before interest and taxes to its interest expense, can be calculated for state and state-controlled enterprises and for registered private firms.[69] On this metric, registered private firms since the mid-1990s have been consistently more creditworthy than the universe of state-owned and state-controlled companies (figure 3.8). As discussed earlier in this chapter, state companies improved their financial performance after the far-reaching economic reforms Premier Zhu Rongji initiated in the mid-1990s. As a result, the gap in interest coverage between private and state firms was essentially eliminated for a few years. But in the last six years shown in figure 3.8, private and state companies diverged dramatically. By 2012, registered private industrial firms had more than twice the interest coverage of state-owned and state-controlled industrial companies. We should thus not be surprised that China's financial institutions, which are increasingly profit oriented, find the private sector an ever more attractive lending market.

But even when loans are classified based on the nature of the majority or dominant owner, private firms' little more than one-third share of loans outstanding is only about half the best estimate that private firms now produce two-thirds of China's GDP (Ma, Shi, and Lan 2013). Even on a flow basis, the one-half share of new loans going to private firms in 2012 was well below the two-thirds share of GDP they produced. Moreover, many private firms lack any access to bank credit. Thus it is still accurate to say that relative to their contribution to GDP state firms have greater access to bank credit than private firms.

But state firms' greater access to credit may reflect not only a residual pro-state bias on the part of banks or small private firms' lack of collateral, but also state policies that systematically exclude private firms from entering some of the most capital-intensive sectors in the economy. If this were the case, the share of loans going to private companies would be less than their contribution to output even if banks were not biased and lack of collateral was not an impediment. The best examples of state-dominated capital-intensive industries are telecommunications, where a handful of state-controlled companies enjoy an

---

68. See note 52 for an explanation of why the financial performance of registered private firms is a good proxy for the financial performance of the broader universe of private firms, including firms in other registration categories where the majority or dominant owner is private.

69. Because Chinese statistical and banking authorities do not publish data on principal repayments by enterprises, it is not possible to calculate debt servicing capacity.

Figure 3.8   Interest coverage ratio of state and private industrial enterprises, 1996–2012

operating income/interest expense

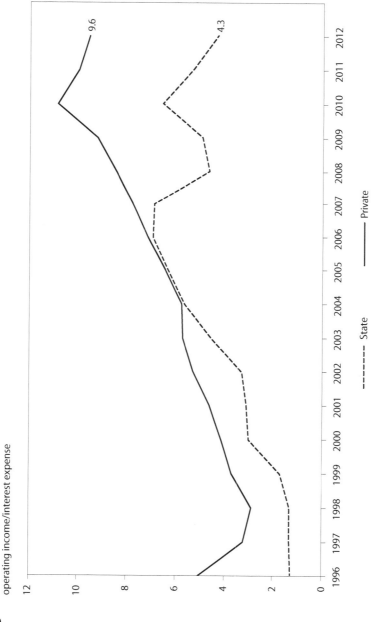

Note: State enterprises are state-owned enterprises and shareholding companies in which the state is the majority or dominant owner. Private enterprises are registered private enterprises. Operating income was calculated by adding interest expense to earnings before corporate income tax.

Sources: National Bureau of Statistics of China (2013c, 475–93); National Bureau of Statistics of China, www.stats.gov.cn (accessed on February 28, 2014).

oligopoly on the key basic services; electric power generation and distribution, where all the significant players are state owned; and the oil and gas industry, where three state firms—the China National Petroleum Corporation (the parent of the publicly listed PetroChina), the China Petroleum and Chemical Corporation (Sinopec), and CNOOC—have complete control of both onshore and offshore exploration and extraction of oil and natural gas and dominant shares of downstream activities such as refining and distribution.[70] Thus licensing and other regulatory barriers may be more important obstacles for private businesses than credit access.

The foregoing analysis of credit flows and the price of credit is based on bank lending. But in recent years increasingly large amounts of credit have been extended through nonbank financial intermediaries. Thus the People's Bank has begun to publish a series identified as social finance, which in addition to bank lending includes entrusted loans, trust loans, bankers' acceptances, the issuance of corporate bonds and equity, and loans extended by microfinance companies. By 2013, bank loans accounted for only 57 percent of social finance. Does the flow of credit to firms of varying ownership types through the nonbank components of social finance differ from these flows through the banking system?

Data on the funds flowing to firms of various ownership types through the issuance of bonds and equity and through borrowing from microfinance companies are reasonably good and are detailed in the next sections. Information on the flow of funds through trust and entrusted loans and bankers' acceptances is less complete. Most analyses assume credit through these channels flows primarily to real estate and to local government platform companies. Real estate developers, which are mostly private, are thought to have relied heavily on loans from the shadow banking system beginning in 2010, as regulators increasingly instructed banks to curtail their lending to the property sector. Similarly, as the central government gained an increased understanding of the amount of borrowing from banks by local government platform companies, it sought to dissuade banks from extending large amounts of additional credit, leading some of these companies to seek funding outside regular lending channels, most notably from trust companies. Lending to government platform companies, of course, is considered lending to state enterprises.

A large share of bankers' acceptances appears to be issued to private companies. Issuance of this form of credit is concentrated in manufacturing, wholesaling, and retailing, all lines of business where private firms predominate. Two-thirds of the bankers' acceptances go to small and medium-size firms, which also suggests that private rather than state enterprises are the predominant recipients (People's Bank of China Monetary Policy Analysis Small Group 2014, 28). According to Yanglee, a web portal providing data on the Chinese trust sector, in the third quarter of 2013, new collective trust products

---

70. As noted earlier in this chapter, one important exception to the control of downstream activities by the national oil companies is gas distribution.

funding privately managed industrial and commercial enterprises equaled RMB27.162 billion, accounting for 74 percent of all collective trust products financing industrial and commercial enterprises.[71]

Entrusted loans are mainly used by group companies to move cash between subsidiaries, which increases the speed at which money moves around the economy but does not generate money supply growth. Since almost all group companies are state owned, entrusted loans do not usually affect the allocation of funds across business units of different ownership types.[72]

Bond and Equity Financing

While bank lending to the private sector and household businesses has expanded over the past 10 or more years and private firms appear to have substantial access to bankers' acceptances and trust loans, corporate bond financing remains the almost exclusive domain of state-owned and state-controlled companies. In 2012 and 2013 the value of bonds issued by private nonfinancial enterprises in China's domestic bond market reached RMB261 billion and RMB385 billion, respectively. These amounts accounted for only 7 and 10 percent, respectively, of the total value of nonfinancial corporate bonds issued in those years.[73] Similarly, while a few private firms, notably real estate companies, have been able to issue bonds in the Hong Kong market, state firms appear to dominate bond issuance there as well. Thus while the domestic bond market is a slightly widening financing channel for private nonfinancial enterprises, there is a long way to go before the share of funds private companies raise there is comparable to their share of bank lending. However, bond financing constitutes a relatively small share of social finance, about 10 percent in 2013.

China has two stock markets, Shanghai and Shenzhen, which began formal operations in late 1990 and early 1991, respectively. In the very early years, state firms dominated initial public offerings in both markets. Selection of individual firms eligible to list was a top-down process initially directed by the State Planning Commission, which identified the industrial sectors eligible for equity financing. This process included establishing listing quotas for ministries and provincial governments, which not surprisingly favored state-owned companies within their respective jurisdictions (Walter and Howie 2003,

---

71. Available at http://money.163.com/13/1115/02/9DMHU61T00253BOH.html (accessed on February 28, 2014). Collective trust products account for about a quarter of outstanding trust products.

72. Eighty percent of entrusted loans are by conglomerates moving funds across their business units. Dinny McMahon and Lingling Wei, "A Partial Primer to China's Biggest Shadow: Entrusted Loans," May 2, 2014. Available at http://blogs.wsj.com (accessed on May 2, 2014).

73. These data were supplied courtesy of May Yan at Barclays. Barclays' accounting of nonfinancial corporate bond issuance includes enterprise bonds, corporate bonds, medium-term notes, short-term commercial paper, asset-backed securities, and convertible bonds. Private bond issuance includes bonds issued by registered private companies and bonds issued by limited liability corporations and shareholding limited companies where the majority or dominant owner is private.

115–17). As a result, in the early 1990s only a handful of nonstate companies were listed. But by the mid-1990s the share of state firm listings had declined to three-quarters of all listed companies. In 2000 the quota listing system was abolished, and securities firms began to play a larger role in identifying and developing listing candidates. As a result, the share of state companies in the universe of listed companies declined steadily in the 2000s. By 2010 state firms accounted for just under half of all listed companies on the two exchanges (All-China Federation of Industry and Commerce 2012, 101).

The surge in private company listings also reflects the opening of the ChiNext Board at the Shenzhen Stock Exchange in October 2009. This board targets innovative, growth-oriented firms and, because of its lower capital requirement, accommodates smaller firms. Its establishment led to a surge in listings of nonstate companies starting in 2010. At the end of 2012, there were 1,288 listed private companies, accounting for 52 percent of all listed A share companies (All-China Federation of Industry and Commerce 2013, 92).[74] By the end of 2012 in the all-important A share market, there were 953 listed companies in which the state was the sole or dominant shareholder, accounting for 38.5 percent of all listings.[75] But since state companies on average were larger, they accounted for a more significant share of market capitalization—51.4 percent.[76] Nonetheless, the transformation since the opening of the Shanghai and Shenzhen exchanges is remarkable—from complete domination by state companies to a situation in which such companies account for barely half of the market capitalization of listed A share companies. From 2010 through 2013, private firms raised RMB660 billion through initial public offerings in the Shanghai and Shenzhen markets, compared with the state companies' RMB166 billion.[77]

Microfinance

Another institutional development that has increased the flow of credit to the private sector is the emergence of microfinance companies, whose lending is not included in the bank lending data analyzed earlier but, as noted, is an element of social finance. Microfinance in China can be traced to the 1980s,

---

74. Private companies in this source are defined as registered private companies and limited liability and shareholding limited companies where the majority or dominant owner is private.

75. In addition to the A shares, which are priced in RMB and traded in the Shanghai and Shenzhen stock markets, there are about 20 B share listed companies priced in Hong Kong dollars and traded in Shenzhen. The B share market is very small and has had no new listings in over a decade. Private and state firms combined do not account for 100 percent of the listed A share companies since there are a few listed firms where the controlling shareholder is a university, a collective, or foreign.

76. "State-controlled shareholding companies account for half of the A share market value, with a total value of RMB13.71 trillion," *People's Daily,* January 11, 2013. Available at www.sasac.gov.cn (accessed on October 28, 2013).

77. Thomas Gatley, "IPOs: A Narrow But Efficient Funding Channel," *China Update,* February 19, 2014, Gavekal Dragonomics. Available by subscription only at research.gavekal.com (accessed on July 17, 2014).

when a number of international organizations, including the United Nations Development Fund for Women, the International Foundation for Agricultural Development, and the United Nations Family Planning Agency, introduced the methodology there. In the 1990s the number of microfinance projects increased, with notable efforts by the Rural Development Institute of the Chinese Academy of Social Sciences (with funding and technical support from the Ford Foundation and Grameen Bank) and the United Nations Development Program. In the late 1990s rural credit cooperatives began to issue microcredit loans based on provisional regulations issued by the People's Bank. These regulations were finalized in 2001, leading to a further expansion of microcredit loans for rural households (He Guangwen et al. 2009, 20–21).

In 2005 the central bank launched a pilot program in five provinces that by 2008 led the China Banking Regulatory Commission and the People's Bank of China to jointly issue formal Guidelines for Microcredit Companies. This framework allowed individuals, corporate legal entities, and social organizations to invest in setting up microloan companies. By the end of 2009 there were more than 1,300 microfinance companies with loans outstanding of RMB77 billion (China Banking Society 2011, 556).

Beginning in 2010, microfinance expanded much more rapidly. In 2010 alone the number of microcredit companies doubled to 2,600, and credit outstanding increased by more than 150 percent. Microcredit outstanding doubled in 2011. By the end of 2012 there were more than 6,000 microcredit companies that had extended loans amounting to RMB592 billion, almost eight times the amount outstanding three years earlier.[78] While this pales next to the magnitude of credit extended by the formal financial system, microfinance companies have become an important source of funding for private companies and particularly for household businesses.

In part, the recent rapid expansion of microcredit reflects the entry of Alibaba Group Holding Ltd. and other internet companies into the microlending business.[79] Using their massive databases on payment histories and other information, internet firms such as Alibaba in 2010 began offering unsecured loans to their small-business customers through their wholly owned microfinance subsidiaries. While Alibaba has been the pacesetter, other internet companies such as Baidu and JD.com have also begun lending to small businesses (Cui 2013).[80]

---

78. People's Bank of China, "Statistical Report on Microfinance Companies in 2012," February 1, 2013. Available at www.pbc.gov.cn (accessed on February 4, 2013).

79. Alipay was established to operate the e-payment services of Alibaba in 2004 but since 2011 has been a legal entity separate from Alibaba. Starting in March 2014 Alipay became one of four units in a newly established, separate legal entity called Alipay Small and Micro Finance Group. Although a separate legal entity, this group has contractual relationships with Alibaba. In the text of this study I will thus simply use the term "Alibaba" to cover the activities of Alibaba and the Alipay Small and Micro Finance Group.

80. Meng Jing, "WeChat to manage wealth," *China Daily*, January 20, 2014, p. 15.

Investment—A Summary Measure

Changing shares of fixed investment by private and state firms is perhaps the best single measure of the combined effects of their differential performance in terms of both return on assets and access to bank credit, debt and equity markets, and other sources of finance. Fortunately, these data are available for privately controlled and state-controlled companies starting in 2006.[81] Figure 3.9 shows that the share of investment undertaken throughout the economy by state firms fell from just under 50 percent in 2006 and to 34 percent in 2012, while the share of private firms rose from 35 percent to almost 50 percent in the same period.[82] At the outset of reform in 1980, state-owned firms were responsible for 82 percent of all investment.[83] Thus by 2012, state firms' share of fixed asset investment had fallen by more than half.

Interestingly, the state share of investment did rise by 1.6 percentage points in 2009, the only year since 2006 that its share did not decline. This uptick reflects a large increase in infrastructure investment in 2009, a key part of the government's stimulus to offset the effect of the global downturn. Given the size of this infrastructure spending and the state's large role in it as reflected in the large increase in infrastructure-related borrowing through local government investment vehicles, a key question is why the increase in the state share of fixed investment was not even larger. In answering this question it is important to note that the magnitude of infrastructure investment must be estimated. The only official time-series data, compiled by the Ministry of Housing and Urban Development, is restricted to infrastructure investment undertaken by municipal governments.[84] The increase in municipal infrastructure investment in 2009 accounts for well under 10 percent of the overall increase in fixed asset

---

81. The data on which this analysis, the next four paragraphs, and figures 3.8 and 3.9 are based exclude investment by rural households. By definition, this excluded investment is all private, and thus the share of private investment is understated. But the understatement is quite small: 1 percentage point in 2011 (National Bureau of Statistics of China 2012b, 164, 176–77). As is well known, Chinese fixed asset investment data include the value of assets that are purchased. Thus the value of land transactions and the value of mergers and acquisitions are included in fixed asset investment. Ideally, analysis should be based on capital formation—that is, activities that expand the productive capacity of an economy rather than a data series that includes asset sales.

82. The balance of fixed investment, a roughly constant 15 percent, was undertaken by collective firms (accounting for about one-third of the balance) and foreign firms (accounting for about two-thirds of the balance).

83. ISI Emerging Markets, CEIC Database. Available by subscription only at www.ceicdata.com (accessed on July 17, 2014).

84. Thus, for example, the data do not include investment in electric power generation and distribution and in telecommunications, which are typically undertaken by state companies controlled at the national level. Similarly in transport, the ministry's data do not include investment in intercity rail and civil aviation, though they do include local investment in metro systems, roads, and bridges. This series, which starts in 1978, could not be found on the website of the Ministry of Finance but is available from Wind Information System, Economic Database. Available by subscription only at www.wind.com.cn (accessed on July 17, 2014).

Figure 3.9   Fixed investment by ownership, 2006–12

percent of fixed asset investment

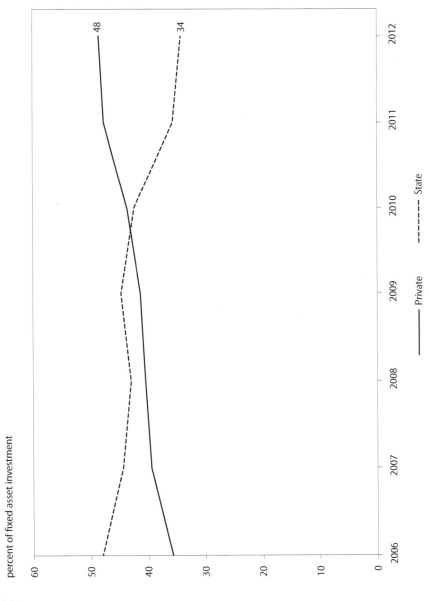

Sources: National Bureau of Statistics of China (2013c, 170–73); National Bureau of Statistics of China, www.stats.gov.cn (accessed on February 28, 2014).

investment that year. Using a broader definition, the increase in infrastructure investment accounts for a little more than a third of the increase in fixed asset investment in 2009.[85] But the combined increase in investment in manufacturing and real estate accounted for more than two-fifths of the increase in fixed asset investment. Private activity heavily dominates manufacturing and real estate investment, partly offsetting the influence of the increasing infrastructure investment on the state share of fixed asset investment. Moreover, state and state-controlled units in 2009 accounted for 86 percent of infrastructure investment, meaning that state infrastructure investment accounted for 30 percent of the overall increase in fixed asset investment (National Bureau of Statistics of China 2010b, 172–73). Taking these various factors into account, the overall increase in state investment in 2009 was only slightly greater than the increase in private investment, so the overall share of investment undertaken by the state rose by less than 2 percentage points.

The same point can be made from another perspective. The outstanding borrowings of local governments, as reported by China's national audit office, rose from RMB5.6 trillion at the end of 2008 to RMB17.8 trillion by the end of June 2013, an increase of RMB12.2 trillion. This rapid increase in local government debt has raised concern both outside and inside China. But compared with fixed asset investment, the borrowing of local governments is not so large. National fixed asset investment from 2009 through 2012 was RMB119 trillion (National Bureau of Statistics of China 2013c, 154). Spending by local governments that was debt financed over the same period is unlikely to have reached more than RMB20 trillion.[86] In short, given the massive increase in fixed asset investment in 2009–12, a substantial increase in local government debt was sufficient to raise the state share of investment only slightly.

Figure 3.10 shows the changing private and state firm shares of fixed investment in China's industrial sector. Here the transformation is even more striking, with private firms' annual investment slightly exceeding that of state firms as early as 2006 and that margin expanding to 45 percentage points by 2012, leaving state firms responsible for only a fifth of fixed investment in industry.

Moreover, disaggregating industrial investment shows that the share of investment by state firms is as high as 20 percent only because of their dominance of investment in electricity, gas, water, and to a much lesser degree

---

85. Following the scope of infrastructure used by the World Bank in its analytical work, I estimate infrastructure investment as the sum of fixed asset investment in the production and supply of electricity, gas, and water; information transmission, computer services, and software; management of water conservancy, environment, and public facilities; and transport, storage, and post. For 2003 through 2011, these data—disaggregated into state, collective, and private (all based on the concept of control outlined in box 2.1) are available in National Bureau of Statistics of China (2012b, 164–66).

86. This estimate is based on an average maturity of local government debt of three years, the assumptions that all loans due during this period were repaid rather than rolled over, and that no more than 90 percent of the gross debt issued in 2009–12 was spent.

Figure 3.10 Fixed investment in industry and manufacturing by ownership, 2006–12

percent of fixed asset investment

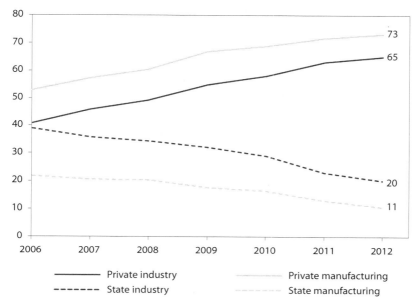

Legend:
——— Private industry
- - - - - State industry
——— Private manufacturing
- - - - - State manufacturing

Sources: National Bureau of Statistics of China (2013c, 170–73); National Bureau of Statistics of China, www.stats.gov.cn (accessed on February 28, 2014).

mining.[87] State firms in 2012 accounted for 70 percent and 46 percent, respectively, of all investment in utilities and mining. As previously noted, however, government-owned utilities are not uncommon in market economies, so the relatively elevated state share of investment in utilities is not strong evidence that China is following a model of state capitalism. But, as shown in the figure, by 2012 the share of investment of state firms in manufacturing, which accounts for four-fifths of value added in industry, had fallen to only 11 percent, while the share of investment in manufacturing by private firms stood at 73 percent (National Bureau of Statistics of China 2013c, 54, 170–71). Thus in manufacturing, private firms are now investing almost seven times more than state firms.

Figures 3.9 and 3.10 reflect very different paces of transformation. The explanation is that investment in infrastructure and a broad range of public services—education, health, social security, social welfare, water conservancy, environment, and public facilities—are included in the data underlying figure 3.9 but not in figure 3.10. The state dominates investment in infrastructure

---

87. Both utilities and mining are components of industry in China's system for classifying components of GDP.

and public services, so the transformation of investment by ownership in figure 3.10 is substantially less than in figure 3.9. The same point can be made from another angle—the potential importance of retained earnings as a source of investment finance. As detailed earlier in this chapter, retained earnings have financed two-thirds of all investment undertaken from 2000 through 2011 by nonfinancial corporations but are not a significant source of finance in infrastructure and the many public service areas in which state investment dominates. The superior financial performance of private firms and their increasing access to credit are clearly reflected in the fact that private sector investment in industry by 2011 was more than two and a half times that of state firms.

Role of the Party in the Private Sector

Perhaps the analysis in this chapter overstates the role of the market and private sector in the economy because it has not to this point addressed the role of the Communist Party in private businesses. Is it possible that, while the party-state has given up its dominant direct ownership over wide swaths of the economy, it exercises control increasingly by recruiting entrepreneurs into the party and then either influencing or controlling the activities of these entrepreneurs' private firms?

Recruitment of entrepreneurs into the party began in the mid-1980s but was banned in August 1989 following the crackdown on demonstrators in Tiananmen Square on June 4. In part, entrepreneurs were excluded because they were prominent supporters of the predominantly student demonstrators (Dickson 2008, 71). While new party members were not recruited for several years after 1989, the massive downsizing and privatization of state-owned companies in the second half of the 1990s led to an increase in so-called red capitalists since the managers of the newly privatized firms were typically their former managers, most of whom were already party members (Dickson 2008, 83). But in July 2001 Party General Secretary Jiang Zemin gave a speech calling for the party to represent advanced social productive forces, advanced culture, and the greatest majority of the people (the "three represents" (三个代表)). This speech substantially expanded the mandate beyond the party's traditional aim of representing the Chinese proletariat (Dickson 2008, 77) and paved the way for a renewed recruitment of entrepreneurs into the party. According to surveys by Chinese organizations, about a third of private entrepreneurs were members of the party by 2006, a substantial increase from a fifth in 2000, the year before Jiang's speech (Dickson 2008, 70).

Bruce Dickson carried out extensive surveys to evaluate the motivation for entrepreneurs to join the party and also analyzed the party's motives in recruiting them. Entrepreneurs' motives for joining the party are simple—to gain economic benefits and political power. Political connections, for example, could make it easier to obtain loans or avoid enforcement of worker safety and environmental regulations. Private businessmen also believed that membership might allow them "to avoid the interference of party and government organizations in their business affairs" (Dickson 2008, 94). About one-third of the entrepreneurs that have become so successful that they are listed on Rupert Hoogewerf's annual compilation of China's wealthiest people, the Hurun China Rich List, are party members. Many are or aspire to become delegates to the National People's Congress (NPC) or the Chinese People's Political Consultative Conference (CPPCC), in part because these positions confer prestige and in part because "delegates have regular and recurring access to decision makers and the opportunity to influence laws and regulations" (Dickson 2008, 171–72).

Rich entrepreneurs who have been recruited to the party and have become delegates to the NPC or CPPCC make no secret of their attempts to advance their business interests in these political bodies. Shortly after the conclusion of the 2014 NPC, a number of the more than 100 delegates to these bodies who were renminbi billionaires were asked what proposals they made at the meetings and whether they were related to their business interests. Zong Qinghou—founder and chairman of the Wahaha Group, the second richest person on the 2013 Hurun China Rich List (net worth RMB115 billion, or $18.7 billion), and an NPC deputy from Zhejiang Province—responded that he had introduced one formal proposal and made 14 suggestions, "most related to my business." Similarly, chairman of the New Hope Group Liu Yonghao, the seventeenth richest person on the Hurun list (net worth RMB34 billion, or $5.5 billion) and an NPC deputy from Sichuan Province, acknowledged that the three proposals he made were "all closely related to my business."[88]

The literature suggests the party's motivation to recruit entrepreneurs is twofold. First, as the legitimacy of the party has come to depend increasingly on the growth that generates higher living standards and as the private sector has become the primary source of economic growth, the party wants the private sector to become a partner in modernizing the economy. Second, the party fears that entrepreneurs will organize outside of the party, perhaps by aligning with pro-democracy political activists, as appeared to be the case in 1989. Thus Dickson labels the strategy of recruiting entrepreneurs to the party as one of "co-opting the capitalists." Dickson concludes, "Party building in the private sector has been more successful at promoting the firms' interests than exerting party leadership" over the private sector (2008, 111).

Christopher McNally has elaborated on this theme based on case studies of several private enterprises in Sichuan Province (McNally 2011). The entrepreneurs he studied all cultivated ties with local party and government officials, leading McNally to characterize China's economic model not as one of market capitalism or state capitalism but rather as one of "connections" (关系) capitalism. In the absence of a strong legal system and well-established property rights, entrepreneurs cultivate ties with local officials to protect their business interests. Like Dickson, McNally sees connections capitalism as a mecha-

---

88. "Billionaires speak out on reform roles," *China Daily*, March 13, 2014, p. 6.

nism "to create channels by which wealthy entrepreneurs can enter political institutions and exert political influence" (2011, 10). Connections capitalism, McNally maintains, has "changed the nature of the CCP's political constituency and its basis of legitimacy" and as a result "private business interests are gaining political leverage" (2011, 21).

Despite the research just summarized, which indicates that private entrepreneurs are using the party to advance their commercial interests, some believe that the Chinese government and the Chinese Communist Party have substantial control over private enterprises. Indeed, in the extreme they assert that there is no such thing as a private enterprise in China and that the party controls everything.[89] The obvious weakness in this argument is that it fails to explain the systematic differences in economic performance between state and private firms. This study has already shown the following:

- private firms have increasingly displaced state firms as the dominant source of output in most of manufacturing, mining, construction, wholesaling and retailing, and catering;

- private industrial firms consistently make more productive use of capital, as reflected in a much higher return on assets;

- private firms are responsible for virtually all of the growth of employment in urban China since reform began; and

- private firms are now the most important contributor to China's still growing exports.

Those who believe that the state and party exert as much control over private firms as they do over state firms—that is, burdening the former with noncommercial objectives—need to explain this divergent performance. In the absence of such an explanation, the sensible conclusion is that private sector firms in China are significantly more market oriented than their state counterparts and, for the most part, behave in ways similar to commercially motivated firms in market economies. The exceptions are few and obvious—for example, the self-censorship by private internet and media companies.

China's economic rise in the reform era is largely the story of the expanding role of markets and private enterprise. The transformation of production arrangements from collective to private was most rapid in agriculture. The transformation in manufacturing and construction was much more gradual but in many ways more profound since these sectors accounted for a much larger share of GDP than agriculture and they were in some ways more inextricably linked to the system of economic planning that China adopted from the Soviet Union in the 1950s. But by 2011 the share of manufacturing and construction output originating in state-owned and state-controlled firms

---

89. This was a verbal statement at an off-the-record meeting at the International Monetary Fund in February 2014 by someone not employed by the IMF.

had declined to only one-fifth and one-third, respectively; initially output was entirely produced by state or collective firms, with the latter controlled by governments at the local level. The transformation of production arrangements in public utilities and services presents a more complex picture. Power generation and distribution remain state monopolized, but private firms are making inroads in water and gas supply in many cities. Some services, notably retailing and catering, are now dominated by private firms, but broad swaths of the service sector, including finance, basic telecommunications, and almost all social services, remain largely in the domain of the state. The importance of the private sector to China's economy is also reflected in labor markets, where private firms account for all of the growth of employment since 1978.

The rise of private enterprise in manufacturing, construction, and portions of the service sector was an evolutionary process, not the outcome of a big-bang privatization. Private enterprise started in 1978 from a tiny base, fueled by household savings and loans from family and friends rather than funds borrowed from the formal financial system. But the higher return on assets earned by these private enterprises allowed them to expand their capital stock rapidly and increasingly displace less efficient state-owned firms from their initially dominant positions in many product lines in manufacturing and in the components of the service sector that were open to private firms. Government policy, initially hostile to private firms, became more favorable, starting with the promulgation of the Provisional Regulations on Private Enterprises in 1988 and continuing with the Company Law, adopted in 1994 and revised in 2006. These provided a regulatory environment that was more conducive to the growth of the private sector, first by allowing private firms with eight or more employees, later by allowing private limited liability firms, and finally by allowing single-person limited liability companies. After the mid-1990s, banks increasingly found private firms to be better credit risks than state-owned companies so that on average in 2010–12 private firms' share of loans to enterprises was 52 percent compared with an average of 32 percent for state firms.

Nonetheless, China's transition to a market economy is incomplete. Competition in important segments of the service sector is quite limited. A few key prices remain administered rather than market determined, distorting the allocation of resources and slowing economic growth. And, while improving, the share of bank lending going to private firms is still far below the contribution that these firms make to China's economic growth. The reforms that China must undertake to complete its transition to a market economy are the subject of the next chapter.

4

Implementing the Reform Agenda

China has fundamentally transformed from an economy in which key prices were administered and a large share of resources was allocated through bureaucratic planning to one in which almost all prices are determined in competitive markets and private firms, focused on profitability, undertake a large and still growing share of investment. As laid out in a key decision of the Chinese Communist Party at the Third Plenum of the 18th Party Congress in November 2013, China's current reform agenda includes eliminating remaining price controls, which distort resource allocation, and reducing regulatory barriers that impede the entry of private firms into the few domains, mostly in services, where state firms retain near complete control.[1] The key prices that will be decontrolled include those for various forms of energy, foreign exchange, and the cost of capital. Distortions of these prices over the past decade have favored the development of the industrial sector at the expense of services and contributed to an expansion of profits at the expense of wages.

If implemented, these reforms will substantially rebalance China's economic growth. Looked at from the production perspective, they will lead to more moderate growth of industry and a much more robust expansion of the service sector. From the income perspective, reforms will gradually increase the wage share of GDP while reducing the profit share of GDP. From the expenditure perspective, reforms will lead to more moderate growth of investment and more robust growth of private consumption expenditure. From a domestic

---

1. Chinese Communist Party Central Committee, "Decision on Major Issues Concerning Comprehensively Deepening Reforms," November 15, 2013. Available at www.gov.cn (accessed on December 17, 2013).

saving-investment balance perspective, the promised more-market-determined exchange rate should reduce government intervention in the foreign exchange market and thus promote continued appreciation of the renminbi over the medium term.[2] That appreciation should largely offset the higher growth of productivity in the production of tradable goods and lead to a continued modest current account surplus as a share of China's GDP.

State Firms Drag Down Growth

The analysis in chapter 3 shows that the footprint of state firms as measured by their share of output, employment, and investment has shrunk dramatically since 1978. Moreover, there is scant evidence that the global economic crisis and its immediate aftermath slowed this shrinkage. The accounting explanation for this long-term trend is very straightforward. First, the productivity of state industrial firms, as measured by return on assets, has consistently lagged that of private industrial firms and has also fallen in absolute terms since roughly the middle of the 2000s. The higher return of private industrial firms translates into a higher level of retained earnings, which in turn finances much of the investment underlying their superior growth performance. A similar pattern occurs in services. As noted in chapter 3, the return on assets of state service firms in 2008 (the only year for which reasonably comprehensive data are currently available) was only 3.4 percent, only half the level of nonstate firms.[3] Second, starting at least a decade ago banks began to allocate a larger share of their loans to private firms. On both counts, investment by state firms accounts for a declining share of national investment, the growth of output of state firms is slow relative to that of private firms, and employment in state firms continues to fall, not only as a share of total employment but in absolute numbers as well.

The key theme of this chapter is that state firms are an increasing drag on China's growth, even as they are contributing a declining share of national output because of their relatively low and declining return on assets. Consequently, economic reform should now focus on opening up the portions of the economy that remain off-limits for private firms, including foreign firms. The Third Plenum decision addresses this directly in several ways. First, the decision declares that the market should be the decisive force in the allocation of resources, a substantial elevation of its role compared with previous party documents. Second, it elevates the role of the nonstate sector to

---

2. The depreciation of the renminbi in the early months of 2014 is most likely an attempt by the authorities to disrupt the carry trade that sought to take advantage of the combination of higher domestic interest rates in China plus a steadily appreciating currency. This carry trade has led to significant inflows on the capital and financial account. However, over the medium term appreciation is likely to resume in order to offset the continued growth in the production of export goods. In the absence of this appreciation, over the medium term China's exports likely would become supercompetitive on global markets, leading to a large and growing trade and current account surplus.

3. See note 53 in chapter 3.

parity with the state sector. This also marks a substantial departure from prior party documents, which acknowledged that the private sector was an important contributor to growth but stopped well short of placing the private sector on a par with the state-owned economy. Third, the decision calls repeatedly for a level playing field, competitive markets, and restriction of state monopoly ownership to natural monopolies.

Figure 4.1 clearly captures why state industrial firms are a drag on China's growth. With the exception of 2010, the return on assets of these firms since 2007 has been less than their cost of capital.[4] Moreover, because the return on assets of state-owned service firms in 2008 was only half that of nonstate firms and profit margins of state firms in the service sector have since fallen even more than profit margins of state industrial firms (see figure 1.2), it seems very likely that the returns on assets of these firms also remain substantially below the returns of private service sector firms. In short, there is a substantial misallocation of capital, which, if corrected, would allow China to sustain relatively rapid economic growth with a smaller share of resources devoted to investment, one of the key rebalancing objectives of China's political leadership.

Some analysts argue that the widening gap between the return on assets of state and private firms since 2007 is due in large part to cyclical factors. Jon Anderson, for example, points out that state firms are concentrated in mining and heavy manufacturing and that these industries are more cyclical than light manufacturing activities such as textiles, information technology, electronics, and food processing, where private firms dominate. Since China is at the end of a commodity boom and growth is slowing, he argues, it should not be surprising to find that the return on assets of state firms has fallen. Indeed, he argues that "there's nothing in the numbers to suggest that SOEs are (i) significantly worse than the rest of the economy or (ii) in urgent need of aggressive reforms" (Anderson 2013b).

But this sanguine view of state-owned enterprises is not supported by an examination of the relative performance of state and private firms in one of China's most important heavy industries—steel. As shown in figure 4.2, state-owned and state-controlled firms in this industry in the first half of the last decade achieved a return on assets that was roughly the same as the average return of all firms in the steel industry. But in 2006 and 2007, returns of state steel firms fell while returns for the industry as a whole rose; after 2007 returns of state firms fell more rapidly than industry average returns. By 2012, the return on assets of state firms had fallen by 6.5 percentage points compared

---

4. Typically the cost of capital for firms is calculated as a weighted average of the cost of debt and the cost of equity, the latter measured by the return that an investor would expect from holding a company's shares. But in China few companies are listed on the stock exchanges, and the corporate bond market is extremely small. Thus, other than retained earnings, most capital in the corporate sector comes from bank loans. So the interest rate on a one-year loan is assumed to be a reasonable estimate of the cost of capital. To the extent that state firms rely on funds from nonbank lenders in the shadow banking sector, where interest rates for borrowers are typically higher, the approach adopted here understates the degree to which the return on assets falls below the cost of capital.

Figure 4.1   Return on assets versus cost of capital for industrial firms, 1997–2012

percent

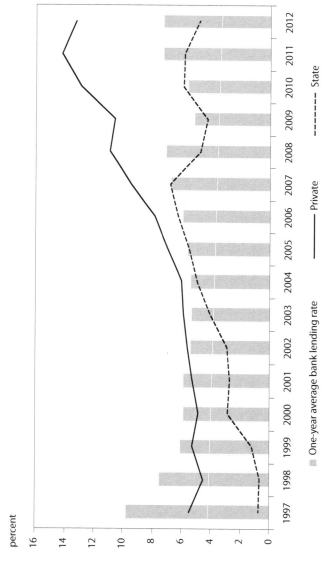

■ One-year average bank lending rate   — Private   ----- State

Note: Total profits are earnings before corporate income tax. The annual one-year average lending rate was calculated using the quarterly weighted average lending rate between 2009 and 2012. Prior to 2009, the one-year benchmark lending rate was used.

Sources: National Bureau of Statistics of China (2013c, 475–93); ISI Emerging Markets, CEIC Database.

Figure 4.2 Return on assets of ferrous metal smelting and pressing by ownership, 2001–12
(percent)

total profits/total assets

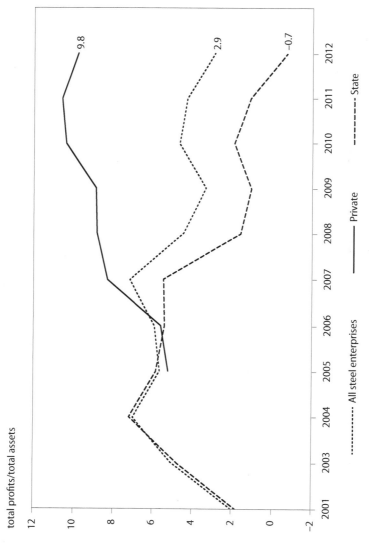

.... All steel enterprises   ———— Private   – – – – State

Notes: Total profits are earnings before corporate income tax. No data were available for 2002.

Sources: National Bureau of Statistics of China (2013c, 475–93); National Bureau of Statistics of China, www.stats.gov.cn (accessed on February 28, 2014).

with 2005 to a negative 0.7 percent, while average returns in the industry fell by less than 3 percentage points, to 2.9 percent. The mediocre performance of state firms is even more apparent when one compares their returns with those of registered private steel companies. These firms, which produced about a quarter of the output of the ferrous metals sector, earned a return on assets of 10.6 percent in 2011, which was 10 times the return on assets of state firms.[5] Moreover, private firms managed to double their return on assets between 2005 and 2011. Not until the downturn in the steel industry deepened further in 2012 did the returns of private firms weaken, falling slightly to 9.8 percent. Thus at least through 2012, private steel firms largely escaped the adverse effects of China's economic slowdown while state steel firms were bleeding.

This analysis strongly suggests that cyclical factors are not the major determinant of the declining performance of state firms vis-à-vis their private counterparts in the steel industry. There is a large and still growing productivity differential between state and registered private firms in China's preeminent heavy industry. Private steel firms are more nimble than state firms, adjusting more successfully to changing demand conditions. Whether this same pattern holds in other cyclical industries is an important topic for future research.

The Opportunity in Services

China's service sector offers the greatest opportunities for the next wave of expansion of the private sector for two reasons. First, as demonstrated in chapter 3, the state firms' share of output in industry has already fallen by two-thirds compared with 1978, and in many branches of industry, more efficient private firms have almost entirely displaced state firms. In manufacturing, private firms already account for three-quarters of investment, while the state share has fallen to barely over 10 percent. Thus there are limited efficiency gains from further increasing the private sector's presence in manufacturing (Yao 2013). The state is likely to continue to exercise complete control of electric power distribution, so the opportunity for expansion of private activity in thermal power likely will be limited to power generation. Except in wholesale and retail trade, hotels, and catering, state firms continue to dominate the service sector. The Third Plenum decision signals that the state is prepared to reduce its role in important services that are not a natural monopoly, such as telecommunications.

The second reason China's service sector offers the greatest opportunity for the next wave of expansion is that it is relatively underdeveloped. An Asian Development Bank study shows that the share of GDP originating in services in China throughout the reform era is substantially below the share predicted

---

5. As noted in chapter 3, state and state-controlled steel firms produced 37 percent of steel output in 2011. Foreign firms produced 13 percent of output and registered private firms produced 26 percent. The residual of 24 percent was produced by limited liability companies in which the majority or dominant owner was private and possibly by collective firms.

based on the relationship between the growth of per capita GDP and the share of the service sector in GDP for 12 Asian economies. Similarly, the share of employment in the service sector in China is also less than the predicted share (Park and Shin 2012, 14–17).

The lagging performance of China's service sector is also apparent in the time path of the growth of service output. At the outset of the reform program, China's service sector was particularly small, reflecting the heavy-industry bias that characterized economic planning and resource allocation before 1978. But as the government began to reduce the scope of economic planning and to increasingly liberalize product prices and factor markets, the pace of expansion of the service sector far outstripped the growth of GDP, pushing up its share of GDP from an average of 22 percent in 1979–81 to 42 percent by 2002 (National Bureau of Statistics of China 2012b, 45). Thus China's growth pattern in the first two decades of the reform era was consistent with the widely observed pattern in which sustained economic growth is accompanied by a rising share of services in GDP.

But in the third decade of reform, three factor price distortions substantially slowed the relative growth of service output. First, starting from as early as 2002, China's currency became increasingly undervalued. This undervaluation of the renminbi was a significant contrast with the first two decades of economic reform, when the renminbi was substantially overvalued, and from the mid-1990s until 2001, when the value of the renminbi was close to an equilibrium level. Renminbi undervaluation raised the profitability of production of tradable goods. Since tradable goods in China are overwhelmingly manufactures, currency undervaluation led to increasing investment in manufacturing at the expense of services and a slowing in the relative pace of growth of service output (Goldstein and Lardy 2009, 10, 59).

A second factor price distortion contributing to the stagnation of the service share of GDP was the central bank's adoption of a low interest rate policy beginning in 2004. The central bank fixed the ceiling on the nominal interest rate that banks could pay on deposits so low that, taking inflation into account, the real return to savings became negative (figure 4.3). This policy was a distinct change from earlier years, when the bank adjusted the nominal deposit rate ceiling so that the real rate was always in positive territory, regardless of the rate of inflation. As a result, the average real deposit rate starting in 2004 was an average of 330 basis points lower than it had been from 1997 through 2003. Competition among banks meant that the resulting lower cost of bank funding was passed on to bank borrowers. As reflected in figure 4.4, this pushed down the average real cost of borrowing over the next seven years to only 3.2 percent, a decline of 300 basis points compared with the average real cost in 1997–2003.[6] Since manufacturing is more capital intensive than services, this declining cost of capital also increased the profitability of manufacturing relative to ser-

6. The real cost of borrowing is the nominal interest rate adjusted for inflation as measured by the consumer price index.

Figure 4.3 Real deposit rate, January 1997–2013

percent

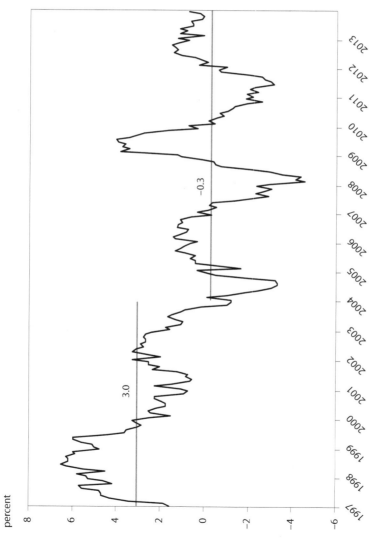

Note: For 1997–2012, the real deposit rate is calculated as the difference between the one-year benchmark savings deposit rate and the consumer price index. After July 2012, it is calculated as the difference between 1.1 times the one-year benchmark deposit savings rate and the consumer price index.

Sources: People's Bank of China, www.pbc.gov.cn; National Bureau of Statistics of China, www.stats.gov.cn (accessed on February 28, 2014); ISI Emerging Markets, CEIC Database.

Figure 4.4   Real lending rate, January 1997–2013

percent

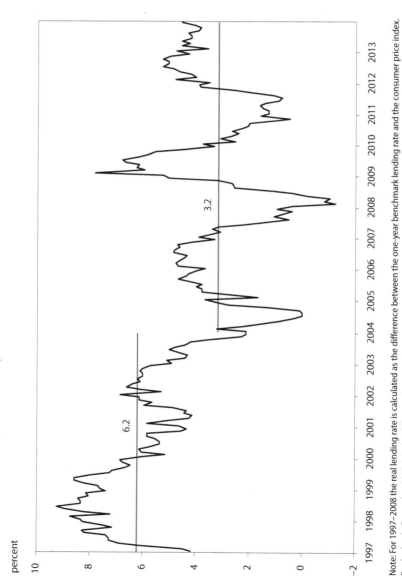

Note: For 1997–2008 the real lending rate is calculated as the difference between the one-year benchmark lending rate and the consumer price index. Beginning in December 2008, it is the difference between the weighted average lending rate and the consumer price index.

Sources: People's Bank of China, www.pbc.gov.cn (accessed on February 28, 2014); National Bureau of Statistics of China, www.stats.gov.cn; ISI Emerging Markets, CEIC Database.

vices and tilted investment even more strongly into the manufacturing sector. Because on average service industries are more labor intensive than manufacturing, the bias toward manufacturing as opposed to service investment, in turn, contributed to a reduction in the wage share of GDP and thus a decline in the private consumption share of GDP as well.[7]

A third factor contributing to the relative stagnation of service output after 2002 was a change in government policy on energy pricing. In 2003, in response to a sharp rise in the global price of crude oil and coal, the new Hu Jintao-Wen Jiabao government abandoned the policy of full-cost pricing of electricity and fuels that had been implemented in the late 1990s under the leadership of President Jiang Zemin and Premier Zhu Rongji. Instead, when periodically the international price of crude oil or coal rose sharply, these costs were not fully reflected in the prices either of refined petroleum products or of electricity, leading to large financial losses for refiners and power generators and implicit subsidies for users of energy. Since about three-fourths of all energy in China is consumed in manufacturing, this policy also constituted a subsidy for manufacturing (Lardy 2012, 84–86, 103–104, 106–12).

Largely as a result of these three factor price distortions, the growth of service output slowed dramatically relative to GDP after 2002. Between 2002 and 2007–08, the service share of GDP stagnated at 42 percent. Subsequently, its share rose very gradually, reaching 46 percent of GDP by 2013. So in the first two decades of economic reform, the service share of output rose by an average of 1 percentage point of GDP per year, but in the next 11 years, when distortions in the pricing of foreign exchange, energy, and capital became important, the pace of expansion was only 4 percentage points cumulatively (National Bureau of Statistics of China 2013b, 21).

Another important reason for the slow growth of services since 2002 is the highly restrictive government policy on the entry of private firms into much of the sector. This policy is much more restrictive than it is in manufacturing. An OECD survey of 40 countries ranks China as the most restrictive in terms of barriers to entry in services the OECD identifies as networked sectors (gas, electricity, road freight, postal services, and telecommunications) and second most restrictive in professional services and retail. Where 6 is the most restrictive score possible, China scored 5.4 and 4.5, respectively. India's scores were much lower, at 3.6 and 1.3. Brazil, with scores of 2.4 and 1, has even lower barriers to entry in services.[8] While this OECD survey is based on data from 2008, barriers to entry in Chinese services likely remain relatively high.

These barriers reduce competition and appear to account for a substantial share of the difference between the growth of total factor productivity (TFP)

---

7. The wage share of GDP declined from 53.6 percent of GDP in 2002 to 47.0 percent in 2011, according to the most recent flow of funds data (National Bureau of Statistics of China 2012b, 82–83; 2013c, 80–81).

8. Organization for Economic Cooperation and Development, Product Market Regulation Database. Available at www.oecd.org (accessed on November 14, 2013).

in services and that in manufacturing. Carsten Holz (2006) studied the growth of TFP over the first two decades of economic reform and found that annual TFP growth in nontradable goods, a proxy for services, was 2.6 percent, while annual TFP growth in tradables, a proxy for manufacturing, was 4.1 percent. A more recent study, by several economists at the Hong Kong Institute for Monetary Research focusing on 2001–10, estimated the annual TFP growth for the whole economy, the tradable sector, and the nontradable sector at 3.7 percent, 4.9 percent, and 2.4 percent, respectively. While productivity in services lags that in manufacturing in most economies, He Dong and his colleagues (2012, 9–10, 12) find that the differential in China is substantially greater than in developed market economies and "in line with those of fast-growing emerging economies such as Korea during 1990–97 before it accelerated liberalization of services after the Asian financial crisis."

A similar result emerges from an analysis from the middle of the last decade, which shows a huge 13-fold gap in aggregate TFP between China and the United States. But in manufacturing, the gap was only 1.3 times, leading to the conclusion that "most of the differences in aggregate productivity, and therefore living standards, between China and the United States have to be rooted in the inefficiency in the nonmanufacturing sectors—mostly domestically oriented services and agriculture" (Ahuja 2013, 202–203). The International Monetary Fund estimates that deregulation of services would have a substantial payoff, increasing TFP growth in the economy by more than 1 percentage point annually (IMF 2013b, 22).

The difference in the restrictions on private activity in services versus industry is clearly reflected in differing trends in the sectors' sources of investment. As shown in chapter 3 (see figure 3.10), the share of investment in industry by state and private firms was roughly equal, at about 40 percent in 2006.[9] But by 2012, private firms accounted for 65 percent of all industrial investment, while the share of investment by state firms had fallen to only 20 percent. By contrast, as reflected in figure 4.5, the state share of investment in services was much more elevated in the middle of the last decade and has declined much more slowly. By 2012, state firms were still responsible for 45 percent of service investment, twice their share of investment in industry and four times their share of investment in manufacturing. Private firms' share of investment in services has increased quite slowly since 2006 and by 2011 stood at only 36 percent.

The private share of investment in services could increase quite substantially even if the state remains the dominant investor in components that governments dominate in most market economies: education, health, science, water conservancy and public facilities, and public management. In 2011 state investment in these public services accounted for 40 percent of state investment in services. If private investment by private enterprises had completely

---

9. 2006 is the first year for which industrial investment data based on the nature of the majority or dominant owner are available.

Figure 4.5   Investment in services by firm ownership, 2006–12

percent of fixed asset investment

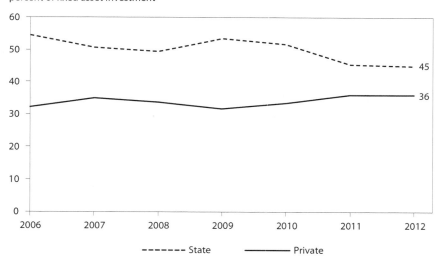

Sources: National Bureau of Statistics of China (2013c, 170–73); National Bureau of Statistics of China, www.stats .gov.cn (accessed on February 28, 2014).

displaced state investment from the remaining components of services in 2011, the private share of investment in all services would have been 63 percent rather than 36 percent, an increase of three-quarters.[10]

The potential for an expanded role for private firms is especially large in modern services, where state firms have an elevated role. Modern services include information technology, financial services, leasing and business services, and technical services, while traditional services include wholesale and retail, hotels and catering, transportation and storage, personal services, and public services such as education and health.[11] A number of studies have shown that modern services have strong positive spillover effects to the rest of the economy. Moreover, modern services are not the natural monopolies or social services that governments commonly choose to closely regulate or provide directly. The share of investment in modern services undertaken by China's state and private companies is 46 percent and 34 percent, respectively.

Information on investment by ownership in the four components of modern services is presented in table 4.1. The state share of investment both in information transmission, software, and information technology (IT) and

10. The private share of services would have been 27 percentage points (= 60 percent of 45 percent) higher than the observed 36 percent.

11. "Technical services" is my label for the component of the service sector identified as "scientific research, technical services, and geological prospecting."

Table 4.1   Investment in modern services by firm ownership, 2012
         (percent)

	State	Private
Total	46	34
Information transmission, software, and information technology	60	19
Financial intermediation	60	22
Leasing and business services	35	43
Technical services	49	35

Source: National Bureau of Statistics of China (2013c, 170–73).

in financial intermediation is a relatively high 60 percent. Within the IT, software, and IT services category, the state accounts for fully three-quarters of all investment in telecommunications and transmission services, half of all investment in internet and related services, and just under a third in software and IT. Private and foreign firms account for the balance of investment, with the private share of investment reaching almost a third in internet and related services and almost half in software and IT. In contrast, the state dominates investment in all the subcomponents of financial intermediation (banking, capital markets, and insurance) except for a small residual category of other financial services where the private share approaches one-half (National Bureau of Statistics of China 2013c, 172). The only modern service where private investment exceeds state investment is leasing and business services. Where data are available, the return on assets of state firms in modern services is far below that of nonstate firms, suggesting that further liberalizing the barriers to their entry would enhance China's economic growth.[12]

Financial Sector Reform

Given private firms' substantially higher returns on assets, reforms of the financial sector that improve the flow of funds to them should be growth enhancing. The most important reforms are the gradual liberalization of deposit rates and the formation of more private banks. China's central bank has long set benchmark rates for both deposits and loans. While banks have been free to price loans upward from these rates since November 2004 and downward since July 2013, deposit rates are much more tightly controlled. Until June 2012 the central bank allowed banks no upward flexibility on deposit rates. Since then it has allowed banks to pay as much as 10 percent over the benchmark rates on deposits of various maturities. When this change was made, the benchmark rate on a one-year deposit, for example, was 3 percent; thus the maximum banks could offer was 3.3 percent.

---

12. The 2008 economic census shows that in the software industry the return on assets of state and state-controlled firms was 6 percent, while in nonstate firms it was 9.1 percent. In computer services, returns were 6.1 percent and 11.0 percent, respectively, for the two ownership categories.

There seems little doubt that liberalization would lead to higher deposit rates. First, when the central bank first allowed 10 percent upward flexibility in June 2012, almost all banks immediately floated their one-year deposit rates up to the maximum. Second, beginning in 2012, banks increasingly competed to retain customer funds by offering unregulated wealth management products that typically paid 100 to 150 basis points more than bank deposits of the same duration. Third, China's largest internet firms, notably Alibaba Holdings Ltd. and Tencent Holdings Ltd., are beginning to offer financial services that compete with state banks. Alibaba, in cooperation with Tianhong Asset Management Co. Ltd., created Yu'e Bao, a wealth management service.[13] By November 2013 it had attracted deposits of more than RMB100 billion, and deposits jumped to RMB500 billion by mid-February 2014.[14] Yu'e Bao is essentially a money market account. Funds in these accounts can be transferred back to Alipay at any time to pay for online purchases, so they are similar to bank demand deposits or checkable money market accounts. But the interest rates the internet firms pay on these accounts are up to ten times those that Chinese banks pay on demand deposits, where the central bank ceiling on interest rates still applies (Cui 2013). In early 2014 competitive pressures from these internet companies led banks to also float their interest rates on longer-term deposits to 1.1 times the benchmark rates for those maturities.[15]

Since Chinese banks are funded overwhelmingly by deposits, implementing the Third Plenum decision to liberalize deposit rates will further raise their cost of funds. The banks, in turn, will pass along a portion of this increase to their customers. In short, if banks have to pay higher rates on their liabilities, they will seek to earn higher rates on their assets. Given that, on average, state firms' return on assets is already less than the average loan rate, higher rates would presumably lead more state firms to reduce their demand for loans. Even if their demand for loans did not decline, banks likely would curtail lending to them. Conversely, the many private firms that have had no or limited access to bank loans and rely to some degree on informal credit markets, where interest rates are typically several times those charged by banks, would be an obvious new market for bank lending. Thus it seems likely that deposit rate liberalization would increase the share of bank lending to private firms, which tend to make much better use of the funds than state firms do. This conjecture is fully consistent with the experience of deposit rate liberalization in other economies, which has generally led to increased lending to firms

13. In October 2013 Alibaba invested RMB1.18 billion to become the controlling shareholder in Tianhong Asset Management Co. Ltd., with a 51 percent equity stake. Chen Jia, "Now securities and Internet firms look to linkups," *China Daily*, February 12, 2014, pp. 13–14.

14. "Yu'ebao boosts capital supply for economy," *China Daily*, March 10, 2014, available at www. chinadaily.com.cn (accessed on July 2, 2014).

15. Jiang Xueqing, "Banks strike back at online financial startups," *China Daily*, February 12, 2014, p. 13.

that previously were underserved by the banking system (Feyzioğlu, Porter, and Takáts 2009, 16).

A second reform that would improve the flow of funds to private firms would be to allow the creation of truly private banks that would likely lend an even larger share of their funds to private companies than do China's existing banks and provide additional competition with China's predominantly state-owned banks. China has long had a few banks that arguably are private. And the extent of private ownership in shareholding banks, city commercial banks, and rural banks is higher than many recognize. Private and collective capital accounted for 41 percent of the total equity of shareholding banks, 54 percent of city commercial banks, and 73 percent of rural banks at the end of 2012 (China Banking Regulatory Commission 2013, 38).[16] Thus while most rural banks and many city commercial banks may be privately controlled, the state remains the majority or dominant owner of shareholding banks, which account for a much larger share of total bank assets than do either rural banks or city commercial banks.

In 2013, momentum grew to green-light the establishment of more private banks. In its July financial sector guiding opinion, the State Council called for experimentation with private banks.[17] The China Banking Regulatory Commission (CBRC) almost immediately followed up, posting for comment a draft regulation on establishing banks, which included a provision for private banks.[18] Two months later, central bank governor Zhou Xiaochuan, in an important article in the party's *Qiushi* magazine, called for the promotion of private banks and other reforms to increase the financial support for small and microenterprises.[19] He reiterated these themes in the party's newspaper, *People's Daily,* in November.[20] In March 2014 CBRC announced that the State Council had accepted applications for the establishment of five private

---

16. The report gives these percentages for minjian (民间) ownership, a category that includes both private and collective ownership. Collectively owned units (including units that are pure collectives and units in which a collective is the majority or dominant owner of a corporation in another registration category) were less than 4 percent of the total number of corporate units in China at the end of 2011 (National Bureau of Statistics of China 2012b, 27). In banking, collective capital is significant only in rural banks and rural credit cooperatives.

17. State Council Management Office, "Guiding opinion concerning finance supporting economic structural adjustment and upward transformation," July 5, 2013. Available at www.gov.cn (accessed on March 12, 2014).

18. Wang Xiaotian, "Boost for private capital in banking industry," *China Daily*, August 13, 2013, p. 14.

19. Zhou Xiaochuan, "Practice the Party's Mass Line; Promote Inclusive Financial Development," *Qiushi*, September 16, 2013. Available at www.pbc.gov.cn (accessed on May 28, 2014).

20. Zhou Xiaochuan, "Thoroughly Deepen Financial Reform and Opening; Quickly Perfect the Financial Market System," *People's Daily*, November 28, 2013. Available at http://theory.people. com.cn (accessed on May 28, 2014). Large portions of this article were subsequently translated in *China Daily* under the title "Road map for financial reform," December 11 and 18, 2013, p. 11.

banks in four jurisdictions: Zhejiang and Guangdong Provinces, Tianjin, and Shanghai.[21] Interestingly, applicants for the first five private banking licenses include Tencent and Alibaba.

Power of the Chinese State in Perspective

How powerful is the Chinese state? Stephen Green, a well-regarded analyst at Standard Chartered Bank, believes that "China has a large and powerful government sector. It is one of the world's most powerful bureaucracies in terms of employment, income, ownership of the means of production, and regulatory powers."[22] Yet on some criteria this assessment exaggerates the power of the Chinese state.

First, the size of the Chinese government and party bureaucracy is surprisingly modest (table 4.2). In this respect, the Chinese Communist Party is similar to previous Chinese dynasties as far back as the Han, which ruled the vast Chinese empire with a modestly sized civil service (Maddison 1998, 21). Total government employment in 2011 was 42.3 million.[23] This number includes employment in all government offices at central, provincial, and local levels that are mainly controlled by and financed by the government. It is inclusive of not only those working directly in government agencies and organizations but also those employed in institutions (事业单位), a category that includes educational institutions, hospitals and clinics, research organizations, and so forth, almost all of which in China come under the purview of and are financed by the government. It also includes those employed in Chinese Communist Party organizations (中国共产党机关).[24] Government employment excludes workers producing goods and services in enterprises (企业) that are mainly owned or controlled by the government.

Forty-two million is a large number; indeed, it exceeds the population of many sovereign states. But government workers in all states are primarily involved in the provision of services ranging from public safety to health and education. Since the delivery of most of these services is very labor intensive, more populous countries inevitably have larger bureaucracies. Thus the standard practice of the International Labor Organization and other agencies analyzing the size of government bureaucracies is to express the number of

---

21. "CBRC Vice-Chairman Ju Qingmin discusses trial work on private banks," March 11, 2014. Available at www.cbrc.gov.cn (accessed on February 11, 2014).

22. Stephen Green, "China—Dreaming of Economic Reform in 2013." January 7, 2013. Standard Chartered Global Research.

23. This is the sum of reported employment in state agencies and organizations, state institutions, state nonprofit organizations, and a tiny residual "other" category. An identical number can be derived by subtracting state enterprise employment from total state employment (National Bureau of Statistics of China and Ministry of Human Resources and Social Security 2011, table 4-1).

24. Employment in party positions is relatively small, 561,000 in 2011 or 1.3 percent of the total.

Table 4.2 Public sector employment, 1999–2011 (millions of workers)

Year	Public sector employment	Public enterprise employment[a]	Government and party bureaucracy employment[b]
1999	96.5	59.8	36.8
2000	94.3	57.3	37.0
2001	90.2	53.3	36.9
2002	86.9	50.3	36.6
2003	83.4	46.9	36.5
2004	83.0	45.8	37.2
2005	80.5	42.9	37.6
2006	81.0	42.9	38.1
2007	81.6	42.9	38.7
2008	82.1	42.7	39.5
2009	77.6	37.6	40.0
2010	79.0	37.8	41.2
2011	87.4	45.1	42.3

a. Includes employment in state-controlled shareholding companies (国有控股企业) and traditional state-owned enterprises (国有企业).

b. Includes employment in public institutions (事业单位) and agencies (机关).

Note: A program to corporatize certain public institutions accelerated in 2011. There appears to be some double counting in the original sources for the 2011 data. Thus public sector and public enterprise employment in 2011 is probably overstated.

Sources: National Bureau of Statistics of China and Ministry of Human Resources and Social Security (2006–13); National Bureau of Statistics of China Population and Employment Statistics Office (2012; 2013, 262).

government employees relative to the population of the country in question. When scaled this way, China has only 31 government and party employees per thousand residents. The number of civil servants per thousand residents in France is 95, in the United States, 75, and in Germany, 53.[25]

Of course, a bureaucracy's size is also a function of a country's per capita income. High-income countries typically provide more services to their populations, and this almost always involves a larger civil service. So comparisons with countries closer to China's level of economic development are more appropriate. Government employment per thousand residents is 38 in both Mexico and Turkey and 32 in South Africa. In short, in government employment relative to population, China does not rank particularly high, even when those employed by the party are included.

Including employment in state-owned enterprises, China's total public sector employment in 2011 was a much higher 87.4 million, accounting for 11

---

25. International Labor Office (ILO), ILO LABORSTA Database, 2010. Available at http://laborsta.ilo.org (accessed on November 1, 2013). The US number would be even higher if it included workers in the post office, which is considered a quasi-government agency, employees of government-sponsored enterprises such as the Federal National Mortgage Association (Fannie Mae) and the Federal Home Loan Mortgage Corporation (Freddie Mac), and government contract workers.

percent of China's economically active population.[26] This is significantly less than the 15 percent and 14 percent figures for the United States and Germany, respectively, and far below France's 24 percent. Compared with countries closer in per capita income, China's 11 percent figure is higher than the 9 percent level in both Thailand and South Africa but slightly below Malaysia's 13 percent and Turkey's 12 percent.[27] Yet no one is charging that the government bureaucracies in Malaysia and Turkey are among the world's most powerful.

Moreover, employment in state-owned enterprises has been falling, and by 2011 was 25 percent less than in 1999 and accounted for only 13 percent of urban employment.

Neither does the Chinese state look so powerful on the second metric, income—that is, fiscal revenues relative to GDP. At the outset of reform, consolidated central and local government revenue accounted for 31 percent of GDP, a relatively high share for China's level of economic development at the time. But as firms were able to retain an increasing share of their profits rather than remitting them to the Ministry of Finance, government revenues relative to GDP shrank. By 1995, fiscal revenues were the equivalent of only 10 percent of GDP, one of the lowest ratios in the world. Various tax reforms, notably the expansion of the scope of the value-added tax starting in 1994, have boosted the ratio of government revenues to GDP. But in 2011 the ratio was only 22 percent (National Bureau of Statistics of China 2013b, 72), compared against the 28 percent average for emerging markets and developing economies. China's government revenue relative to GDP is identical to that of Mexico, 2 percentage points below that of Malaysia, and 5 percentage points below that of South Africa.[28] Thus, there is little evidence in the fiscal data of the overwhelming power of China's bureaucracy.

The case that the Chinese state is one of the world's most powerful in terms of the ownership of the means of production is closer to the mark than the claims with respect to employment and income. But this study has already presented evidence that the state's power in this domain is shrinking. This is reflected in the declining share of industrial output produced by state and collective firms, from 100 percent of output in 1978 to about one-quarter in 2012. State and collective firms controlled all of the country's productive capital in the industrial sector as reform was getting under way, and one can infer from the production data that its share of productive assets has dropped precipitously since. Second, the investment data examined in chapter 3 show that state firms' share of investment in industry has been declining since 1980,

---

26. The economically active population is the sum of employed workers and unemployed workers.

27. International Labor Office (ILO), ILO LABORSTA Database, 2010. Available at http://laborsta.ilo.org (accessed on November 1, 2013).

28. Data for government revenue as a share of GDP for countries other than China and for the average of emerging market and developing economies is from the IMF, World Economic Outlook database, April 2013. Available at www.imf.org (accessed on November 1, 2013).

while that of private firms has been rising. By 2011, private firms' investment was almost three times that of state firms in absolute terms, and the ratio is higher when private foreign firms' share of investment is taken into account. Given this large and increasing disparity, the state's share of total productive assets must be falling as the private sector's share is rising.

Figure 4.6 provides a more precise measure of the share of productive assets owned by state firms in industry, with a further disaggregation into its three components: manufacturing, mining, and utilities. Not surprisingly given trends in the state share of output of manufactured goods, state ownership of assets in manufacturing has declined by more than half, from 60 percent in 1999 (the first year for which these data are available) to only 25 percent by 2012. In mining the decline is much less, only a quarter, and the decline in the state share in utilities, from 91 percent to 88 percent, is negligible. The share of industrial assets the state controls is simply the weighted average of its three components; the decline from 69 percent in 1999 to only 38 percent in 2012 was a little more than two-fifths. All of these data exclude the assets of below-scale firms, which are disproportionately private and so somewhat overstate state companies' share of assets. While the state share of manufacturing assets is declining, the one-quarter remaining in state hands undoubtedly puts China at the top of any global ranking of state ownership of manufacturing assets.[29]

Assessing the regulatory powers of states is more difficult since there is no commonly accepted, widely available metric. The OECD's Product Market Regulation Survey includes a component called "use of command and control regulation," which provides a starting point. China is rated a 3 on a scale of 0 to 5, a rating it shares with South Africa and Chile. Among those countries with greater use of command and control are India and Greece, both with a score of 5, and Brazil, Russia, Belgium, Israel, Turkey, and Indonesia, all with a score of 4. The remaining 29 countries are all judged to have less pervasive government command and control regulation. The limits of the OECD survey are that it was last completed in 2008, the vast majority of countries included in the survey are high-income developed economies, and the questionnaire on which the scores are based is quite limited.[30] But one clear finding is that China exercises less government command and control than the other BRIC group members (Brazil, Russia, and India). Thus the OECD study also fails to support claims of the power supremacy of Chinese bureaucracy.

---

29. Net assets of state-controlled manufacturing firms in China at year-end 2011 were RMB7.3 trillion, or $1.1 trillion. An OECD study reports that the total value of state-owned enterprises in 27 OECD countries that responded to a survey was $1.4 trillion. Of this amount, only 7 percent, or $100 billion, was accounted for by manufacturing firms (Christiansen 2011, 7–8, 15).

30. The survey has only about a dozen very limited questions covering five specific sectors. For example, in the retail sector one question is whether shop opening hours are regulated. For professional services, one question is whether the government regulates the profession's advertising and marketing. Available at www.oecd.org/economy/pmr (accessed on July 17, 2014).

Figure 4.6 State control of net assets by sector, 1999–2012

percent of total net assets

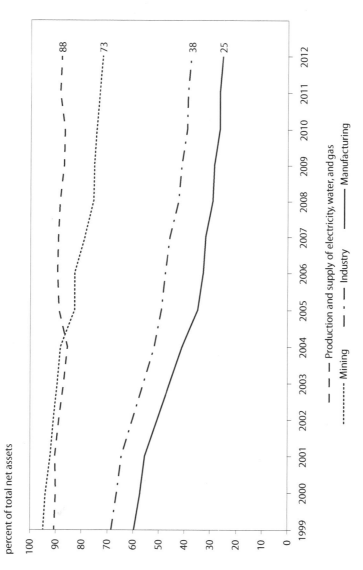

Sources: National Bureau of Statistics of China (2013c, 475–85); National Bureau of Statistics of China, www.stats.gov.cn (accessed on February 28, 2014).

It might be useful to examine not just the pervasiveness but also the effectiveness of regulations, which the OECD survey does not. As a first approximation, it appears that the regulatory power of China's central government in the economic domain is strong primarily when its objectives align well with the interests of provincial and local governments. When this alignment is lacking, Beijing struggles to achieve its regulatory objectives. The difficulties the central government has had in engineering consolidations in the steel and automobile industries and in enforcement of environmental regulations illustrate this point.

The government since 2003 has sought to consolidate steel production in a smaller number of technologically efficient and profitable large enterprises (Naughton 2009). They provided explicit support to three large steel mills—Baogang, Angang, and Wugang—in an attempt to create what some call national champions. Simultaneously, the central government sought to shut down low-tech and small-scale steel mills. The initial government efforts produced little result, so in April 2007 the National Development and Reform Commission negotiated and signed specific compliance contracts with provincial government leaders in the 10 biggest steel-producing provinces calling for the closure of steel mills with 78 million metric tons of steel capacity. This plan, too, failed; local governments actually increased their investment in steel production (Naughton 2009). In 2009 the State Council launched another steel consolidation campaign that sought to increase the share of national steel production of the top five steel producers to 45 percent by 2011.[31]

None of these campaigns achieved its objective. When the first campaign was launched in 2003, China had 4,100 steel companies; 485 of these companies were state owned (National Bureau of Statistics of China 2004, 518, 528). By 2011 the number of steel firms had expanded to 6,742; 312 of these companies were state owned (National Bureau of Statistics of China 2012b, 502, 512). Thus the government had achieved a one-third reduction in the number of state owned firms. But it had no ability to control private firms, the numbers of which expanded from 3,600 in 2003 to more than 6,200 in 2011.[32] Local governments had no interest in blocking the entry of these profitable private firms into the industry since they hired local workers and paid tax revenues, a share of which accrued to the local government. The result, already noted in chapter 1, was that the share of production of the top handful of steel firms actually shrank rather than expanded.[33]

---

31. State Council, "Steel Sector Adjustment and Revitalization Plan," March 20, 2009. Available at www.gov.cn (accessed on November 12, 2013).

32. About two-thirds of these are registered private firms; the balance are limited liability companies or shareholding limited companies in which the majority or dominant owner is private.

33. By 2011 the share of the top five steel producers was only 30 percent, far short of the goal of 45 percent.

The central government's efforts to consolidate the vehicle industry likewise illustrate the weakness of Beijing's regulatory powers. China has long had an exceptionally large number of assembly plants, in part because almost every province has sought to develop its own production capacity. In 1995, for example, China had 122 assembly plants producing only 1.45 million units, meaning the average annual volume per firm was only 12,000 vehicles. Only 15 of these plants produced cars, but given national output of 326,000 cars, output per plant was far below the level that would capture economies of scale. "As a result China had the most fragmented motor vehicle industry in the world."[34] The central government since 1994 has repeatedly sought to consolidate the industry. The goal was to create three or four globally competitive auto producers by 2010.[35] This effort was not entirely successful. While a few assembly plants now do account for a much larger share of auto production than was the case 20 years ago, the majority of these plants are joint ventures between state and foreign firms. There are still many domestic automakers producing relatively high-cost, low-quality vehicles. As a result, the market share of domestic passenger cars peaked at 31 percent in 2010, fell to 27 percent in 2013, and then to less than 23 percent in the first two months of 2014. Moreover, exports of these brands are tiny. "The country that boasts the world's biggest car market, unlike Japan and Korea before it, thus far has failed to produce a national champion of its own that can compete globally."[36] While some argue that China has sought to promote economic growth through industrial policies that are more far reaching than those in post–World War II Japan and Korea, so far these policies have achieved limited success in China's auto industry.

The long-term deterioration of China's environment is also due in part to the weakness of the Chinese state. With a population about five times that of the United States, China's central environmental protection bureaucracy employs only one-sixth of the workers the United States does; spending on environmental protection is woefully inadequate; and there is no central environmental agency or commission that is even "capable of convening the full range of ministries necessary to resolve many complex environmental challenges that cross bureaucratic boundaries" (Economy 2010, 277). The increasing importance the central government attaches to addressing environmental issues was reflected in the upgrading to cabinet level of the previous National Environmental Protection Administration and its renaming as the Ministry of Environmental Protection in 2008. But despite this enhanced status, the ministry lacks jurisdiction over local environmental protection bureaus, which

34. Eric Thun, "Going Local: Foreign Investment, Local Development, and the Chinese Auto Sector," unpublished manuscript, May 2001.

35. State Council, "Notice concerning the promulgation of the 'auto industry policy,'" March 12, 1994. Available at http://chinafindlaw.cn (accessed on February 5, 2014).

36. Tom Mitchell, "Chinese carmakers yet to make their marque," *Financial Times*, February 14, 2014, p. 13; Tom Mitchell, "Chinese branded cars suffer sales fall," *Financial Times*, March 11, 2014, p. 11.

local governments control. These local governments typically prioritize economic growth over environmental protection. As a consequence, levels of funding are frequently so modest that one local bureau official responsible for enforcement of environmental regulations reported that he was unable to carry out required quarterly inspections of every factory in his district since "he lacked regular access to a car and thus could not get himself to the factories to perform the inspections" (Economy 2010, 115).

The examples of the steel and auto industries and environmental protection all suggest that the regulatory power of the state is weak when the objective is to accomplish something positive, like reshaping the ownership structure of an industry or enforcing environmental regulations. But state regulatory power can also be exercised in a negative direction, for example by imposing difficult licensing and other requirements to prevent the formation of new businesses. The Third Plenum document released in November 2013 calls specifically for the deepening of the reform of the "administrative examination and approval system" (行政审批制度), going so far as to call for the elimination of examination and approval in areas where the market can effectively regulate itself.

Premier Li Keqiang launched this policy in May 2013, shortly after taking office. He announced the goal of reducing government interference in the market and called specifically for a one-third reduction within one year in the number of items that required examination and approval by the State Council.[37] By the end of the year the State Council had either eliminated or transferred to lower administrative levels its examination and approval authority over about 300 items. Among those eliminated are the minimum capital requirements of RMB30,000, RMB100,000, and RMB5,000,000 to register a limited liability company, an individual limited liability company, and a shareholding limited corporation, respectively.[38] The latter reform has stimulated a surge of 43 percent in new company registrations in the first quarter of 2014 compared to the first quarter of 2013, when the capital requirements were in effect. Most of the new companies are small and thus presumably private.[39]

These administrative reforms are likely to improve China's rankings in the World Bank's survey of the ease of doing business. In 2013, China ranked 96th out of 189 countries, essentially unchanged from its ranking of 93rd in 2007. In two components of the index, starting a business and ease of getting

---

37. Li Keqiang, "Speech at a videoconference meeting of the State Council on transforming and mobilizing the functions and powers of the bureaucracy," May 14, 2013. Available at www.gov.cn (accessed on January 23, 2014).

38. "Li Keqiang convenes a State Council Standing Committee meeting to dispose and carry out a reform of the company registered capital registration system to lower the cost of starting a business and stimulate social investment activity," October 27, 2013. Available at www.gov.cn (accessed on January 24, 2014).

39. Chen Dun, "Starting out with nothing, reaping rich rewards in the market," *China Daily*, May 20, 2014, p. 17.

construction permits, China ranked near the bottom, at 158th and 185th, respectively.[40] These rankings suggest that new business formation in China is weak.

However, these World Bank rankings seem detached from reality. In 2002 China had 2.6 million registered private businesses with registered capital of RMB2.48 trillion, employing 32.5 million workers. By 2012 these numbers had shot up to 10.9 million, RMB31.1 trillion, and 113 million, respectively.[41] Over the same period the number of household businesses rose from 23.8 million, employing 47.4 million workers, with capital of RMB378 billion, to 40.6 million businesses, employing 86.3 million workers, with capital of RMB1.98 trillion (All-China Federation of Industry and Commerce 2013, 26, 30). In short, Chinese entrepreneurs created 25 million businesses in 10 years, discrediting the World Bank's contention that China is among the most difficult countries in the world to start a new business. Similarly, it is hard to credit the World Bank's assertion that it is very difficult to get a construction permit in a country where new starts (including homes, offices, and commercial buildings) rose from 428 million square meters in 2002 to over 2 billion square meters in 2013 (National Bureau of Statistics of China 2011a, 196; 2014a).

In sum, the evidence does not seem to support the view that the Chinese state exercises extraordinary regulatory power. The OECD survey of product market regulation shows that China makes less use of command and control than Brazil, India, and Russia, which with China make up the BRIC group. The central government is frequently unable to effectively use its regulatory power to reshape industries or enforce environmental regulations when its objectives are not aligned with those of local governments. And while the state has substantial power to regulate a broad range of activities through the formal administrative examination and approval system, this power has not impeded the extraordinarily rapid registration of new private businesses that now produce about two-thirds of China's GDP, up from nothing when reform began.

Debating the Role of the Market

Even as the rise of competitive markets since 1978 has increasingly allowed private firms to displace state firms over broad swaths of manufacturing and

---

40. International Finance Corporation and World Bank, *Doing Business*, available at www.doing-business.org (accessed on January 23, 2014). "Starting a business" measures the number of procedures, time, and cost for a small and medium-size limited liability company to start up and formally operate.

41. The data on the number of private businesses include branches. But based on a count excluding branches—that is, based on the concept of enterprise legal person—the growth of registered private businesses follows a similarly robust trajectory, from 1.3 million in 2001 to 5.9 million in 2012. The numbers in the text for 2002 and 2012 are for registered private businesses. In addition, in 2012 there were about 635,000 limited liability companies and shareholding limited companies where the majority or dominant owner was private (National Bureau of Statistics of China 2013c, 27–29).

to some extent in services, there has been a continuing, active debate in China concerning the degree to which the market should guide China's economic development. In the early years of reform, Chen Yun, who by the mid-1950s was the fifth ranked leader of the Chinese Communist Party and had served as minister of commerce and a member of the State Planning Commission, was a proponent of contracting down to the household and expanding the role of rural markets, price incentives, and private plots to stimulate agricultural production. These policies were similar to those he had advocated in the early 1960s to encourage rural recovery from the agricultural disaster induced by Mao's Great Leap Forward (Lardy and Lieberthal 1983). While he supported the role of the market and liberalized prices in agriculture and light industry, Chen had severe reservations about enhancing the role of market forces in other parts of the economy, particularly the heavy industrial sector. By the early 1980s Chen articulated the view that the market was like a bird that needed to be constrained by a cage, that is, the plan. If the plan was all encompassing, the cage would be too small and the bird would suffocate, an outcome Chen opposed. But if there was no plan, the bird would fly away—in other words, the market would be all powerful, leading potentially to economic imbalances such as excess investment and inflation, which could be avoided if the plan was given primacy over the market. Thus Chen was an advocate for market liberalization, but within a carefully and narrowly defined sphere (Bachman 1985, Vogel 2011).

By the mid-1980s Chen had clearly lost this debate, as the party approved an expansion of the role of the market far beyond the limits he favored and the role of the plan was substantially reduced, as analyzed in chapter 1. But the debate on the role of the market resurfaced in the mid-2000s, when some Chinese economists criticized what they regarded as China's excessively market-oriented economic reforms. The most prominent of these critics was Liu Guoguang, director of the Institute of Economics in the Chinese Academy of Social Sciences in the early 1980s, who wrote extensively on the relationship between plan and market and later served as president of the Academy. In 2006, long after he had retired, he wrote that the excessive reliance on the market was contributing to rapidly increasing income inequality and that the Chinese Communist Party would lose power if it did not rein in market reforms.[42]

In the wake of the global financial crisis, internal critics of the market-centric model gained new strength (Freeman and Yuan 2011). Previously, it had been difficult for these critics, sometimes identified as the new leftists, to gain much traction against the widespread view that China should emulate the American market-oriented economic model, particularly its increasingly deregulated financial system. But the clear US origins of the global crisis provided new ammunition for Chinese critics to challenge the presumed superiority of the US market-based, deregulated financial system. Many of them argued that

---

42. Richard McGregor, "Challenging change: why an ever fiercer battle hinders China's march to the market," *Financial Times*, February 28, 2006, p. 11.

China should preserve a large role for state-owned enterprises, in part because their profits could be redistributed to alleviate growing income inequality (Kelly, Rasmussen, and Ek 2012, 24). Even some mainstream Chinese economists argue publicly that large state-owned enterprises should continue to play a leading role in China's future economic growth (Hu Angang 2012).

At the other end of the economic spectrum, more reform-oriented economists in China have used the phrase "the state advances while the private (sector) retreats" (国进民退) to criticize what they see as the resurgence of the state in response to the global financial crisis and the waning of the market-oriented reform impetus of earlier years. This group believes China's continued growth is threatened by the large claim that inefficient state enterprises have on resources (Kroeber 2012, 17). These economists championed the market-oriented economic reform agenda that was adopted by the party in November 2013.

While the debate in China over the appropriate role of the market is likely to continue, I anticipate that it will influence only the pace of reform, not its direction. In the coming decade, the role of the market is likely to further expand, in line with the vision laid out in the Third Plenum decision, for several reasons.

First, the rationales that were once and sometimes are still advanced in China to support a large and continuing role for state-owned enterprises are substantially less compelling than they were a decade or two ago. At one time it was argued that state-owned enterprises were essential to absorbing new entrants into the labor force, providing housing and a broad range of social services to their employees, and thus maintaining social stability. Similarly, it was argued that state-owned firms made disproportionate contributions to government fiscal revenue and that any reform that led to a smaller role for state-owned firms could significantly erode the government's fiscal position. Finally, some have argued that state-owned firms are an important source of innovation that will drive China up the technology ladder to higher and higher levels of per capita income. None of these arguments is very compelling.

As pointed out in chapter 3, employment in state and collective firms, which in 1978 accounted for all urban employment, today accounts for less than a fifth.[43] The absolute number of workers in state firms has been falling for years and by 2011 was not much more than estimates of the number of workers who lost their jobs in the downsizing of the state sector in the second half of the 1990s. In addition, the growth of China's labor force has slowed dramatically. In 1995–2010 the labor force grew at almost 1 percent per year. This pace is slowing to 0.3 percent in 2011–15, and over the next five years the labor force will actually shrink by 0.2 percent per year (World Bank 2012,

---

43. This figure includes firms in services and industry and incorporates both traditional state-owned firms and corporatized firms in which the state is the sole, majority, or dominant shareholder, plus employment in collective firms, which may be partially controlled or owned by local governments.

9). So the challenge of labor force absorption is commensurately less. Taking both these factors into account, the case for retaining a large role for state firms to provide employment and thus contribute to the maintenance of social stability is extremely weak.

State companies once did provide both highly subsidized housing to more than 90 percent of their employees (including retirees), comprising half of all urban residents, and an array of free social services. For example, in the mid-1990s state-owned enterprises operated more than 18,000 schools with an enrollment of 6.1 million students, requiring 600,000 teachers and staff. Hospitals built, run, and paid for by state firms accounted for one-third of all hospital beds in China (Lardy 1998, 51). The cost of providing these services amounted to about 40 percent of the wage bill of a typical state firm (Broadman 1995, 9). The traditional dual role of state-owned firms as production units and providers of housing and social services was once an argument for maintaining a large role for state-owned firms.

But when the government began its campaign to downsize state-owned companies in the second half of the 1990s, it also launched programs that accelerated the sale of enterprise housing units to their employees and curtailed firm-provided social services. The sale of public housing on an experimental basis began as early as 1982 and picked up speed in 1988, when the National Housing Reform Plan was adopted. The principal goal was to encourage private ownership of housing (Zhang 2001, 69–70). Privatization accelerated significantly after mid-1998, when the state announced "the termination of the administratively planned housing distribution system," which led state enterprises to sell off virtually all of their housing units to their employees, typically at relatively low prices (Ye, Song, and Tian 2010, 274). Through these reforms, housing has largely become a commodity allocated through the market.

The contribution of state firms to state fiscal resources has also eroded substantially. As already noted, state firms' remission of profits to the Ministry of Finance was a key source of fiscal revenue at the outset of and in the early years of reform but diminished rapidly in the 1980s and was completely eliminated after 1993. Since then, the growth of fiscal revenue relative to GDP, as private businesses became increasingly important, shows that the Chinese government is perfectly capable of taxing private firms. It does so largely through the value-added tax and the corporate income tax, which are paid by all enterprises, regardless of ownership.

Finally, there is scant evidence that state firms are an important source of innovation in China. Indeed, the opposite may be the case. An analysis of listed Chinese state-owned companies shows that average research and development expenditures relative to sales revenue was well under 2 percent and falling in 2009–12, while 10 leading private companies had much higher and rising research and development expenditures, reaching 4.5 percent of sales revenue by 2012 (Ma, Shi, and Lan 2013, 30). The best macro evidence on the relative innovation performance of state firms was reviewed in chapter 3. A number of studies summarized there showed that state firms have lagged in the growth of total factor productivity throughout the reform era. If state firms have an advantage in innovation, it should be reflected in higher growth of productivity than firms with other forms of ownership. It is not.

State firms are almost entirely absent from some of the most dynamic segments of the Chinese economy. Internet businesses, such as ecommerce, are perhaps the best example. China's e-tail revolution is being driven entirely by private firms, notably Taobao (Alibaba's online auction house), Tmall (Alibaba's online mall), and Tencent's Paipai. These three firms account for an enormous share of China's e-tailing market, which has been growing by more than 100 percent annually since 2003 and now accounts for a larger share of retail market transactions than e-tailing does in the United States (Dobbs et al. 2013, 1, 3).

These private internet firms also are exploiting the internet to make inroads into businesses traditionally dominated by state-owned companies. The increasing range of financial services offered by leading internet companies such as Alibaba poses an increasing competitive challenge to China's state-owned banks. Another example is Weixin (WeChat in English), an online chat platform introduced by Tencent at the beginning of 2011. It attracted more than 300 million users within two years of its introduction, crowding out a considerable portion of the traditional mobile phone text-message business offered by China's three state-owned telecom companies (Ma, Shi, and Lan 2013, 25).

A second reason to anticipate that the role of the market will continue to expand is the growing recognition by the party that the role of state must evolve in order to respond to increasingly urgent popular demands for cleaner air and water, safer food supplies, a stronger social safety net, and more inclusive economic growth. To meet these rising demands and new objectives, the state will need to cede a greater role for the market in resource allocation and to concentrate its own limited resources on providing the public goods and services that the market cannot supply.

Premier Li has expressed the critical need for this evolution in State Council documents, and it is one of the most important points endorsed by the Central Committee at its Third Plenum in the fall of 2013.[44] The plenum decision called for a "reduction of the direct role of the government in the allocation of resources" and the promotion of resource allocation "based on market principles, market prices, and market competition. The duties and functions of the government are mainly to maintain macroeconomic stability, strengthen and improve the provision of public services, guarantee fair competition, strengthen market supervision and management, safeguard market order, and

---

44. "Premier Li Keqiang convenes a State Council Standing Committee meeting on research to promote strengthening government provision of public goods and on plans to strengthen urban infrastructure construction," July 31, 2013. Available at www.gov.cn (accessed on February 14, 2014). State Council, "Guiding opinion concerning strengthening the government's provision of services to society," September 30, 2013. Available at www.gov.cn (accessed on February 14, 2014).

promote sustainable development."[45] So the state will continue to play a major role in the development of China's infrastructure and "will maintain control and operation of natural monopolies," presumably meaning public utilities such as supply of water and electricity and certain forms of transportation such as rail.[46] But it will eliminate its monopoly of other sectors and shift its attention increasingly to improving the environment, providing stronger and better-enforced regulations to improve food safety, and providing more subsidized housing and higher-quality health care and education, especially to underserved rural residents and migrants in urban areas. This shift can help to ensure more inclusive economic growth, another major party objective.

A third reason to anticipate that the role of the market will continue to expand is an increasingly broad consensus in China that the growth model of the past decade is dysfunctional and that continuing on the path of investment-driven growth entails unacceptably high risks for the Chinese Communist Party. China's bank-financed stimulus program, which started in the fourth quarter of 2008, has resulted in a large increase in the ratio of private credit to GDP. Including off–balance sheet credit and credit extended by nonbanks, this ratio has jumped by over 60 percentage points, from a little over 120 percent in 2008 to almost 200 percent by the end of 2013. Jon Anderson (2013a, 15) notes this increase is "one that is not only huge by Chinese historical standards but also places China near the top of the emerging market league tables in terms of the five-year increase in credit penetration." A number of analysts have pointed out that this increase is of a magnitude that has been observed in other countries before they have encountered financial crises, typically triggered by a sudden stop in credit growth or the collapse of an asset bubble.

There are several reasons to believe that the probability of such a crisis in China is low. First, all of the credit is domestic in origin, meaning China is not vulnerable to a sudden stop in foreign funding, as occurred in several countries at the time of the 1997 Asian financial crisis. Second, China's bank credit boom is largely financed by deposits rather than through the wholesale interbank market, which is more vulnerable to sudden stops. Most notably, China's systemically important financial institutions finance their loans entirely from deposits. These deposits are very "sticky" in all financial systems, but especially so in China, where the range of alternative financial assets available to households is quite limited. Third, there is almost no securitization of bank assets, a practice that contributed significantly to the financial crisis in the United States. Fourth, China has a national saving rate of around 50 percent, far and away the highest in the world, which makes financing a large credit buildup more feasible. Finally, it should be noted that, due to its very strong external position, China is not vulnerable to the capital outflows that have in a number

---

45. Chinese Communist Party Central Committee, "Decision on Major Issues Concerning Comprehensively Deepening Reforms," November 15, 2013. Available at www.gov.cn (accessed on December 17, 2013).

46. Ibid., section 2.

of emerging market economies accompanied the so-called tapering in the pace of asset purchases by the US Federal Reserve. Several of these economies have been forced to raise interest rates in an attempt to reduce these outflows but are likely to suffer slower growth as a result.

While China's current high ratio of credit to GDP may not lead to a financial crisis, there is little doubt that the pace of credit expansion must soon begin to moderate to one that is less than the growth of nominal GDP so that the ratio of credit to GDP first plateaus and then falls. This deleveraging process will be painful for firms that have become more highly leveraged in recent years, particularly for those that are generating a return on assets that is less than their cost of capital. As noted in chapter 3, this is particularly a problem for state firms. Moreover, it is likely to be a more severe problem than might be anticipated simply by comparing the average return on assets of these firms with the cost of capital. The average returns of state firms as a group are pulled up by the outsized profits of a few state-owned companies such as China Mobile, CNOOC, and the China National Tobacco Corporation, so the median return of state firms is likely lower than the average. Consequently, many state firms will find deleveraging a painful process.

Moderation in credit growth, other things being equal, is likely to lead to slower growth. But if the party is successful in changing China's growth model, other things will not remain the same, and the impacts of a slowdown in growth can be at least partially ameliorated. As the reforms endorsed by the party at the Third Plenum are implemented, two results can be expected. First, more credit should flow to the private sector, where returns are much higher than for state firms. There is room for some expansion of the private sector even in manufacturing, where the most progress has been made. There are still tens of thousands of state manufacturing firms at the provincial and local levels that have returns less than the cost of capital. Unless increased competitive pressure leads to increased productivity, these firms should shrink or exit as the cost of capital rises. But, as noted above, the more substantial opportunities for the expansion of the private sector are in large swaths of the service sector, where competition has been much more limited and productivity of state firms particularly low. As reforms lead to a larger share of investment flowing to more productive private enterprises, particularly in services, the slowdown in growth will be proportionately less than the reduction in the share of investment in GDP.

Second, the reforms are likely to increase the pace of growth of private consumption relative to GDP growth. More rapid growth of the service sector, which is more labor intensive, will lead to more rapid growth of employment and wages, thus increasing the wage share of GDP. And higher real interest rates on household deposits will lead to an increase in household disposable income. These trends should be positive for consumption growth, thus partially offsetting the slowdown associated with a lower share of resources flowing to investment.

This process will take the better part of a decade, will involve significant transition costs, and will be opposed by the interest groups that have benefited disproportionately from the imbalanced growth of the past. But a party that has staked its legitimacy on delivering sustained growth of incomes and rising living standards for China's population is likely to act on the reform blueprint it adopted in the fall of 2013.

Appendices

Appendix A

Alternative Measures of Private Sector Credit

Measuring the flow of credit to the private sector in China is a challenge. Data for the early years of the reform period are limited, and even since more data have become available, interpreting them requires a detailed understanding of the central bank's loan classification and accounting system. The People's Bank of China did not regularly publish any data on credit to the private sector until 1987, when the *Almanac of China's Finance and Banking* included a data series that went back to 1980. But this series aggregated lending to individual businesses and lending to urban collective enterprises (China Banking Society 1987, II-24–II-25).[1] As discussed in the text, collective firms, particularly in the early years of reform, usually were closely linked with local governments. For this reason collective firms are not treated as part of the private sector in this book, and these early data are not reported in this appendix.[2] The publication of separate data on loans to individual businesses began in 1988 in the *Almanac of China's Banking and Finance* (China Banking Society 1988, 58–59). When registered private businesses were allowed, the scope of the series, shown in table A.1, was expanded to include data on loans to private enterprises as well as to individual businesses (私营及个体短期贷款). This three-decade-long

---

1. The almanac, while technically compiled by the China Banking Society, is widely regarded as an official publication of the People's Bank of China. For example, in the 2013 edition, Jin Zhongxia, the director of the bank's Financial Research Institute, is identified as the chairman of the Compilation Committee for the almanac.

2. Loans outstanding to urban collectives and individual businesses at year-end 1980 were RMB7,829 million (China Banking Society 1987, II-24–II-25); thus loans to individual businesses accounted for only 0.3 percent of these loans.

Table A.1   Short-term loans to private and individual businesses, 1980–2009

Year	Millions of renminbi	Percent of total loans
1980	23	0.01
1981	47	0.02
1982	55	0.02
1983	150	0.04
1984	1,056	0.22
1985	1,065	0.17
1986	1,064	0.13
1987	1,547	0.16
1988	1,930	0.16
1989	3,280	0.23
1990	4,020	0.23
1991	4,920	0.23
1992	6,760	0.26
1993	10,860	0.33
1994	15,590	0.38
1995	19,620	0.39
1996	27,980	0.46
1997	38,660	0.52
1998	47,160	0.55
1999	57,908	0.62
2000	65,460	0.66
2001	91,804	0.82
2002	105,877	0.81
2003	146,159	0.92
2004	208,149	1.17
2005	218,075	1.12
2006	266,757	1.18
2007	350,766	1.34
2008	422,382	1.39
2009	712,101	1.78

Sources: China Banking Society (1988, 58–59; 1990, 152–53; 1996, 429; 2006, 389; 2008, 402); ISI Emerging Markets, CEIC Database.

series, discontinued in 2009, remains the longest running series on credit to the private sector. The series shows short-term loans outstanding at year end to private enterprises and individual businesses. These loans grew from only 0.01 percent of total loans outstanding in 1980 to 1.78 percent by 2009, or RMB712 billion in loans outstanding.

These data understate the amount of credit flowing to the private sector for two reasons. First, the series includes only short-term loans. Second, the series only accounts for loans to registered private enterprises and individual household businesses. There is a significant subset of firms that are majority owned by private individuals but not registered as private enterprises.[3]

Data on lending to private firms and individual businesses inclusive of medium- and long-term loans (second set of columns of table 3.9) comes from the All-China Federation of Industry and Commerce in its annual report on the nonstate economy. This data series is identified as "lending to narrow nonstate enterprises" (侠义内资民营贷款) and goes back to 2002.[4] Incorporating both short- and long-term loans, the series shows that other studies' exclusive focus on short-term loans to private enterprises consistently understates the flow of credit to the private sector. For some years in which data on both metrics are available, the short-term series understates the flow of credit to the private sector by a factor of about ten.

The third set of columns in table 3.9 shows lending to household businesses (住户经营性贷款). Beginning in 2004, the People's Bank of China released quarterly data on household business borrowing as part of a series on the sources and uses of credit funds of financial institutions by sector (金融机构本外币信贷收支表 (部门)). The series consists primarily of lending to agricultural households and individual businesses. Total household business borrowing as a share of total loans doubled over the past decade, reaching nearly 10 percent of total loans, or RMB6.9 trillion, at the end of 2013. The key differences between this series and the second series are that this lending includes agricultural households and excludes lending to most registered private businesses.

It is tempting to combine the series on lending to household businesses and the series on lending to private enterprises and individual businesses to gain a broader picture of lending to the private sector. But data on lending to household businesses also include lending to a small subset of private enterprises known as noncorporatized private enterprises (非公司私营企业).[5] Thus the two series are partially overlapping, and adding them would involve some degree of double counting. One result is that it is difficult to disaggregate private enterprise loans. Even if this were not the case, both series still understate the size of bank lending to the private sector by only including lending to registered private firms, thus ignoring lending to limited liability companies where the majority or dominant owner is private.

---

3. In 2012 there were 5,917,718 registered private enterprise legal persons. In the same year there were 6,552,049 enterprise legal persons majority owned by private individuals (National Bureau of Statistics of China 2013c, 27–29). This implies that there are 634,331 limited liability companies and shareholding limited companies where the majority or dominant owner is private.

4. These are loans to private enterprises and individual businesses (私营个体).

5. Noncorporatized private enterprises tend to be smaller enterprises; many incorporated prior to the time the Company Law took effect in 1994. Noncorporatized private enterprises include private enterprises registered under the Provisional Regulations of the People's Republic of China on Private Enterprises (1988), the Law on Wholly Individually Owned Enterprises (2000), or the Law on Partnership Enterprises (1997, revised 2006).

Fortunately, the People's Bank of China in 2011 began releasing data on enterprise lending based on the concept of control (see box 2.1), and these data are the source for figures 3.6 and 3.7. Loans outstanding to registered private enterprises and to limited liability companies and shareholding limited companies where the majority or dominant owner is private (私人控股企业) for 2009–12 are shown in table A.2. In 2012 these loans reached RMB14.2 trillion, 30 percent higher than lending to private enterprises and individual businesses based on registration status (table 3.9). Thus loans outstanding at the end of 2012 to limited liability companies and shareholding limited companies where the majority or dominant owner is private can be derived as RMB3.2 trillion, just over one-fifth of loans outstanding to the broader universe of private enterprises.[6]

Even the series on enterprise loans based on control does not give a full account of lending to the private sector. First, the various series examined so far do not fully capture loans to households. Business loans to households were shown in the third set of columns in table 3.9, which includes lending to agricultural households. But even more important are consumption loans to households (住户消费性贷款), shown in table A.3. Data on consumption loans to households were first reported in 1997 alongside household business loans in the sources and uses of credit funds of financial institutions by sector (金融机构本外币信贷收支表　(部门)). Consumption loans include lending to individuals primarily for travel, school tuition, home mortgages, and automotive financing. Consumption loans to households have risen from only 0.2 percent of all bank loans outstanding in 1997 to 18 percent by the end of 2013.

Loans to individuals to purchase residential property (个人住房贷款) have consistently accounted for about three-fourths of all consumption to households. The People's Bank of China reports loans to individuals to purchase residential property in its quarterly monetary policy report. This type of mortgage loan has grown from less than 0.2 percent of total loans outstanding in 1997 to 12.5 percent by the end of 2013. Looking at the data on mortgage loans is especially important to understanding the direction of bank credit during the stimulus. Loans to individuals to purchase residential property doubled between the beginning of 2008 and the end of 2010 and were responsible for 15 percent of all new bank loans over the period. These data highlight the fact that households were in fact one of the major beneficiaries of the stimulus-induced bank credit boom.

Combining enterprise loans to private-controlled enterprises, consumption loans to households, and business loans to rural households gives a much

---

6. This confirms that privately controlled limited liability companies and shareholding limited companies, on average, are larger than registered private companies. These firms account for about 10 percent of all privately controlled companies but account for over a fifth of all bank lending to privately controlled companies.

Table A.2   Loans outstanding to private-controlled enterprises, 2009–12

Year	Total enterprise loans (billions of renminbi)	Loans to private-controlled enterprises (billions of renminbi)	Loans to private-controlled enterprises (percent of total)
2009	25,006	6,587	26
2010	30,292	9,116	30
2011	35,017	11,731	34
2012	39,283	14,216	36

Sources: China Banking Society (2011, 322; 2012, 369; 2013, 367–68).

Table A.3   Consumption loans to households, 1997–2013
(billions of renminbi)

Year	Total loans	Consumption loans	Of which: housing mortgage loans to individuals
1997	7,491	17	13
1998	8,652	46	43
1999	9,373	140	136
2000	9,937	427	338
2001	11,231	699	560
2002	13,129	1,068	827
2003	15,900	1,574	1,180
2004	17,736	1,988	1,600
2005	19,469	2,194	1,840
2006	22,529	2,405	1,982
2007	26,169	3,273	2,697
2008	30,339	3,721	2,980
2009	39,968	5,533	4,330
2010	47,920	7,506	5,624
2011	54,795	8,872	6,456
2012	62,991	10,436	7,500
2013	71,896	12,972	9,000

Sources: People's Bank of China, www.pbc.gov.cn (accessed on February 11, 2014); ISI Emerging Markets, CEIC Database.

broader picture of the flow of bank credit to the private sector, shown in table A.4. Bank credit to the private sector was RMB27.6 trillion in 2012, representing 44 percent of total outstanding loans from China's banking system, up from 35 percent in 2009.

Table A.4 Total bank loans outstanding to the private sector, 2009–12 (billions of renminbi)

Year	Total loans to private economy	Loans to private-controlled enterprises	Household consumption loans	Business loans to rural households
2009	13,857	6,587	5,533	1,737
2010	18,816	9,116	7,506	2,194
2011	23,188	11,731	8,872	2,585
2012	27,614	14,216	10,436	2,962

Sources: People's Bank of China, www.pbc.gov.cn (accessed on May 29, 2014); China Banking Society (2011, 322; 2012, 369; 2013, 367–68); Wind Information Database.

Appendix B

State versus Private Borrowing Costs

The *Economist* in its special issue on state capitalism writes, "State-owned companies in China pay interest of only 1.6 percent when they borrow from state banks, but private ones are charged 4.7 percent—if they can get a loan at all."[1] These numbers are not specifically attributed but appear to have been taken from a study of Unirule Institute of Economics, a Beijing research organization. Unirule reports that on average from 2000 through 2007 state-owned firms paid 1.6 percent per annum on bank loans while the rate of interest paid by firms with other types of ownership—everything from collectives to private and foreign firms—was the market rate of 4.68 percent.[2] Unirule, in turn, cites a study by Liu Xiaoxuan and Zhou Xiaoyan (2011).[3] For several reasons, it appears that the Liu and Zhou study is flawed and cannot be relied on to assess the interest rates that state and private firms pay on bank loans.

First, 1.6 percent is an implausibly low number for an average lending rate in the 2000–2007 timeframe. During this period, China's central bank set benchmark interest rates for loans of various maturities and imposed strict limits on the degree to which bank lending rates could diverge from these

---

1. "The Rise of State Capitalism: The Emerging World's New Model," *Economist*, January 21, 2012, p. 15.

2. Unirule Institute of Economics, "The Nature, Performance, and Reform of the State-Owned Enterprises," (April 12, 2011), p. 46. Available at www.unirule.org (accessed on January 3, 2014).

3. Liu and Zhou do not give the 4.68 percent market rate used by Unirule in its analysis. Rather, they give specific rates across all different ownership categories. Unirule takes the Liu and Zhou 1.6 percent interest rate for state firms (including state-controlled shareholding firms) and then takes the weighted average of the Liu and Zhou lending rates to all other types of firms and labels that the market rate.

benchmarks. For the years in question, the lower bound on the interest rate banks could charge on a loan of any maturity was 0.9 times the benchmark interest rate for that maturity.[4] The weighted average benchmark lending rate on loans with maturities over six months and up to and including one year during 2000–2007 was 5.7 percent.[5] Taking into account the maximum discount from the benchmark, the lowest possible average lending rate on a one-year loan was 5.1 percent. One-year loans are the most common loans made by Chinese banks. Given the structure of benchmark interest rates for loans of other maturities, 5.1 percent can be regarded as the lower bound on the average interest rate charged on bank loans during this period.[6] Perhaps banks occasionally violated the rules and lent at rates below 5.1 percent, but the average lending rate to state-owned firms over this period could not possibly have been 1.6 percent, an amount equal to only one-third of the lower bound of 5.1 percent calculated above.

Second, Liu and Zhou's interest rate numbers are not based on borrowing rates reported by firms or lending rates reported by banks. Rather, they are calculated based on financial information in the National Bureau of Statistics of China's annual Industrial Survey Firm-Level Database. The authors calculate the effective interest rate paid by firms by dividing a measure of interest paid by a measure of firm liabilities. There appear to be two flaws in this calculation. The first flaw is the denominator should include only interest-bearing liabilities. Instead, Liu and Zhou have used total liabilities. But firms in all economies have significant noninterest-bearing liabilities such as payables and accrued taxes. China is not an exception. While the Industrial Survey Firm-Level Database does not provide information on the share of firm liabilities that are noninterest bearing, this number can be calculated for the roughly 2,000 A share listed companies. In 2012, interest-free liabilities of these firms accounted for a little over half of all liabilities for firms of all ownership types.[7] Thus if the liability structure of A share listed companies is representative of

---

4. Prior to 1999 the benchmark rate was the lower bound for all loans. Beginning in 1999 banks could make loans to large enterprises as low as 0.9 times the benchmark, and beginning in 2004 banks could make loans to all enterprises as low as 0.9 times the benchmark.

5. The central bank adjusted the benchmark rate several times over the eight-year period. The weights are the length of time each specific rate was in effect.

6. The interest rate benchmarks on loans with maturities over one year and up to and including three years, over three years and up to and including five years, and over five years are about 20, 30, and 50 basis points higher, respectively, than the benchmark rate cited in the text. The benchmark interest rate on loans with maturities of six months or less is about 25 basis points lower than the benchmark interest rate on loans over six months up to and including one year. Given the modest differential in the benchmark rates across the maturity spectrum, it is extremely unlikely that the weighted average benchmark lending rate on loans could be significantly less than 5.7; more likely it would be slightly higher.

7. Calculated from data in Wind Information Systems, Economic Database. Available by subscription only at www.wind.com.cn (accessed on July 17, 2014).

the larger universe of Chinese firms, the interest rates calculated by Liu and Zhou appear to be understated by a little more than 100 percent.

The second flaw is that the numerator in the interest rate calculation should be interest expense (利息支出). Instead, the authors use financing costs (财务费用). Financing costs are the sum of interest paid less interest received, plus exchange rate losses, plus handling fees paid to financial institutions. For reasons that are not clear, finance costs for private firms in 2006, for example, were one-quarter greater than interest expense, while for state firms the two numbers were almost the same (National Bureau of Statistics of China 2007, 147). Thus the use of financing costs rather than interest expense possibly leads Liu and Zhou to overestimate by one-quarter the interest rate that private firms pay on their bank loans.

In short, Liu and Zhou's methodology has several flaws. First, it results in an interest rate on loans to state companies that implies a massive violation of central bank rules, something that has never been suggested in the financial press in China. Second, the use of total liabilities rather than interest-bearing liabilities results in a significant understatement of the average interest rate that firms of all ownership types pay on bank loans. Third, the use of financing costs rather than interest expense appears to bias upward the calculated interest rate paid by private firms relative to state firms.

References

Ahuja, Ashvin. 2013. De-Monopolization toward Long-Term Prosperity in China. In *China's Economy in Transition: From External to Internal Rebalancing*, edited by Anoop Singh, Malhar Nabar, and Papa N'Diaye. Washington: International Monetary Fund.

All-China Federation of Industry and Commerce. 2011. *Report on Non-state-owned Economy in China, No. 8 (2010–2011)*. Beijing: Social Sciences Academic Press (China).

All-China Federation of Industry and Commerce. 2012. *Report on Non-state-owned Economy in China, No. 9 (2011–2012)*. Beijing: Social Sciences Academic Press (China).

All-China Federation of Industry and Commerce. 2013. *Report on Non-state-owned Economy in China, No. 10 (2012–2013)*. Beijing: Social Sciences Academic Press (China).

All-China Federation of Industry and Commerce and China Nonstate (Private) Economy Research Association. 2011. *China Private Economy Yearbook (2008.6–2010.6)*. Beijing: All-China Federation of Industry and Commerce Publishing House.

All-China Federation of Industry and Commerce and China Nonstate (Private) Economy Research Association. 2013. *China Private Economy Yearbook (2010.6–2012.6)*. Beijing: All-China Federation of Industry and Commerce Publishing House.

Anderson, Jon. 2012. How to Think About China: Part 2—State, Market . . . or What? Emerging Advisors Group (October 16). Available by subscription only at www.emadvisorsgroup.com (accessed on July 17, 2014).

Anderson, Jon. 2013a. Hard Thinking on China's Traps, Reforms and the Plenum. Emerging Advisors Group (November 4). Available by subscription only at www.emadvisorsgroup.com (accessed on July 17, 2014).

Anderson, Jon. 2013b. State Enterprises Are Awesome. Emerging Advisors Group (November 6). Available by subscription only at www.emadvisorsgroup.com (accessed on July 17, 2014).

Bachman, David M. 1985. *Chen Yun and the Chinese Political System*. University of California Institute of East Asian Studies, China Research Monograph no. 29. Berkeley: Institute of East Asian Studies.

Batson, Andrew. 2014. How to Fix China's State Sector. *Ideas* (March 3). Gavekal Dragonomics. Available by subscription only at research.gavekal.com (accessed on July 17, 2014).

Beijing Normal University. 2003. Report on the Development of China's Market Economy 2003. Available at www.china.org.cn/english/2003chinamarket/79497.htm (accessed on May 31, 2013).

Brandt, Loren, Chang-tai Hsieh, and Xiaodong Zhu. 2008. Growth and Structural Change in China. In *China's Great Economic Transformation,* edited by Loren Brandt and Thomas G. Rawski. Cambridge: Cambridge University Press.

Brandt, Loren, Thomas G. Rawski, and John Sutton. 2008. China's Industrial Development. In *China's Great Economic Transformation,* edited by Loren Brandt and Thomas G. Rawski. Cambridge: Cambridge University Press.

Bremmer, Ian. 2010. *The End of the Free Market: Who Wins the War Between States and Corporations?* New York: Penguin.

Broadman, Harry. 1995. *Meeting the Challenge of Chinese Enterprise Reform.* World Bank Discussion Paper No. 283 (April). Washington: World Bank.

Cai Fang and Kam Wing Chan. 2009. The Global Economic Crisis and Unemployment in China. *Eurasian Geography and Economics* 50, no. 5 (September–October): 513–31.

Cai Fang, Albert Park, and Yaohui Zhao. 2008. The Chinese Labor Market in the Reform Era. In *China's Great Economic Transformation,* ed. Loren Brandt and Thomas G. Rawski. Cambridge, UK: Cambridge University Press.

China Banking Regulatory Commission. 2013. *2012 Annual Report.* Available at www.cbrc.gov.cn (accessed on September 17, 2013).

China Banking Society. 1987. *Almanac of China's Finance and Banking 1986.* Beijing: China Financial Publishing House.

China Banking Society. 1988. *Almanac of China's Finance and Banking 1988.* Beijing: China Financial Publishing House.

China Banking Society. 1990. *Almanac of China's Finance and Banking 1990.* Beijing: China Financial Publishing House.

China Banking Society. 1995. *Almanac of China's Finance and Banking 1995.* Beijing: China Financial Publishing House.

China Banking Society. 1996. *Almanac of China's Finance and Banking 1996.* Beijing: China Financial Publishing House.

China Banking Society. 2006. *Almanac of China's Finance and Banking 2006.* Beijing: China Financial Publishing House.

China Banking Society. 2008. *Almanac of China's Finance and Banking 2008.* Beijing: China Financial Publishing House.

China Banking Society. 2011. *Almanac of China's Finance and Banking 2011.* Beijing: China Financial Publishing House.

China Banking Society. 2012. *Almanac of China's Finance and Banking 2012.* Beijing: China Financial Publishing House.

China Banking Society. 2013. *Almanac of China's Finance and Banking 2013.* Beijing: China Financial Publishing House.

China's State-Owned Assets Supervision and Administration Commission. 2011. *China's State-Owned Assets Supervision and Administration Yearbook 2011.* Beijing: China Economics Publishing House.

Christiansen, Hans. 2011. *The Size and Composition of the SOE Sector in OECD Countries.* OECD Corporate Governance Working Papers no. 5. Paris: Organization for Economic Cooperation and Development. Available at www.oecd-ilibarary.org (accessed on July 17, 2014).

Conway, Paul, Richard Herd, Thomas Chalaux, Ping He, and Jianxun Yu. 2010. *Product Market Regulation and Competition in China*. OECD Economics Department Working Papers no. 823 (December). Paris: Organization for Economic Cooperation and Development. Available at www.oecd-ilibrary.org (accessed on July 17, 2014).

Cui Ernan. 2013. Internet Firms Burst into Banking (December 11). Gavekal Dragonomics. Available by subscription only at research.gavekal.com (accessed on July 17, 2014).

Dickson, Bruce J. 2008. *Wealth into Power: The Communist Party's Embrace of the Private Sector*. Cambridge, UK: Cambridge University Press.

Dobbs, Richard, Yougang Chen, Gordon Orr, James Manyika, Michael Chui, and Elsie Chang. 2013. China's e-tail revolution: Online shopping as a catalyst for growth (March). McKinsey Global Institute. Available at www.mckinsey.com (accessed on July 17, 2014).

Dollar, David, and Shang-Jin Wei. 2007. *Das (Wasted) Kapital: Firm Ownership and Investment Efficiency in China*. IMF Working Paper 07/9 (January). Available at www.imf.org (accessed on January 25, 2007).

Dougherty, Sean, Richard Herd, and Ping He. 2007. Has a private sector emerged in China's industry? Evidence from a quarter of a million Chinese firms. *China Economic Review* 18, no. 3: 309–34.

Economy, Elizabeth. 2010. *The River Runs Black: The Environmental Challenge to China's Future*. Second edition. Ithaca, NY: Cornell University Press.

Fan Gang and Nicholas Hope. 2013. The Role of State-Owned Enterprises in the Chinese Economy. In *US-China Economic Relations in the Next Ten Years: Toward Deeper Engagement and Mutual Benefit*. Hong Kong: China-US Exchange Foundation. Available at www.Chinausfocus.com (accessed on May 23, 2013).

Fernald, John, Israel Malkin, and Mark Spiegel. 2013. *On the Reliability of Chinese Output Figures*. FRBSF Economic Letter March 25. Federal Reserve Bank of San Francisco. Available at www.frbsf.org (accessed on April 14, 2014).

Feyzioğlu, Tarhan, Nathan Porter, and Elöd Takáts. 2009. *Interest Rate Liberalization in China*. IMF Working Paper 09/171 (August). Washington: International Monetary Fund. Available at www.imf.org (accessed on October 15, 2013).

Freeman, Charles W. III, and Wen Jin Yuan. 2011. *China's New Leftists and the China Model Debate after the Financial Crisis*. Report of the CSIS Freeman Chair in China Studies (July). Washington: Center for Strategic and International Studies.

Garnaut, Ross, Ligang Song, Stoyan Tenev, and Yang Yao. 2005. *China's Ownership Transformation: Process, Outcomes, Prospects*. Washington: International Finance Corporation.

Goldstein, Morris, and Nicholas R. Lardy. 2009. *The Future of China's Exchange Rate Policy*. Washington: Peterson Institute for International Economics.

Haggard, Stephan, and Yasheng Huang. 2008. The Political Economy of Private Sector Development in China. In *China's Great Economic Transformation*, edited by Loren Brandt and Thomas G. Rawski. Cambridge, UK: Cambridge University Press.

Hamid, Javed, and Stoyan Tenev. 2008. Transforming China's Banks: The IFC's Experience. *Journal of Contemporary China* 17, no. 56 (August): 449–68.

Hanemann, Thilo, and Daniel H. Rosen. 2012. *China Invests in Europe: Patterns, Impacts and Policy Implications*. New York: Rhodium Group.

He Dong, Wenlang Zhang, Gaofeng Han, and Tommy Wu. 2012. *Productivity Growth of the Non-Tradable Sectors in China*. Hong Kong Institute for Monetary Research Working Paper No. 08 (March). Available at www.hkimr.org (accessed on December 19, 2013).

He Guangwen, Du Xiaoshan, Bai Chengyu, and Li Zhanwu. 2009. *China Microfinance Industry Assessment Report*. Beijing: China Association of Microfinance.

Holz, Carsten. 2006. Measuring Chinese Productivity Growth, 1952–2005. Unpublished manuscript.

Hsueh, Roselyn. 2011. *China's Regulatory State: A New Strategy for Globalization.* Ithaca, NY, and London: Cornell University Press.

Hu Angang. 2012. State enterprises are a bellwether of China's economic rise. *Red Flag Manuscripts* no. 19. Available at www.qstheory.cn/hqwg/2012/201219/201210/t20121011_185632.htm (accessed on September 18, 2013).

Hu Xiaoyi. 1996. Reducing State-Owned Enterprises' Social Burdens and Establishing a Social Security System. In *Policy Options for Reform of Chinese State-Owned Enterprises,* edited by Harry Broadman. World Bank Discussion Paper no. 335 (June). Washington: World Bank.

Huang Jikun, Keijiro Otsuka, and Scott Rozelle. 2008. Agriculture in China's Development: Past Disappointments, Recent Successes, and Future Challenges. In *China's Great Economic Transformation,* edited by Loren Brandt and Thomas G. Rawski. Cambridge, UK: Cambridge University Press.

Huang Yasheng. 2008. *Capitalism with Chinese Characteristics.* Cambridge, UK: Cambridge University Press.

Huang Yiping. 2010. China's great ascendancy and structural risks: consequences of asymmetric liberalization. *Asian-Pacific Economic Literature* 24, no. 1 (May): 65–85.

IFC (International Finance Corporation). 2007. *Reforming Collateral Laws and Registries: International Best Practices and the Case of China.* Washington. Available at www.ifc.org (accessed on February 18, 2014).

IMF (International Monetary Fund). 2013a. *Regional Economic Outlook: Asia and Pacific.* IMF World Economic and Financial Surveys (March). Washington.

IMF (International Monetary Fund). 2013b. *People's Republic of China: 2013 Article IV Consultation* (July). Washington. Available at www.imf.org (accessed on July 22, 2013).

Jefferson, Gary H., and Thomas G. Rawski. 1994. Enterprise Reform in Chinese Industry. *Journal of Economic Perspectives* 8, no. 2 (spring): 47–70.

Kelly, David, Amanda Rasmussen, and Erlend Ek. 2012. SOE Policy Debate: Six Tribes. *China Economic Quarterly* 16, no. 4 (December): 23–28.

Kroeber, Arthur. 2012. Role of the state sector: still in retreat but getting bigger. *China Economic Quarterly* 16, no. 4 (December): 17–22.

Lardy, Nicholas R. 1978. *Economic Growth and Distribution in China.* Cambridge, UK: Cambridge University Press.

Lardy, Nicholas R. 1983. *Agriculture in China's Modern Economic Development.* Cambridge, UK: Cambridge University Press.

Lardy, Nicholas R. 1984. Consumption and Living Standards in China, 1978-83. *China Quarterly,* no. 100 (December): 849-65.

Lardy, Nicholas R. 1985. State Intervention and Peasant Opportunities. In *Chinese Rural Development: The Great Transformation,* edited by William L. Parish. Armonk, NY: M. E. Sharpe, Inc.

Lardy, Nicholas R. 1998. *China's Unfinished Economic Revolution.* Washington: Brookings Institution Press.

Lardy, Nicholas R. 2002. *Integrating China into the Global Economy.* Washington: Brookings Institution Press.

Lardy, Nicholas R. 2012. *Sustaining China's Economic Growth after the Global Financial Crisis.* Washington: Peterson Institute for International Economics.

Lardy, Nicholas R., and Kenneth Lieberthal. 1983. *Chen Yun's Strategy for China's Development: A Non-Maoist Alternative.* Armonk, NY: M. E. Sharpe.

Lee, John. 2012. China's Corporate Leninism. *American Interest* 7, no. 5 (May/June): 36–45.

Li Bo and Wang Jue. 2006. Marketization of Trade. In *Assessing the Extent of China's Marketization,* edited by Li Xiaoxi. Burlington, VT: Ashgate.

Li, Cheng. 2012. *The Political Mapping of China's Tobacco Industry and Anti-Smoking Campaign.* Brookings Institution John L. Thornton China Center Monograph Series, no. 5. Washington.

Liang, Zai, and Zongdong Ma. 2004. China's Floating Population: New Evidence from the 2000 Census. *Population and Development Review* 30, no. 3 (September): 467–88.

Lieberthal, Kenneth, and Michel Oksenberg. 1988. *Policy Making in China: Leaders, Structures, and Processes.* Princeton: Princeton University Press.

Lin, Justin Yifu, Fang Cai, and Zhou Li. 1996. *The China Miracle: Development Strategy and Economic Reform.* Hong Kong: The Chinese University of Hong Kong Press.

Lin, Li-Wen, and Curtis J. Milhaupt. 2013. We Are the (National) Champions: Understanding the Mechanisms of State Capitalism in China. *Stanford Law Review* 65, no. 4 (April): 697–760.

Liu Xiaoxuan and Zhou Xiaoyan. 2011. An Examination of the Allocation Relationship between Financial Resources and the Real Economy. *Finance Research* no. 2: 57–70. Available at www.cnki.net (accessed on January 9, 2014).

Ma Jun, Audrey Shi, and Shan Lan. 2013. Deregulation and Private Sector Growth (September 13). Deutsche Bank Markets Research. Available at china.db.com (accessed on July 17, 2014).

Maddison, Angus. 1998. *Chinese Economic Performance in the Long Run.* Paris: Organization for Economic Cooperation and Development.

McGregor, James. 2010. China's Drive for "Indigenous Innovation": A Web of Industrial Policies (July). Global Intellectual Property Center, Global Regulatory Cooperation Project, US Chamber of Commerce, and APCO Worldwide. Available at www.uschamber.com (accessed on September 23, 2013).

McGregor, James. 2012. *No Ancient Wisdom, No Followers: The Challenges of Chinese Authoritarian Capitalism.* Westport, CT: Prospecta Press.

McGregor, Richard. 2010. *The Party: The Secret World of China's Communist Rulers.* New York: Harper.

McNally, Christopher A. 2011. China's Changing Guanxi Capitalism: Private Entrepreneurs between Leninist Control and Relentless Accumulation. *Business and Politics* 13, no. 2: 1–28. Available at www.bepress.com (accessed on October 14, 2013).

Mihaljek, Dubravko. 2010. *Domestic Bank Intermediation in Emerging Market Economies during the Crisis: Locally Owned Versus Foreign Owned Banks.* BIS paper no. 54 (December). Available at www.bis.org (accessed on September 18, 2012).

Ministry of Finance. 2013. *Report on the Implementation of the Central and Local Budgets in 2012 and on Draft Central and Local Budgets for 2013* (March 5). Available at www.npc.gov.cn (accessed on May 6, 2013).

National Bureau of Statistics of China. 1982. *China Statistical Yearbook 1981.* Beijing: China Statistics Press.

National Bureau of Statistics of China. 1983. *China Statistical Yearbook 1983.* Beijing: China Statistics Press.

National Bureau of Statistics of China. 1985. *China Statistical Yearbook 1985.* Beijing: China Statistics Press.

National Bureau of Statistics of China. 1986. *Chinese Statistical Yearbook 1986.* Beijing: China Statistics Press.

National Bureau of Statistics of China. 1990. *Chinese Statistical Yearbook 1990.* Beijing: China Statistics Press.

National Bureau of Statistics of China. 1991. *China Statistical Yearbook 1991.* Beijing: China Statistics Press.

National Bureau of Statistics of China. 1992. *China Statistical Yearbook 1992.* Beijing: China Statistics Press.

National Bureau of Statistics of China. 1995. *Chinese Statistical Yearbook 1995*. Beijing: China Statistics Press.

National Bureau of Statistics of China. 1997. *China Statistical Yearbook 1997*. Beijing: China Statistics Press.

National Bureau of Statistics of China. 1998. Report on the Results of the First National Census of Work Units (February 24). Available at www.stats.gov.cn (accessed on February 4, 2013).

National Bureau of Statistics of China. 2000. *China Statistical Yearbook 2000*. Beijing: China Statistics Press.

National Bureau of Statistics of China. 2001a. Regulations Concerning the Classification of Enterprise Registration Types (October 10). Available at www.stats.gov.cn (accessed on August 7, 2013).

National Bureau of Statistics of China. 2001b. *China Statistical Yearbook 2001*. Beijing: China Statistics Press.

National Bureau of Statistics of China. 2004. *China Statistical Yearbook 2004*. Beijing: China Statistics Press.

National Bureau of Statistics of China. 2005a. *China Statistical Yearbook 2005*. Beijing: China Statistics Press.

National Bureau of Statistics of China. 2005b. Report on Important Data from the First National Economic Census. Available at www.stats.gov.cn (accessed on December 20, 2005).

National Bureau of Statistics of China. 2006. *China Statistical Yearbook 2006*. Beijing: China Statistics Press.

National Bureau of Statistics of China. 2007. *China Statistical Abstract 2007*. Beijing: China Statistics Press.

National Bureau of Statistics of China. 2010a. *China Economic Census Yearbook 2008*. Beijing: China Statistics Press. Available at www.stats.gov.cn (accessed on January 13, 2014).

National Bureau of Statistics of China. 2010b. *Chinese Statistical Yearbook 2010*. Beijing: China Statistics Press.

National Bureau of Statistics of China. 2010c. *Statistical Report on National Economic and Social Development in the People's Republic of China in 2009* (February 25). Available at www.stats.gov.cn (accessed on February 28, 2013).

National Bureau of Statistics of China. 2011a. *China Statistical Yearbook 2011*. Beijing: China Statistics Press.

National Bureau of Statistics of China. 2011b. *Statistical Report on National Economic and Social Development in the People's Republic of China in 2010* (February 28). Available at www.stats.gov.cn (accessed on February 28, 2013).

National Bureau of Statistics of China. 2012a. *China Statistical Abstract 2012*. Beijing: China Statistics Press.

National Bureau of Statistics of China. 2012b. *China Statistical Yearbook 2012*. Beijing: China Statistics Press.

National Bureau of Statistics of China. 2012c. *Statistical Report on National Economic and Social Development in the People's Republic of China in 2011* (February 22). Available at www.stats.gov.cn (accessed on February 28, 2013).

National Bureau of Statistics of China. 2013a. *Statistical Report on National Economic and Social Development in the People's Republic of China in 2012* (February 22). Available at www.stats.gov.cn (accessed on February 28, 2013).

National Bureau of Statistics of China. 2013b. *China Statistical Abstract 2013*. Beijing: China Statistics Press.

National Bureau of Statistics of China. 2013c. *China Statistical Yearbook 2013*. Beijing: China Statistics Press.

National Bureau of Statistics of China. 2014a. *Statistical Report on National Economic and Social Development in the People's Republic of China in 2013* (February 24). Available at www.stats.gov.cn (accessed on February 28, 2014).

National Bureau of Statistics of China Population and Employment Statistics Office. 2012. *China Population and Employment Statistical Yearbook 2011*. Beijing: China Statistics Press.

National Bureau of Statistics of China Population and Employment Statistics Office. 2013. *China Population and Employment Statistical Yearbook 2012*. Beijing: China Statistics Press.

National Bureau of Statistics of China and Ministry of Human Resources and Social Security. 2011. *China Labor Statistical Yearbook 2010*. Beijing: China Statistics Press.

National Bureau of Statistics of China and Ministry of Human Resources and Social Security. 2012. *China Labor Statistical Yearbook 2011*. Beijing: China Statistics Press.

National Bureau of Statistics of China and Ministry of Human Resources and Social Security. 2013. *China Labor Statistical Yearbook 2012*. Beijing: China Statistics Press.

National Development and Reform Commission. 2011. The Twelfth Five-Year Program Outline of the People's Republic of China for Economic and Social Development. Available at www.ndrc.gov.cn (accessed on October 1, 2013).

Naughton, Barry. 2003. How Much Can Regional Integration Do to Unify China's Markets? In *How Far Across the River? Chinese Policy Reform at the Millennium*, edited by Nicholas C. Hope, Dennis Tao Yang, and Mu Yang Li. Redwood City, CA: Stanford University Press.

Naughton, Barry. 2007. *The Chinese Economy: Transitions and Growth*. Cambridge, MA: MIT Press.

Naughton, Barry. 2009. Loans, Firms, and Steel: Is the State Advancing at the Expense of the Private Sector? *China Leadership Monitor* 30: 1–10.

Naughton, Barry. 2014. Reform Retreat and Renewal: How Economic Policy Fits into the Political System. Unpublished manuscript, March.

Nee, Victor, and Sonja Opper. 2012. *Capitalism from Below: Markets and Institutional Change in China*. Cambridge, MA: Harvard University Press.

OECD (Organization for Economic Cooperation and Development). 2000. *Reforming China's Enterprises*. Paris.

OECD (Organization for Economic Cooperation and Development). 2005. *China*. OECD Economic Surveys (September). Paris.

OECD (Organization for Economic Cooperation and Development). 2010. *China*. OECD Economic Surveys (February). Paris.

Oi, Jean C., and Han Chaohua. 2011. China's Corporate Restructuring: A Multi-step Process. In *Going Private in China: The Politics of Corporate Restructuring and System Reform*, edited by Jean C. Oi. Stanford: Walter H. Shorenstein Asia-Pacific Research Center Books.

Park, Donghyun, and Kwanho Shin. 2012. *The Service Sector in Asia: Is It an Engine of Growth?* ADB Economics Working Paper Series, no. 322 (December). Manila: Asian Development Bank.

People's Bank of China Monetary Policy Analysis Small Group. 2011a. *Report on Implementation of Monetary Policy, First Quarter 2011* (May 3). Available at www.pbc.gov.cn (accessed on May 3, 2011).

People's Bank of China Monetary Policy Analysis Small Group. 2011b. *Report on Implementation of Monetary Policy, Second Quarter 2011* (August 10). Available at www.pbc.gov.cn (accessed on August 12, 2011).

People's Bank of China Monetary Policy Analysis Small Group. 2011c. *Report on Implementation of Monetary Policy, Third Quarter 2011* (November 16). Available at www.pbc.gov.cn (accessed on January 3, 2014).

People's Bank of China Monetary Policy Analysis Small Group. 2012. *Report on Implementation of Monetary Policy, Fourth Quarter 2011* (February 15). Available at www.pbc.gov.cn (accessed on February 15, 2012).

People's Bank of China Monetary Policy Analysis Small Group. 2014. *Report on Implementation of Monetary Policy, Fourth Quarter 2013* (February 8). Available at www.pbc.gov.cn (accessed on February 15, 2014).

Prosterman, Roy, Keliang Zhu, Jianping Ye, Jeffrey Riedinger, Ping Li, and Vandana Yadav. 2009. *Secure Land Rights as a Foundation for Broad-Based Rural Development in China* (November). NBR Special Report no. 18. Seattle: National Bureau of Asian Research.

Qian Yingyi and Wu Jinglian. 2003. China's Transition to a Market Economy: How Far Across the River? In *How Far Across the River? Chinese Policy Reform at the Millennium,* edited by Nicholas Hope, Dennis Tao Yang, and Mu Yang Li. Redwood City, CA: Stanford University Press.

Qu Yanfang and Jiang Xiaohua. 2006. Labor Flow and Market Determination of Wage Rates. In *Assessing the Extent of China's Marketization,* edited by Xiaoxi Li. Burlington, VT: Ashgate.

Rawski, Thomas G. 2011. Is China's Development Success Transferable? In *Reform and Development: What Can China Offer to the Developing World?* edited by Ho-Mou Wu and Yang Yao. London and New York: Routledge.

Roach, Stephen. 2014. *Unbalanced: The Codependency of America and China.* New Haven, CT: Yale University Press.

Song Ligang. 2005. Interest Rate Liberalization in China and the Implications for Non-State Banking. In *Financial Sector Reform in China,* edited by Yiping Huang, Anthony Saich, and Edward Steinfeld. Cambridge, MA: Harvard University Asia Center.

State Council. 1993. Notice on Accelerating the Pace of Reform of the Grain Distribution System (February 15). Available at www.chinabaike.com (accessed on January 16, 2014).

State Council. 2000. Law on Wholly Individually Owned Enterprises. Available at www.gov.cn (accessed on February 8, 2013).

State Council. 2005. Guidelines on Encouraging, Supporting, and Guiding the Development of the Individual, Private, and Other Nonpublic Economic Sectors (August 8). Available at www.gov.cn (accessed on August 7, 2013).

State Council. 2006a. Outline of the National Medium- and Long-Term Program on Scientific and Technological Development (2006–2020) (February 9). Available at www.gov.cn (accessed on August 7, 2013).

State Council. 2006b. Company Law. Available at www.gov.cn (accessed on February 8, 2013).

State Council. 2011. Provisions on Individual Commercial Businesses. Available at www.gov.cn (accessed on February 8, 2013).

State Council. 2014. Small and Micro Enterprises Receive a Large Reduction in Their Income Taxes (April 3). Available at http://china.caixin.com (accessed on July 17, 2014).

State Council Management Office. 2006. Guiding Opinion on Promoting the Adjustment of State-Owned Capital and the Reorganization of State-Owned Enterprises (December 5). Available at www.gov.cn (accessed on October 1, 2012).

State Council Leading Small Group Office on the Second National Economic Census and the National Bureau of Statistics of China. 2009. *Report on the Important Data from the Second National Economic Census* (December 25). Available at www.stats.gov.cn (accessed on February 4, 2013).

State Planning Commission. 1956. *First Five-Year Plan for Development of the National Economy of the People's Republic of China in 1953–57.* Beijing: Foreign Languages Press.

State Planning Commission. 1984. *The Sixth Five-Year Plan of the People's Republic of China for Economic and Social Development (1981–1985).* Beijing: Foreign Languages Press.

Tsai, Kellee S. 2002. *Back-Alley Banking: Private Entrepreneurs in China.* Ithaca, NY: Cornell University Press.

Tsai, Kellee S. 2007. *Capitalism without Democracy: The Private Sector in Contemporary China*. Ithaca, NY: Cornell University Press.

US-China Economic and Security Review Commission. 2010. *2010 Report to Congress*. Washington.

US-China Economic and Security Review Commission. 2011. *2011 Report to Congress*. Washington.

US-China Economic and Security Review Commission. 2012. *2012 Report to Congress*. Washington.

Vogel, Ezra. 2011. *Deng Xiaoping and the Transformation of China*. Cambridge, MA: Harvard University Press.

Walter, Carl, and Fraser J. T. Howie. 2003. *Privatizing China: The Stock Markets and Their Role in Corporate Reform*. Singapore: John Wiley and Sons (Asia).

Walter, Carl, and Fraser J. T. Howie. 2011. *Red Capitalism: The Fragile Financial Foundation of China's Extraordinary Rise*. Singapore: John Wiley and Sons (Asia).

Wolfe, Adam, and Jorund Aarsnes. 2011. China's Banking Sector: The Big Payback (March 23). Roubini Global Economics. Available at www.roubini.com (accessed on March 31, 2011).

World Bank. 1982. *World Development Report 1982*. New York: Oxford University Press.

World Bank. 1995. *Reform of State-Owned Enterprises*. Washington: World Bank.

World Bank. 2012. *China 2030*. Conference edition. Washington: World Bank.

Wu Jinglian and Zhao Renwei. 1987. The Dual Pricing System in China's Industry. *Journal of Comparative Economics* 11, no. 3 (September): 309–18.

Yao, Rosealea. 2012. The Slow Retreat of China's State Sector (May 24). Gavekal Dragonomics. Available by subscription only at research.gavekal.com.

Yao, Rosealea. 2013. Finding Investments Future (May 16). Gavekal Dragonomics. Available by subscription only at research.gavekal.com (accessed on July 17, 2014).

Ye, Jian-ping, Jia-ning Song, and Chen-guang Tian. 2010. An Analysis of Housing Policy during Economic Transition in China. *International Journal of Housing Policy* 10, no. 3: 273–300.

Young, Alwyn. 2000. The Razor's Edge: Distortions and Incremental Reform in the People's Republic of China. *Quarterly Journal of Economics* 95, no. 4 (November): 1091–1135.

Zhang Tianzuo, ed. 2011. *Yearbook of Chinese Township and Village Enterprises and Agricultural Processing Industry*. Beijing: Chinese Agricultural Press.

Zhang, Xing Quan. 2001. Redefining State and Market: Urban Housing Reform in China. *Housing, Theory and Society* 18: 67–78.

Index

cost of capital
    calculation, 125n
    versus return on assets for industrial firms,
        126f
credit, 157–162. *See also* loans
credit cooperatives, rural, 31, 114
creditworthiness, of registered private firms,
        109
crude oil, response to rise in global price, 132.
        See also oil and gas
Cultural Revolution (1966–76), 13, 39, 60, 70
culture, state role, 82
currency. *See* renminbi

debt-to-equity ratio, of state firms, 44
decentralization, of production tasks, 60
Deng Xiaoping, 39
deposits
    central bank data on, 7b
    real rate, 1997–2013, 130f

economic planning, evolving role of, 38–41
economic sectors, barriers to entry to, 81, 132
education, state control of, 82
electric power
    generation, 81, 111
    state control of distribution, 128
employment. *See also* migrant workers; urban
        employment
    private firms' role in, 82–89
    in public sector, 44, 138
        1999–2011, 139t
    in state firms, 148
ENN, 78
enterprise loans
    flow, by ownership, 2010–12, 105f
    stock, by ownership, 2009 and 2012, 106f
enterprises
    classification system, 64t
    measurement of number, 93n
    state, 48b
entrepreneurs, recruitment into Communist
        Party, 119–120
environmental protection, 144–145
equity financing, 112–113
Europe, private Chinese firms investment in,
        89
exports
    from China, 37
    private firms' role in, 82–89
    sources by ownership status, 1995–2013,
        87f
    of vehicles, 144
ExxonMobil, 29

family businesses. *See* individual businesses
farms. *See* agriculture
ferrous metal ore
    mining, 24
    smelting, return on assets by ownership,
        2001–12, 126f
financial sector
    investments, by firm ownership, 2012, 135t
    private firms and, 94, 134–135
    private versus public control, 79
    reform, 135–138
    state control of, 82, 137
    state firms in, 30
financial services, on internet, 114, 150
financing costs, 165
First Five-Year Plan (1953–57), 12, 13, 38–39
five-year labor contracts, 18
five-year plans, 38–41. *See also* First Five-Year
        Plan; Second Five-Year Plan; Third Five-
        Year Plan; Sixth Five-Year Plan; Twelfth
        Five-Year Plan
fixed asset investment
    by ownership, 2006–12, 116f
    national, 117
    state firms' share of, 115
foreign banks, share of assets in, 20
foreign direct investment, 1
    and China private sector, 59, 88
    law governing, 69
foreign exchange market, 31, 124
foreign firms, competition in China domestic
        market, 37
foreign investment, and private firm
        registration, 67–68
foreign retailers, 80
Fortune Global 500, Chinese companies
        included in, 24
free markets
    agricultural sales in, 61
    rural, 13

GDP
    of China, disaggregating, 48b
    China's share of global, 1
    decline in private consumption share, 132
    fiscal revenues relative to, 11, 22, 140
    ratio of credit to, 152
    service sector share, 129
        2002–08, 132
global financial crisis, marketcentric model
        critics and, 147–148
government
    analysis of bureaucracy size, 138–139

agriculture, 60–62
industry, construction, and services, 62–82

Paipai, 150
partnership enterprises, private, 63, 65t
People's Bank of China Monetary Analysis
    Small Group, 21, 30, 31, 35, 108, 111, 135,
      159
    Almanac of China's Finance and Banking, 157
    data on bank lending, 104
    data on credit flow to private sector, 99
    data on enterprise lending based on
      control, 160
    Guidelines for Microcredit Companies, 114
per capita income, 1
per capita rural income growth, 1957–78, 60
permanent employment, phaseout in state-
    owned enterprises, 18
petroleum sector. *See* oil and gas
PetroChina, profit margins, 27
pharmaceuticals, price fixing, 14
pillar industries, state control, 54
policy lending, by state-owned banks, 103
pollution reduction targets, in Twelfth Five-
    Year Program, 40n
price controls
    fuel, 14
    products subject to, in 2001, 14
    reforms to eliminate, 123
price-setting power, state firms' lack of, 26
prices, 3, 11
    dual-track, 43
    fixed, and central planning, 12
    formation in reform era, 1978–2003, 14, 15t
    world market, China's leadership and, 13
primary industry, employment in, 85n
private banks, reforms for creating, 137. *See
    also* banking system
private economic activity
    in late 1970s, 11
    state policy toward, 4
private firms, 2, 64t
    access to bank credit, 109
    classification system, 65t
    discrimination against, 90
    expansion potential in modern services,
      134–135
    in heavy industry, 24
    industrial investment by, 133
    interest coverage ratio, 110f
    loans to
      1980–2013, 101t
      2009–12, 161t
      2010 and 2012, 104
      short-term, 1980–2009, 158t

in manufacturing, versus state firms, 118
noncorporatized, 159, 159n
registered
    2002–12, 70t
    subcategories, 63
restrictive policy on entry to services sector,
    132
retained earnings for expansion financing,
    99
rise of, 122
role in generating employment and exports,
    82–89
by sector, 2009, 72
in service sector, 71
in steel, local governments and, 143
stock market listings, 113
urban employment in 2011, 85n
in water supply, 78
private industrial firms, 68
private limited liability companies, 63, 65t, 66
private partnership enterprises, 63, 65t
private sector
    alternative credit measures, 157–162
    alternative measures of value-added
      industrial output, 2003 and 2007, 74t
    bank loans outstanding to, 2009–12, 162t
    Communist Party role, 119–122
    contribution of foreign-owned firms to, 69
    credit availability, 105
    data on credit flow to, 99
    defining, 71
    employment growth, 19
    financing, 94
    state policy evolution toward, 89–93
private sector growth, 59–122
    explaining, 89–122
    ownership structure changes, 60–82
      agriculture, 60–62
      construction, 79
      industry, construction, and services,
        62–78
      services, 79–80
      wholesale and retail trade, 80–82
private shareholding limited companies, 63,
    65t
private sole proprietorship enterprises, 63,
    65t, 90
privatization
    of housing, 149
    of state-owned firms, 45
producer goods, price formation in reform era,
    1978–2003, 15t
product markets, 12–16
productivity, of state and private firms, 95

profit margins, 27
profits, 49
Sixth Five-Year Plan (1981–85), 39
Smithfield Foods, 88
social finance, 111, 112
social insurance schemes, urban migrant
    workers ineligibility for, 19
sole proprietorship enterprises, private, 63, 65t
specialized banks, 31. *See also* banking system
sports, state role, 82
State Administration of Foreign Exchange
    (SAFE), 8b
state capitalism, ix, 4, 5, 23, 24, 48, 51, 100,
    108, 118, 120, 163
state-controlled shareholding companies, 46,
    48b, 47b, 51n, 113n
State Council. *See also* State-owned Assets
    Supervision and Administration
    Commission (SASAC)
    Office for Economic Restructuring, 49
    opinion on adjustment of state capital,
        53–54
    private banks experimentation, 137
    36 Articles directive, 91, 92
State Development and Planning
    Commission, 16n, 39
state enterprises. *See* state firms
state firms, 2, 48b
    average return, 152
    debt-to-equity ratio of, 44
    employment, 148
    housing subsidies, 149
    industrial investment by, 133
    industrial output, 76
    lending to, 107
    in manufacturing, versus private firms, 118
    market power of, 48
    negative impact on economic growth,
        124–128
    outstanding loans, 104
    return on assets in, 97
    share of investment, 117–118
    subsidies to, 33–35
state fiscal resources, state firms and, 149
State Grid Corporation, 50
state industrial firms, losses, 1978–2012, 28,
    28n, 33, 34t, 35, 38, 44–46, 132
state joint ownership enterprises, 47b, 62
state nonfinancial corporations, profit
    margins, 2000–2013, 29, 29t
State-owned Assets Supervision and
    Administration Commission (SASAC),
    24, 47b, 48–50
    company diversification, 51

creation, 3
dividends, from SASAC-affiliated
    companies, 53
emergence, 48–55
financial performance, 55
growth of firms, 57
profits, 2002–13, 56t
subsidiaries, 50–51
state-owned banks, private sector loans from,
    103
state-owned enterprises. *See* state-owned firms
state-owned firms, 47b, 48b, 64t
    average profit margins, 1985–2010, 26, 27t
    downsizing in 1995, 18
    financial losses in 1980s, 44
    gross industrial output, 1978–2011, 75t
    increase in prominence, 50
    interest coverage ratio, 110f
    market power of, 24, 25
    problem of, 3
    privatization of, 45
    profits in 1980s and 1990s, 43
    reform efforts, 43
    service firms share of profiles, 29n
    types, 47–48b
    understating decline, 73
State Planning Commission, 3, 11, 95
    and equity financing eligibility, 112
    and Five-Year Plan, 39
state policy, evolution toward private sector,
    89–93
State Price Bureau, 16n
State Price Commission, 3, 11, 12, 43
    and agriculture prices, 60
    and domestic price of crude oil, 14, 16
state retailers, 80
state sector
    downsizing, 34–35
    employment in, 44
State Tobacco Monopoly Administration, 81
steel industry
    government efforts to consolidate, 143
    production, 24, 76
    state-owned and state-controlled firms'
        return on assets, 125, 128
stimulus program, Chinese state, 5
stock markets, 112, 113n
subsidies, to state firms, 33–35
sugar imports, US tariff rate quotas on, 35
supply and demand, 3
surplus labor, 44

"taking off the red hat" process, 91
Taobao, 150

Other Publications from the
Peterson Institute for International Economics

WORKING PAPERS

Who's Bashing Whom? Trade Conflict in High-Technology Industries   Laura D'Andrea Tyson
November 1992   ISBN 0-88132-106-0
Korea in the World Economy*   Il SaKong
January 1993   ISBN 0-88132-183-4
Pacific Dynamism and the International Economic System*   C. Fred Bergsten and Marcus Noland, eds.
May 1993   ISBN 0-88132-196-6
Economic Consequences of Soviet Disintegration*   John Williamson, ed.
May 1993   ISBN 0-88132-190-7
Reconcilable Differences? United States-Japan Economic Conflict*   C. Fred Bergsten and Marcus Noland
June 1993   ISBN 0-88132-129-X
Does Foreign Exchange Intervention Work?
Kathryn M. Dominguez and Jeffrey A. Frankel
September 1993   ISBN 0-88132-104-4
Sizing Up U.S. Export Disincentives*
J. David Richardson
September 1993   ISBN 0-88132-107-9
NAFTA: An Assessment   Gary Clyde Hufbauer and Jeffrey J. Schott, rev. ed.
October 1993   ISBN 0-88132-199-0
Adjusting to Volatile Energy Prices
Philip K. Verleger, Jr.
November 1993   ISBN 0-88132-069-2
The Political Economy of Policy Reform
John Williamson, ed.
January 1994   ISBN 0-88132-195-8
Measuring the Costs of Protection in the United States   Gary Clyde Hufbauer and Kimberly Ann Elliott
January 1994   ISBN 0-88132-108-7
The Dynamics of Korean Economic Development*   Cho Soon
March 1994   ISBN 0-88132-162-1
Reviving the European Union*
C. Randall Henning, Eduard Hochreiter, and Gary Clyde Hufbauer, eds.
April 1994   ISBN 0-88132-208-3
China in the World Economy   Nicholas R. Lardy
April 1994   ISBN 0-88132-200-8
Greening the GATT: Trade, Environment, and the Future   Daniel C. Esty
July 1994   ISBN 0-88132-205-9
Western Hemisphere Economic Integration*
Gary Clyde Hufbauer and Jeffrey J. Schott
July 1994   ISBN 0-88132-159-1
Currencies and Politics in the United States, Germany, and Japan   C. Randall Henning
September 1994   ISBN 0-88132-127-3
Estimating Equilibrium Exchange Rates
John Williamson, ed.
September 1994   ISBN 0-88132-076-5
Managing the World Economy: Fifty Years after Bretton Woods   Peter B. Kenen, ed.
September 1994   ISBN 0-88132-212-1
Reciprocity and Retaliation in U.S. Trade Policy
Thomas O. Bayard and Kimberly Ann Elliott
September 1994   ISBN 0-88132-084-6
The Uruguay Round: An Assessment*   Jeffrey J. Schott, assisted by Johanna Buurman
November 1994   ISBN 0-88132-206-7

Measuring the Costs of Protection in Japan*
Yoko Sazanami, Shujiro Urata, and Hiroki Kawai
January 1995   ISBN 0-88132-211-3
Foreign Direct Investment in the United States, 3d ed.   Edward M. Graham and Paul R. Krugman
January 1995   ISBN 0-88132-204-0
The Political Economy of Korea-United States Cooperation*   C. Fred Bergsten and Il SaKong, eds.
February 1995   ISBN 0-88132-213-X
International Debt Reexamined*
William R. Cline
February 1995   ISBN 0-88132-083-8
American Trade Politics, 3d ed.   I. M. Destler
April 1995   ISBN 0-88132-215-6
Managing Official Export Credits: The Quest for a Global Regime*   John E. Ray
July 1995   ISBN 0-88132-207-5
Asia Pacific Fusion: Japan's Role in APEC*
Yoichi Funabashi
October 1995   ISBN 0-88132-224-5
Korea-United States Cooperation in the New World Order*   C. Fred Bergsten and Il SaKong, eds.
February 1996   ISBN 0-88132-226-1
Why Exports Really Matter!*
              ISBN 0-88132-221-0
Why Exports Matter More!*   ISBN 0-88132-229-6
J. David Richardson and Karin Rindal
July 1995; February 1996
Global Corporations and National Governments
Edward M. Graham
May 1996   ISBN 0-88132-111-7
Global Economic Leadership and the Group of Seven   C. Fred Bergsten and C. Randall Henning
May 1996   ISBN 0-88132-218-0
The Trading System after the Uruguay Round*
John Whalley and Colleen Hamilton
July 1996   ISBN 0-88132-131-1
Private Capital Flows to Emerging Markets after the Mexican Crisis*   Guillermo A. Calvo, Morris Goldstein, and Eduard Hochreiter
September 1996   ISBN 0-88132-232-6
The Crawling Band as an Exchange Rate Regime: Lessons from Chile, Colombia, and Israel   John Williamson
September 1996   ISBN 0-88132-231-8
Flying High: Liberalizing Civil Aviation in the Asia Pacific*   Gary Clyde Hufbauer and Christopher Findlay
November 1996   ISBN 0-88132-227-X
Measuring the Costs of Visible Protection in Korea*   Namdoo Kim
November 1996   ISBN 0-88132-236-9
The World Trading System: Challenges Ahead
Jeffrey J. Schott
December 1996   ISBN 0-88132-235-0
Has Globalization Gone Too Far?   Dani Rodrik
March 1997   ISBN paper 0-88132-241-5
Korea-United States Economic Relationship*
C. Fred Bergsten and Il SaKong, eds.
March 1997   ISBN 0-88132-240-7
Summitry in the Americas: A Progress Report
Richard E. Feinberg
April 1997   ISBN 0-88132-242-3

Challenges of Globalization: Imbalances and Growth   Anders Åslund and Marek Dabrowski, eds.
July 2008   ISBN 978-0-88132-418-1
China's Rise: Challenges and Opportunities
C. Fred Bergsten, Charles Freeman, Nicholas R. Lardy, and Derek J. Mitchell
September 2008   ISBN 978-0-88132-417-4
Banking on Basel: The Future of International Financial Regulation   Daniel K. Tarullo
September 2008   ISBN 978-0-88132-423-5
US Pension Reform: Lessons from Other Countries   Martin Neil Baily and Jacob Funk Kirkegaard
February 2009   ISBN 978-0-88132-425-9
How Ukraine Became a Market Economy and Democracy   Anders Åslund
March 2009   ISBN 978-0-88132-427-3
Global Warming and the World Trading System
Gary Clyde Hufbauer, Steve Charnovitz, and Jisun Kim
March 2009   ISBN 978-0-88132-428-0
The Russia Balance Sheet   Anders Åslund and Andrew Kuchins
March 2009   ISBN 978-0-88132-424-2
The Euro at Ten: The Next Global Currency?
Jean Pisani-Ferry and Adam S. Posen, eds.
July 2009   ISBN 978-0-88132-430-3
Financial Globalization, Economic Growth, and the Crisis of 2007–09   William R. Cline
May 2010   ISBN 978-0-88132-4990-0
Russia after the Global Economic Crisis
Anders Åslund, Sergei Guriev, and Andrew Kuchins, eds.
June 2010   ISBN 978-0-88132-497-6
Sovereign Wealth Funds: Threat or Salvation?
Edwin M. Truman
September 2010   ISBN 978-0-88132-498-3
The Last Shall Be the First: The East European Financial Crisis, 2008–10   Anders Åslund
October 2010   ISBN 978-0-88132-521-8
Witness to Transformation: Refugee Insights into North Korea   Stephan Haggard and Marcus Noland
January 2011   ISBN 978-0-88132-438-9
Foreign Direct Investment and Development: Launching a Second Generation of Policy Research, Avoiding the Mistakes of the First, Reevaluating Policies for Developed and Developing Countries   Theodore H. Moran
April 2011   ISBN 978-0-88132-600-0
How Latvia Came through the Financial Crisis
Anders Åslund and Valdis Dombrovskis
May 2011   ISBN 978-0-88132-602-4
Global Trade in Services: Fear, Facts, and Offshoring   J. Bradford Jensen
August 2011   ISBN 978-0-88132-601-7
NAFTA and Climate Change   Meera Fickling and Jeffrey J. Schott
September 2011   ISBN 978-0-88132-436-5
Eclipse: Living in the Shadow of China's Economic Dominance   Arvind Subramanian
September 2011   ISBN 978-0-88132-606-2

Flexible Exchange Rates for a Stable World Economy   Joseph E. Gagnon with Marc Hinterschweiger
September 2011   ISBN 978-0-88132-627-7
The Arab Economies in a Changing World, 2d ed.   Marcus Noland and Howard Pack
November 2011   ISBN 978-0-88132-628-4
Sustaining China's Economic Growth After the Global Financial Crisis   Nicholas R. Lardy
January 2012   ISBN 978-0-88132-626-0
Who Needs to Open the Capital Account?
Olivier Jeanne, Arvind Subramanian, and John Williamson
April 2012   ISBN 978-0-88132-511-9
Devaluing to Prosperity: Misaligned Currencies and Their Growth Consequences   Surjit S. Bhalla
August 2012   ISBN 978-0-88132-623-9
Private Rights and Public Problems: The Global Economics of Intellectual Property in the 21st Century   Keith E. Maskus
September 2012   ISBN 978-0-88132-507-2
Global Economics in Extraordinary Times: Essays in Honor of John Williamson
C. Fred Bergsten and C. Randall Henning, eds.
November 2012   ISBN 978-0-88132-662-8
Rising Tide: Is Growth in Emerging Economies Good for the United States?   Lawrence Edwards and Robert Z. Lawrence
February 2013   ISBN 978-0-88132-500-3
Responding to Financial Crisis: Lessons from Asia Then, the United States and Europe Now
Changyong Rhee and Adam S. Posen, eds.
October 2013   ISBN 978-0-88132-674-1
Fueling Up: The Economic Implications of America's Oil and Gas Boom
Trevor Houser and Shashank Mohan
January 2014   ISBN 978-0-88132-656-7
How Latin America Weathered the Global Financial Crisis   José De Gregorio
January 2014   ISBN 978-0-88132-678-9
Confronting the Curse: The Economics and Geopolitics of Natural Resource Governance
Cullen S. Hendrix and Marcus Noland
May 2014   ISBN 978-0-88132-676-5
Inside the Euro Crisis: An Eyewitness Account
Simeon Djankov
June 2014   ISBN 978-0-88132-685-7
Managing the Euro Area Debt Crisis
William R. Cline
June 2014   ISBN 978-0-88132-678-1
Markets over Mao: The Rise of Private Business in China   Nicholas R. Lardy
September 2014   ISBN 978-0-88132-693-2

SPECIAL REPORTS

1   Promoting World Recovery: A Statement on Global Economic Strategy*
     by 26 Economists from Fourteen Countries
     December 1982   ISBN 0-88132-013-7
2   Prospects for Adjustment in Argentina, Brazil, and Mexico: Responding to the Debt Crisis*   John Williamson, ed.
     June 1983   ISBN 0-88132-016-1

WORKS IN PROGRESS

DISTRIBUTORS OUTSIDE THE UNITED STATES

**Australia, New Zealand,
and Papua New Guinea**
Co Info Pty Ltd
648 Whitehorse Road Mitcham VIC 3132
Australia
Tel: +61 3 9210 77567
Fax: +61 3 9210 7788
Email: babadilla@coinfo.com.au
www.coinfo.com.au

India, Bangladesh, Nepal, and Sri Lanka
Viva Books Private Limited
Mr. Vinod Vasishtha
4737/23 Ansari Road
Daryaganj, New Delhi 110002
India
Tel: 91-11-4224-2200
Fax: 91-11-4224-2240
Email: viva@vivagroupindia.net
www.vivagroupindia.com

**Mexico, Central America, South America,
and Puerto Rico**
US PubRep, Inc.
311 Dean Drive
Rockville, MD 20851
Tel: 301-838-9276
Fax: 301-838-9278
Email: c.falk@ieee.org

Asia (*Brunei, Burma, Cambodia, China,
Hong Kong, Indonesia, Korea, Laos, Malaysia,
Philippines, Singapore, Taiwan, Thailand,
and Vietnam*)
East-West Export Books (EWEB)
University of Hawaii Press
2840 Kolowalu Street
Honolulu, Hawaii 96822-1888
Tel: 808-956-8830
Fax: 808-988-6052
Email: eweb@hawaii.edu

Canada
Renouf Bookstore
5369 Canotek Road, Unit 1
Ottawa, Ontario KlJ 9J3, Canada
Tel: 613-745-2665
Fax: 613-745-7660
www.renoufbooks.com

Japan
United Publishers Services Ltd.
1-32-5, Higashi-shinagawa
Shinagawa-ku, Tokyo 140-0002
Japan
Tel: 81-3-5479-7251
Fax: 81-3-5479-7307
Email: purchasing@ups.co.jp
*For trade accounts only. Individuals will find
Institute books in leading Tokyo bookstores.*

Middle East
MERIC
2 Bahgat Ali Street, El Masry Towers
Tower D, Apt. 24
Zamalek, Cairo
Egypt
Tel. 20-2-7633824
Fax: 20-2-7369355
Email: mahmoud_fouda@mericonline.com
www.mericonline.com

United Kingdom, Europe
(*including Russia and Turkey*)**, Africa,
and Israel**
The Eurospan Group
c/o Turpin Distribution
Pegasus Drive
Stratton Business Park
Biggleswade, Bedfordshire
SG18 8TQ
United Kingdom
Tel: 44 (0) 1767-604972
Fax: 44 (0) 1767-601640
Email: eurospan@turpin-distribution.com
www.eurospangroup.com/bookstore

**Visit our website at:
www.piie.com
E-mail orders to:
petersonmail@presswarehouse.com**